Laptops For Seniors

5th Edition

by Nancy C. Muir

for dummies®
A Wiley Brand

Laptops For Seniors For Dummies®, 5th Edition

Published by: **John Wiley & Sons, Inc.**, 111 River Street, Hoboken, NJ 07030-5774, www.wiley.com

Copyright © 2018 by John Wiley & Sons, Inc., Hoboken, New Jersey

Published simultaneously in Canada

For general information on our other products and services, please contact our Customer Care Department within the U.S. at 877-762-2974, outside the U.S. at 317-572-3993, or fax 317-572-4002. For technical support, please visit https://hub.wiley.com/community/support/dummies.

Wiley publishes in a variety of print and electronic formats and by print-on-demand. Some material included with standard print versions of this book may not be included in e-books or in print-on-demand. If this book refers to media such as a CD or DVD that is not included in the version you purchased, you may download this material at http://booksupport.wiley.com. For more information about Wiley products, visit www.wiley.com.

Library of Congress Control Number: 2017952295

ISBN 978-1-119-42026-2 (pbk); ISBN 978-1-119-42029-3 (ebk); ISBN 978-1-119-42021-7 (ebk)

Manufactured in the United States of America

10 9 8 7 6 5 4 3 2 1

Contents at a Glance

Table of Contents

Introduction

Computers for consumers have come a long way in just 35 years or so. They're now at the heart of the way many people communicate, shop, and learn. They provide useful tools for tracking information, organizing finances, and being creative. And, they've become far more portable with all sizes and weights of laptops available.

During the rapid growth of the personal computer, you might have been too busy to jump in and learn the ropes, but you now realize how useful and fun working with a computer can be. In fact, for seniors, the computer opens up a world of activities and contacts that they never had before.

This book can help you get going with your laptop quickly and painlessly.

About This Book

This book is specifically written for mature people like you — folks who are relatively new to using a computer and want to discover the basics of buying a laptop, working with software, and getting on the Internet. In writing this book, I've tried to take into account the types of activities that might interest a 55-plus-year-old who's discovering the full potential of computers for the first time.

Foolish Assumptions

This book is organized by sets of tasks. These tasks start from the very beginning, assuming you know little about computers, and guide you through the most basic steps in easy-to-understand language. Because I assume you're new to computers, the book provides explanations or definitions of technical terms to help you out.

All computers are run by software called an *operating system*, such as Windows. The latest version is Windows 10, Creators Update. This book covers features in the original release of Windows 10 and modifications to those features, as well as new features in the Anniversary Update released in 2016 and the Creators Update released in 2017. Because Microsoft Windows–based personal computers (PCs) — including laptops — are the most common type of computer, this book focuses on Windows 10 functionality.

Beyond the Book

In addition to the material in the print or e-book you're reading right now, this product comes with some access-anywhere goodies on the web. Check out the free Cheat Sheet for a checklist for buying a laptop, computer care and maintenance tips, and Windows keystroke shortcuts. To get this Cheat Sheet, simply go to www.dummies.com and type **Laptops For Seniors For Dummies Cheat Sheet** in the Search box.

Where to Go from Here

Whether you need to start from square one and buy yourself a laptop or you're ready to just start enjoying the tools and toys your current laptop makes available, it's time to get going, get online, and get computer savvy.

1

Get Going!

Chapter **1**

Buying a Laptop

I f you've never owned a laptop and now face purchasing one for the first time, choosing a laptop can be a somewhat daunting experience. There are lots of technical terms to figure out and various pieces of *hardware* (the physical parts of your laptop such as the monitor and keyboard) and *software* (the programs that allow you to use the computer to get things done, such as creating documents and playing games, for example).

In this chapter, I introduce you to the world of activities your new laptop makes available to you, and I provide the information you need to choose just the right laptop for you. Remember as you read through this chapter that figuring out what you want to do with your laptop is an important step in determining which laptop you should buy. You have to consider how much money you want to spend, how you'll connect your laptop to the Internet, and how much power and performance you need from your laptop.

Understand All You Can Do with Laptops

Congratulations — in your life you've been witness to a remarkable revolution. In just a few decades, computers have moved from being expensive behemoths that lived in corporate basements to being personal productivity and entertainment tools. They empower people to connect around the world in unprecedented ways, and they make common tasks much easier to handle.

The following list walks you through some of the things your laptop will enable you to do. Depending on what activities are important to you, you can make a more-informed purchasing choice.

» **Keep in touch with friends and family.** The Internet makes it possible to communicate with other people via email; share video images using built-in video recorders or webcams (tiny video cameras that capture and send your images to others); and make phone and video calls using your laptop and Internet connection with services such as Skype. You can also chat with others by typing messages and sending them through your laptop using a technology called *instant messaging* (IM). These text messages are exchanged in real time, so that you and your grandchild, for example, can see and reply to text or share images immediately. Part 3 of this book explains these topics in more detail.

» **Research any topic from the comfort of your home.** Online, you can find many reputable websites that help you get information on anything from expert medical advice to the best travel deals. You can read news from around the corner or around the world. You can visit government websites to get information about your taxes and Social Security benefits, and go to entertainment sites to look up your local television listings or movie reviews.

» **Address greeting cards, letters, or home inventories.** Whether you're organizing your holiday card list, tracking sales for your home business, or figuring out a monthly budget, computer programs can help. For example, Figure 1-1 shows the Jacquie Lawson e-greeting card site with lots of options for creating electronic cards to send to your friends' email inboxes.

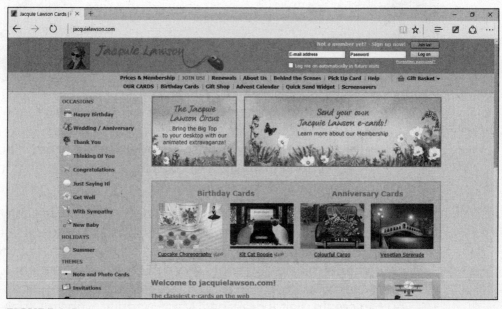

FIGURE 1-1

» **Pursue hobbies such as genealogy or sports.** You can research your favorite teams online (see Figure 1-2) or connect with people who have the same interests. The online world is full of special-interest discussion groups where you can talk about a wide variety of topics with others.

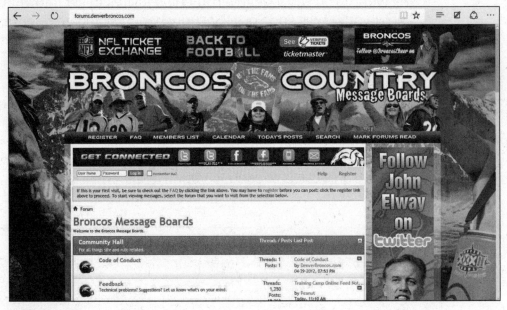

FIGURE 1-2

» **Play interactive games with others over the Internet.** You can play everything from shuffleboard to poker and even participate in action games in virtual worlds.

» **Share and create photos, drawings, and videos.** If you have a digital camera or smartphone, you can transfer photos to your laptop (called *uploading*) or copy photos off the Internet (if their copyright permits it) and share them in emails or use them to create your own greeting cards. If you're artistically inclined, you can create digital drawings. Many popular websites make sharing your homemade videos easy, too. If you have a digital video camera or smartphone and editing software, you can use editing tools to make a movie and share it with others via video-sharing sites such as YouTube or by email. Steven Spielberg, look out!

» **Shop online and compare products easily, day or night.** You can shop for anything from a garden shed to travel deals or a new camera. Using handy shopping site features, you can easily compare prices from several stores or read customer product reviews. Websites such as www.nextag.com list product prices from a variety of vendors on one web page, so you can find the best deals. Beyond the convenience, all this information can help you save money.

» **Manage your financial life.** You can do your banking or investing online and get up-to-the-minute data about your bank account, credit card balances, and investments. And if you're online savvy, you can do this all without fear of having your financial data stolen (see Chapter 15 for more about online safety).

Overview of Hardware

Your computing experience is made up of interactions with hardware and software. The *hardware* is all the tangible computer equipment, such as the body of your laptop containing the monitor, central processing unit, touchpad, and keyboard.

Your laptop hardware consists of

» **A central processing unit (CPU),** which is the very small, very high-tech semiconductor *chip* that acts as the brains of your computer. The CPU is stored in your laptop along with the other nuts and bolts of your computer.

» **A monitor,** which displays images on its screen such as the Microsoft Windows screen, a video you watch from an online entertainment site, or a document in a software program.

Today, more and more laptops sport touchscreen monitors, which allow you to use your finger on the screen to provide input to the computer.

» **A keyboard,** which is similar to a typewriter keyboard. In addition to typing words, you can use a keyboard to give the computer commands such as selecting, copying, and pasting text.

» **A touchpad,** which you also use to give your computer commands. This little device offers a more tactile way to provide input. You move a pointer on the screen by using a built-in pointing device, which might be in the form of a touchpad, or a small button. Slide your fingertip around the touchpad. This moves the pointer around onscreen. You position this pointer on an onscreen button or menu name, for example, and then click the left or right side of your touchpad, which causes an action. You can also tap and drag your fingertip to select text or an object to perform an action on it (such as deleting a file or making a line of text bold). You also have the option of attaching a physical wireless mouse to your laptop; a small transmitter that you place in a USB port on your laptop enables the mouse input.

» **Peripherals,** such as a printer, speakers, webcams, wireless mouse, and headphones. These may or may not come with your laptop when you buy it. Your laptop comes with slots (called *ports*) where you can plug in various peripherals.

Appreciate Software

Software is what makes the hardware work or lets you get things done, such as writing documents with Microsoft Word or playing a game of solitaire. You can install software (also known as *programs*, *applications*, or *apps*) on your laptop or use a version from an online website. Here are a few basics about software:

» **You use software to get your work done, run entertainment programs, and browse the Internet.** For example, Quicken is a financial management program you can use to balance your checkbook or plan for your retirement.

» **Software used to run your computer is called an operating system.** Some examples of operating systems are Apple's OS X for Mac computers and Microsoft Windows. This book deals mainly with Windows 10 Creators Update and the programs it runs.

» **Some programs come preinstalled on your laptop; you can buy and install other programs as you need them.** For example, a computer always has an operating system because the operating system runs all the other programs. Also, some programs are included with a Windows computer, such as WordPad, a simple word- processing program, and Music and Video apps.

» **You can uninstall programs you no longer need.** Uninstalling unwanted programs helps to free up some space on your laptop, which helps it perform better.

» **Software programs called *utilities* exist to keep your laptop in shape.** An *antivirus* program is an example of a utility used to block or spot and erase computer viruses from your system. Your *operating system* also includes some utilities, such as those that optimize your hard drive or restore your system if either one is experiencing problems.

Understand the Difference between a Desktop and Laptop

The fact is that when it comes to performing computing tasks, a desktop and laptop are pretty much identical. They both have an operating system such as Windows 10 or Apple's OS X. They both contain a hard drive where you store data and computer chips that process data, and they both run software and access the Internet.

Where a desktop and laptop differ is their physical appearance, size, and weight. Here's a rundown of the key differences:

» **Appearance:** A desktop computer is typically encased in a tower, into which you plug a separate monitor, keyboard, and mouse. (Some newer models called all-in-ones have the brains of the computer incorporated into a monitor base.) A laptop has all its parts in one unit, as shown in Figure 1-3. The central processing unit (CPU) — chips, monitor, keyboard, and touchpad (a laptop version of a mouse) — all fit in one compact package. Like desktop computers, laptops include slots called ports for plugging in other devices (called peripherals), such as a little toggle that acts as a transmitter for a wireless mouse or printer.

FIGURE 1-3

» **Power source:** A laptop contains a battery that you charge by plugging it into a wall outlet. You can run the laptop off a charged battery or plug the laptop into a wall outlet so battery charge isn't a concern.

» **Portability:** Having a battery and coming in a more compact package makes a laptop more portable (although some larger models are a bit hefty to tote around); a desktop stays put on a desktop as a rule.

» **Extras:** Many laptops today do not include a CD/DVD drive and therefore require an external drive, like the one shown in Figure 1-4, to be attached if you need to install or work with software, music, or videos on DVDs.

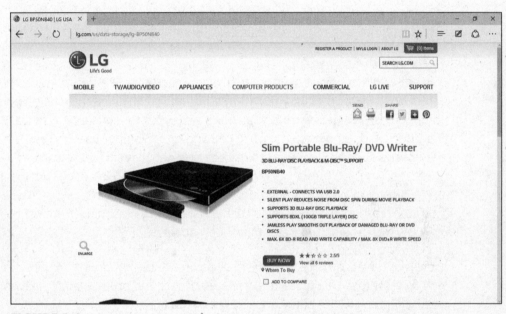

FIGURE 1-4

TIP

If you like the tablet format, consider a 2-in-1 laptop. With these, you can remove a keyboard from the monitor portion of the laptop that then functions as a tablet, or rotate the monitor to rest on the back of the keyboard. The Microsoft Surface is an example of this format.

TABLETS VERSUS LAPTOPS

What's the difference between a laptop and tablet? Tablets, also called *slates,* are more like a hefty pad than a computer. There is no keyboard and no mouse. Instead, you tap the screen to make choices and enter text. The onscreen keyboard is even smaller than a laptop keyboard, but there are physical keyboard and mouse accessories that you can use with tablets to make input (typing text and commands) easier. Tablets also have super battery life at as much as 10 hours — almost a month in standby mode (when you're not actually using them). Tablets connect to the Internet using either Wi-Fi or 3G/4G technologies (Wi-Fi is a network that is in close proximity to you; 3G/4G is what your cell phone uses to connect virtually anywhere). 3G/4G models require that you pay a data usage fee to a mobile phone provider.

Tablets, which are available from many manufacturers (iPad from Apple, the Fire tablet from Amazon, Galaxy from Samsung, and so on), weigh about 1.5 pounds (more or less). Tablets were first planned as devices for consuming media (watching videos and listening to music, to you and me). Whether used to read e-books, play games such as Scrabble, browse the Internet, play music, or watch movies, these devices have proven incredibly popular. Tablets are a big hit with business and educational groups. Applications (called *apps*) range from credit card readers for retail businesses to eReaders such as Kindle and reasonably robust productivity tools such as word processors and spreadsheets.

However, tablets are pretty darn small. If you want a computing solution that's comfortable to work on at a desk for a few hours and pretty easy to take on the road, a laptop still has some advantages over a tablet.

Choose a Laptop

Just as there are many styles of shoes or mobile phones, you can find several styles of laptops. Some are smaller and more portable, whereas others are essentially desktop replacements with large screens and a bit of heft. There are different operating systems installed on laptops to make everything run, and some excel at certain functions such as working with graphics or playing games. Here are some features you should consider when choosing a laptop.

» **Operating system (OS):** An OS is the software that allows you to start and shut down your computer and work with all the other software programs, manage files, and connect to the Internet. Windows is probably the most common computer operating system, and this book focuses mainly on its features.

Mac laptops from Apple are also very popular. These use Apple-specific software including the Mac operating system referred to as OS X. Many software applications written for Windows are also available for the Mac. You can also set up your Mac to run the Windows operating system, which gives you the best of both worlds.

Some computers run on a freely available operating system called Linux, which has functionality similar to Windows. Chromebooks from Google use the Linux-based Chrome operating system and come pre-loaded with lots of Google apps.

» **Laptop design:** A *laptop* is a portable computer, weighing anywhere from two to ten pounds. Touchscreen laptops allow you to tap on items on the screen and use an onscreen keyboard to get things done, or write on the screen with a special stylus called a digital pen. The monitor, keyboard, and touchpad are built into a laptop. Note that if the monitor is damaged, you have to pay quite a bit to have it repaired, or you can hook it up to an external monitor. Laptops are perfect if you want to use your computer mainly away from home or you have little space in your home for a larger computer. Consider design and weight when purchasing a laptop.

» **Laptop variations:** The thinnest and lightest ones (as light as two pounds) are called *ultrabooks*. A 2-in-1 laptop allows you to either rotate the monitor to rest on the back of the keyboard or remove the monitor portion so you can use the laptop like a tablet. When you have removed the physical keyboard from the screen of a 2-in-1, you have to use the touchscreen feature to interact with it. Figure 1-5 shows a 2-in-1 laptop.

FIGURE 1-5

» **Pictures and sound:** If you work with a lot of *visual elements* (for example, photographs, home movies, or computer games), consider a laptop that has a good graphics card. Games often involve sound, so a high-end sound card might also be useful. Laptops with more sophisticated sound and image capabilities are often referred to as *gaming* or *multimedia* models, and they typically require a large-capacity hard drive to handle these functions. Because the capabilities of these cards change all the time, I don't give you exact specifications for what's considered high-end; instead, ask the person you're buying the laptop from whether the system can handle sophisticated sound and graphics.

TIP

One clue that the model has better support for higher-end graphics is if it has a *discrete* graphics card (that is, a card separate from the CPU) versus one built in to the CPU (called *integrated graphics*).

TIP

Tablets such as iPad, Amazon's Fire tablet, and Microsoft Surface offer many computing capabilities, such as reading and working on simple documents, connecting to the Internet to send and receive email, playing games, listening to music, and so on.

However, they have relatively small touchscreens (with a touchscreen, you provide input with your finger or a stylus), onscreen keyboards, which can be a bit challenging to use, no mouse, and often less in the way of file-management capabilities. (With some tablets, such as Surface, you can attach a wireless keyboard or mouse if you like.) If you just want to browse the web, read email, listen to music, and play games, a tablet could be the way to go. If you want a broader range of capabilities with a larger screen size and can handle toting around a machine that weighs a few pounds, a laptop is for you. Many people have both a laptop and a tablet, and it's easy to share files and settings between them. They do complement each other nicely if that approach fits your budget.

Select a Version of Windows

Choosing your laptop's *operating system* (software that runs all the programs and organizes data on your computer) will be one of your first decisions. This book focuses on computers running the current version of Windows, which is called Windows 10 Creators Update. Windows 10 is a departure from the previous Windows operating system, so if you opt for an earlier version of Windows, such as Windows 8, you would need to buy the Windows 8 edition of this book. Note that, depending on your Windows Update settings, updates to Windows may be performed regularly without your instigating them.

Windows 10 comes in several versions, including two versions for home and small business users:

» **Windows 10 Home:** Includes apps such as Music, Video, Weather, People, Camera, and more. If you consider yourself primarily a home user, you should consider this version of Windows 10.

» **Windows 10 Pro:** Is great for small businesses or if you work from home. This version of Windows has ultimate security features and more administrative tools.

Determine Your Price Range

You can buy a laptop for anywhere from about $199 to $5,000 or more, depending on your budget and computing needs. You may start with a base model, but extras such as a larger monitor or larger storage capacity can soon add hundreds to the base price. The key rule of thumb here is to buy just as much computer as you need.

You can shop in a retail store for a laptop or shop online using a friend's computer (and perhaps get his or her help if you're brand new to using a computer). Consider researching different models and prices online and using that information to negotiate your purchase in the store if you prefer shopping at the mall. Be aware, however, that most retail stores have a small selection compared to all you can find online on a website such as Amazon.com and NewEgg.com. In addition, retail stores sometimes carry slightly older models than those available online.

Buying a laptop can be confusing, but here are some guidelines to help you find a laptop at the price that's right for you:

» **Determine how often you will use your computer.** If you'll be working on it eight hours a day running a home business, you will need a better-quality laptop to withstand the use and provide good performance. If you turn on the computer once or twice a week just to check your email, it doesn't have to be the priciest model in the shop.

» **Consider the features that you need.** Do you want (or have room for) a heftier laptop with an 18-inch monitor? Do you need the laptop to run very fast and run several programs at once, or do you need to store tons of data? (Computer speed and storage are covered later in this chapter.) Understand what you need before you buy. Each feature or upgrade adds dollars to your computer's price.

» **Shop wisely.** If you walk from store to store or do your shopping online, you'll find that the price for the same laptop model can vary by hundreds of dollars. See if your memberships in organizations such as AAA, AARP, or Costco make you eligible for better deals. Consider shipping costs if you buy online, and keep in mind that many stores charge a restocking fee if you return a laptop you aren't happy with. Some stores offer only a short time period, such as 14 days, during which you can return a laptop.

» **Buying used or refurbished is an option, though new laptops have reached such a low price point that this may not save you much.** In addition, technology gets out of date so quickly that you might be disappointed buying an older model, which might not support newer software or hardware, such as printers.

» **Online auctions are a source of new or slightly used laptops at a low price.** However, be sure you're dealing with a reputable store or person by checking reviews others have posted about them or contacting the online Better Business Bureau (www. bbb.org). Be careful not to pay by check (this gives a complete stranger your bank account number); instead use the auction site's tools to have a third party handle the money until the goods are delivered in the condition promised. Check the auction site for guidance on staying safe when buying auctioned goods.

TIP

Some websites, such as Epinions, allow you to compare several models of laptops side by side, and others, such as Nextag, allow you to compare prices on a particular model from multiple stores.

Understand Displays

Monitors are the window to your laptop's contents. The right monitor can make your computing time easier on your eyes. The crisper the image, the more impressive your vacation photos or that video of your last golf game will be.

Consider these factors when choosing a monitor:

» **Size:** Monitors for the average laptop user come in all sizes, from tiny 7-inch screens on smaller laptops or tablets to 17-inch models. Laptops with larger screens are typically more expensive.

- » **Image quality:** The image quality on laptop monitors can vary greatly. You will encounter terms such as LCD (*liquid crystal display*), LED (light emitting diode), flat screen, brightness, and resolution when buying your laptop.

  Look for a laptop with an LCD or LED monitor, preferably with a screen that reduces glare.

- » **Resolution:** A monitor's resolution represents the number of tiny dots called *pixels* that form the images you see on the screen. The higher the resolution, the more pixels it contains and the crisper the image. You should look for a laptop that can provide at least a 1366-x-768 pixel resolution.

- » **Touchscreen technology:** Windows 10 provides support for using a touchscreen interface, which allows you to use your fingers to provide input by tapping or swiping on the screen itself. If you opt for a touchscreen device, you can still use your keyboard and mouse to provide input, but touchscreen technology can add a wow factor when performing tasks such as using painting software or browsing around the web or an electronic book (e-book).

Opt for Longer Battery Life

Because you're likely to use your laptop away from home now and then, the amount of time it retains a battery charge can be important. Though many laptops still only last a couple of hours on one charge, newer models are beginning to offer battery lives of eight to twelve hours and technologies to extend battery life even more are evolving at a rapid pace.

Check the battery life rating when looking at a laptop and decide if you might need more hours, for example, to use the laptop on a long train ride, if the power goes out for hours in your area during storms, or for other situations when power just won't be available.

Use USB Ports for Storage or DVDs

In the recent past, most laptops came with a drive where you could insert a disc and play a movie or music. If you buy a software program, it may come on a CD or DVD, so you can use a built-in or external drive to install it.

Today, many new computers, and especially weight-conscious laptops, don't include an optical drive for reading DVDs. However, they do have USB ports. USB ports accommodate a USB stick, a small, plastic-coated gadget that can hold lots and lots of data or a connection to an external drive where you can insert and work with DVDs. Keep in mind that you can download and install software or play videos and music from the *cloud* (that is, via the Internet), so it's possible to get along just fine without the ability to play DVDs. However, some software products still come only on a disc. You can connect an external optical drive to a USB port and load the software on your computer.

TIP

If you want to play the latest optical discs, get a laptop with a Blu-ray player. Blu-ray is a great medium for storing and playing back feature-length movies because it can store 50GB or more, about ten times as much as a DVD.

Choose Features for Faster Performance

Your laptop contains a processor on a computer chip. The speed at which your laptop runs programs or completes tasks is determined in great measure by your computer's processor speed, which is measured in *gigahertz* (GHz). The higher this measurement, the faster the processor. I won't quote the speed you should look for because these chips are constantly getting smaller and more powerful. However, when you shop, know that the higher numbers give the best performance, so factor that into your decision, depending on your needs.

Computers have traditionally used hard drives to store programs and data. In many laptops, a solid state drive (SSD) is used in place of a hard drive. The *access speed* (how fast your computer retrieves data) of solid state drives is much higher than the access speed of hard drives. If you need a laptop that processes information very quickly, look for one with a solid state drive, but be aware that it will be more expensive.

TIP

The capacity for data storage (GB) for solid state drives is generally lower than for hard drives; therefore, the amount of large files you can store on the laptop may be limited.

Another factor involved in performance is whether your processor has multiple cores. *Multiple core* means that two or more processors are involved in reading and executing software instructions as you use your laptop. Most processors today are multiple-core processors, such as the i3, i5, and i7 processor lines from Intel. Those with two processors are called *dual-core;* those with four processors are called *quad-core;* and processors with six cores are referred to as *hexa-core.* The bottom line with cores is that the more you have, the faster your laptop can process instructions because all the cores can work at once. This is what makes multitasking possible. (*Multitasking* is when you're running several programs at once, as when you're playing music, downloading files from the Internet, running an antivirus scan, and working in a word processor — with all of these processes running at the same time.) Be aware that not all software is designed to take advantage of multiple core architecture.

In addition to your processor, computers have a certain amount of working capacity for running programs and accessing frequently used data that can affect performance. You'll see specifications for RAM when you go laptop shopping. RAM, which stands for random access memory, is a measure of the capacity for running programs; the higher the RAM, the more quickly your laptop can juggle multiple tasks, therefore increasing performance. RAM chips come in different types, including DRAM, SDRAM, and the latest version, DDR4. Look for a minimum of 2 gigabyte (GB) of RAM for everyday computing.

Determine How You'll Connect to the Internet

Because so much is online today, you have to decide how you'll connect to the Internet. You can pay a fee to get a broadband connection, such as DSL, satellite, or cable. (Check with AARP to find out if it offers discounted connections in your area.) If you want to set up a wireless connection in your home so you can connect to the Internet or you want to access certain public networks called *hotspots*, you have to be sure to buy a laptop with up-to-date wireless capabilities. Here's how these work:

» **Broadband:** These connections typically come through a DSL (digital subscriber line) or cable modem in your home. In both cases, you pay a fee to a provider, which might be your phone or cable company. DSL works over your phone line but doesn't prohibit you from using the phone when you're online. Cable runs over your cable TV line and is a bit faster than DSL. Satellite broadband is typically used in rural areas without cable or DSL service. These are considered always-on connections, meaning that you don't have to dial up to a phone connection or connect to a wireless network — you're always connected.

» **Dialup:** If you intend to use a dialup connection (that is, connect over your phone line), your computer has to have a dialup modem either built in or external. Dialup connections can be very slow — in fact, in all but remote locations they have been replaced by more current technology. While you're using a dialup connection, you can't use your phone to make or receive calls. I'd discourage you from using dialup unless you absolutely have to.

» **Wireless:** These connections require that you have a computer equipped with wireless capability. You can access the Internet wirelessly through a wireless network connected to a broadband modem in your home, or when you're near a wireless *hotspot* (a place that offers wireless service). Many hotspots are available at public places such as hotels, airports, libraries, and restaurants. You can also subscribe to a Wireless Wide Area Network (WWAN) service from a mobile phone provider to tap into its connection or use a technology called *tethering* to connect via your smart-phone's 3G or 4G connection. Check the laptop model you want to buy to be sure it has the most current wireless technology. There are various techy standards for wireless, such as 802.11a, b, g, or n. The very latest standard to look for is 802.11ac, which delivers better wireless performance.

 See Chapter 13 for more about setting up your Internet connection.

TIP

 Look for laptops that support an up and coming wireless tech-nology called WiGig. WiGig can transfer data to nearby devices (within about 30 feet) about three times faster than Wi-Fi because it runs on the less-traveled 60 GHz frequency.

TIP

Chapter **2**

Setting Up Your Laptop

O nce you unpack your new laptop, you may need help getting it set up. Here I cover the basics: installing and charging your laptop battery; turning the computer on and off; mastering the basic use of your mouse; becoming familiar with some basic keystroke shortcuts; and, if you have a touchscreen, finding out how to interact with it.

Next, you can set up the date and time in your computer's internal clock so they match your time zone and you can apply appropriate daylight saving time settings properly. Finally, you get to work with your user accounts which help you to save individual settings to each account when more than one person is accessing a computer. Windows allows you to create multiple user accounts; each account saves certain settings and allows you to control files and folders separately. Child accounts allow you to have some control over what apps and online content a child can access. When each user logs on with a particular user account, it's like accessing a unique personal computer.

Here, then, are the procedures that you can follow to get going with your laptop.

Install and Charge the Battery

Your laptop comes with a battery that you should insert and charge when you first take the laptop out of the box. The battery is a rect-angular affair (similar to the one shown in Figure 2-1) that slips into the bottom of your laptop.

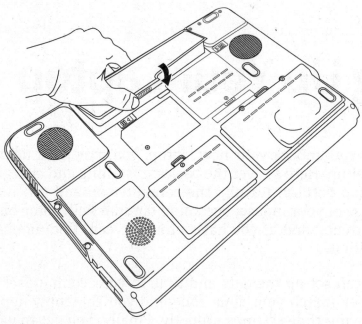

FIGURE 2-1

TIP

Note that tablet models are typically sealed so that your battery is not accessible; if yours is one of those, you don't have to insert a battery; just plug the tablet in to a wall outlet to charge the battery.

It's a good idea to charge your battery completely when you first plug it in, which could take several hours. Follow these instructions to do that:

1. Locate the plug in your laptop packaging. (It's usually a two-piece cable; one half of the cable has a large, boxy transformer on one end that plugs in to the other half.)

2. Plug one end of the cable into a wall outlet and the other into the round power connection port on your laptop. Your user's manual should indicate where this connection is located (usually on the back or near the back of the right or left side of the laptop).

3. When you turn your laptop on (see the next task), you'll find a small icon on the Windows desktop screen in the taskbar (usually called the Battery Meter icon) that looks like a standard battery with a plug next to it. Click this Battery Meter icon to see whether the battery is charged to 100 percent of its capacity. (If you aren't yet sure how to move around the screen and click, see the upcoming task, "Use the Mouse".)

This icon changes to just a battery (no plug) when the computer isn't plugged in; this battery icon indicates visually how much charge your battery has left before it drains. When you hover your mouse over the battery icon, you see the actual percentage of battery life left.

Log on to Windows 10

1. With your laptop charged up, you're ready to turn it on. Start by pressing the power button on your laptop to begin the Windows 10 start-up sequence. When you first turn on a new computer, you should choose Express Settings to set it up.

2. In the resulting Windows 10 Welcome screen, click the screen to reveal the sign-in screen.

Enter your password or PIN, if you've set up one, and then press Enter on your keyboard. (If you haven't set up the password-protection feature for more than one user, you're taken directly to the Windows 10 desktop when you turn on your laptop. If you have more than one user you have to choose the one you want to log on as.) Windows 10 verifies your password and displays the Windows 10 desktop, as shown in Figure 2-2.

Desktop shortcut

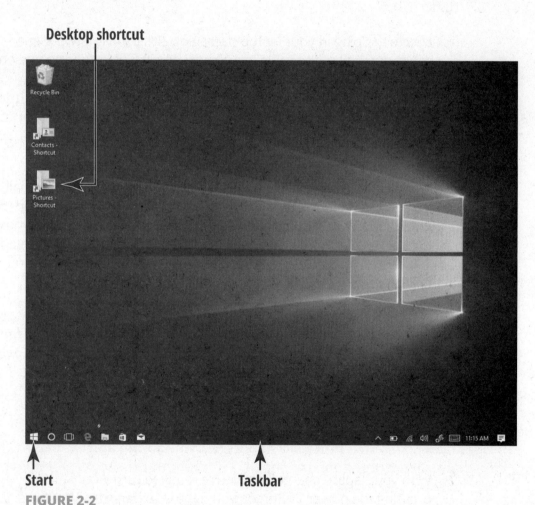

Start   **Taskbar**

FIGURE 2-2

Windows includes a feature called Windows Hello, which allows your computer to take advantage of facial recognition technology. Simply by sitting in front of your computer, you're signed in — in effect, using your face as your password. This feature is currently available only on a limited number of computer models. If you have such a model, you can set up Windows Hello by choosing Accounts in the Settings window and clicking Sign-in Options.

Use the Mouse

Unlike using a typewriter, which sports only a keyboard to enter text into documents, with a non-touchscreen computer, you use both a keyboard and a mouse to enter text and send commands to the computer. On a laptop, the mouse device is in the form of a touchpad, a flat rectangle beneath the keyboard that you maneuver by tapping or sliding your forefinger.

Though you might have used a keyboard before, a mouse might be new to you, and frankly, it takes a little getting used to. (If you know how to use a mouse, just skip this task and move on!) In effect, when you move your finger on the touchpad, a corresponding mouse pointer (a small arrow symbol) moves around your computer screen. You control the actions of that pointer by using the right and left side of the touchpad.

TIP

Can't get the hang of your touchpad? Many users of laptops like to use a wireless mouse instead of the touchpad to provide input to their computers. With a wireless mouse, you move the physical mouse around your desktop with your hand and click the right or left side to perform. There is typically a scroll wheel in the middle of a wireless mouse you can use to scroll through a document. You can buy a wireless mouse at any office supply store, plug the small transmitter into a USB port of your laptop, and then use the mouse instead of the touchpad. Throughout this book, when I say mouse, you can assume that either your built-in touchpad or a wireless mouse will work with the steps provided.

Here are the main functions of a mouse and how to control them:

» **Click:** When people say "click," they mean that you should move your mouse pointer over the command or item you want to select or activate and press and release the left side of the touchpad.

Clicking has a variety of uses. You can click while you're in a document to move the *insertion point,* a little line that indicates where your next action will take place. For example, in a letter you're writing, you might click in front of a word you already typed and then type another word to insert it into the sentence. Clicking is also used in various windows to select check boxes or radio buttons (also called *option buttons*) to turn features on or off, to choose a command in a menu, or to select an object such as a picture or table in your document.

» **Right-click:** If you click the right side of the touchpad, Windows displays a shortcut menu that's specific to the item you clicked. For example, if you right-click a picture, the menu that appears gives you options for working with the picture. If you right-click the Windows desktop, the menu that appears lets you choose commands that display a different view or change desktop properties.

» **Click and drag:** To click and drag, you move your mouse pointer over an item on the screen, press and continue to hold down the left side of the touchpad, and then move your finger to another location (this is the dragging motion). For instance, you can click in a document and drag your finger up, down, right, or left to highlight contents of your document. This highlighted text is *selected,* meaning that any action you perform, such as pressing the Delete key on your keyboard or clicking a button for bold formatting, is performed on the selected text. In another example, if you click a file in the File Explorer window (see Chapter 3), you can drag it to another location on your computer.

» **Scroll:** Many touchpads allow you to swipe down the right side with your finger to scroll through a document or website on your screen. Just swipe down to move through pages going forward, or swipe up to move backward in your document.

Work with a Touchscreen

Windows 10 was designed to work with a touchscreen computer, though not all computers include a touchscreen feature.

If you do own a touchscreen laptop, placing and moving your finger on the screen replaces the movement of a mouse. You can tap the screen to select something, to activate features with buttons, and to make a field active so you can enter content. Windows 10 also offers an onscreen keyboard that touchscreen users can work with to enter text with the tap of a finger.

You can also use your finger to swipe to the right, left, up, or down to move from one item to another (for example, from one web page to another, one page to another in an e-reader, or from one photo to the next in the Photos app) or to move up or down on a page.

Windows 10 also offers some gestures you can make with your fingers, such as moving your fingers apart and then pinching them together to minimize (shrink) elements on your screen, or swiping down from the top of the screen to close an app.

Use Shortcuts

A *keyboard shortcut* refers to a key or combination of keys that you press and hold to perform an action. Many shortcuts involve the Windows key (the key near the bottom-left corner of your keyboard that sports the Windows logo). For example, you can press and hold the Windows key plus A (Win+A) to display the Action Center.

In Windows 10, keyboard shortcuts can be very helpful to those who don't have a touchscreen computer. Table 2-1 lists some handy shortcuts to know.

TABLE 2-1 **Common Windows 10 Keyboard Shortcuts**

Key(s)	Results
Windows key	Displays the Start menu
Win+S	Opens Cortana
Win+X	Displays the desktop menu
Win+C	Opens Cortana in Listening mode
Win+L	Displays the Lock Screen
Win+A	Displays the Action Center
Win+E	Displays File Explorer
Win+I	Displays the Settings window
Win+Tab	Displays Task View

Use the Function Keys

On a laptop computer, you might find that in order to save space, some shortcut functions, such as muting sound or brightening your screen, are accessible by using function keys. Here are the basics of function keys:

» Function keys run across the top of your laptop keyboard, labeled F1, F2, and so on.

» You'll find a key labeled Fn (for Function) near the bottom of your keyboard.

» By pressing and holding down the Function key (Fn) and a numbered function key (F1, for example), you can perform actions such as controlling your built-in speaker's volume.

» The functions assigned to your laptop's keys vary depending on the model and manufacturer. Check your user's manual to find out the specific functions assigned to your keyboard.

TIP

You'll typically find small icons on your function keys that give you a clue about what the keys do. For example, pressing both the function key that has a little light bulb icon and the up arrow key will brighten your screen. Pressing a function key with double, right-pointing arrows (like those you see on a music player) may move you to the next track in an audio file.

Set the Date and Time

1. The calendar and clock on your computer keep good time, but if you travel, for example, you might have to provide the correct date and time for your current location. Click the Start button and then click Settings.

2. Click Time & Language in the Settings window that appears, as shown in Figure 2-3.

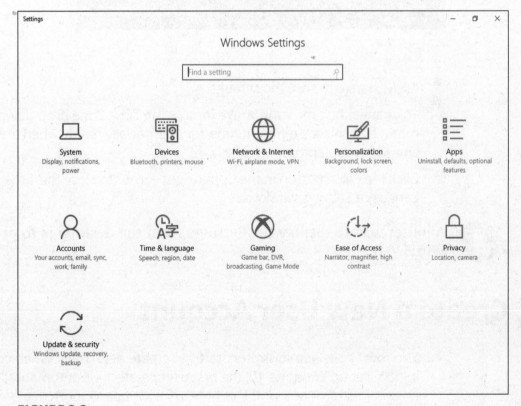

FIGURE 2-3

3. In the Time & Language screen, set the Set Time Automatically toggle to Off, and then click the Change button under Change Date and Time.

4. In the Change Date and Time screen (see Figure 2-4), with Date & Time selected in the left panel, use the various drop-down fields to make different selections. For example, click the year field and choose a different year.

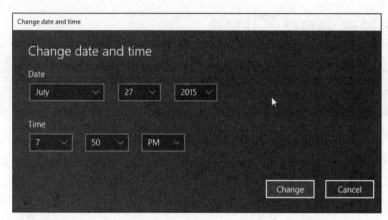

FIGURE 2-4

5. Click Change to save the settings.

6. To change the time zone you're in, click the Time Zone drop-down menu and select a different time zone, especially handy when travelling with your laptop.

7. Click the Close button in the upper-right corner to close the Time & Language Settings window.

 Another way to display the Settings from the desktop is to press Win+I.

TIP

Create a New User Account

1. You must have administrator status to create new users. When you initially set up Windows 10, the first user created will automatically be an administrator account. This time, try a keyboard shortcut to get to the Settings window. Press Win+I.

2. Click Accounts.

3. In the Accounts screen shown in Figure 2-5, click Family & Other People and then click the Add Someone Else to this PC button (it has a plus sign on it).

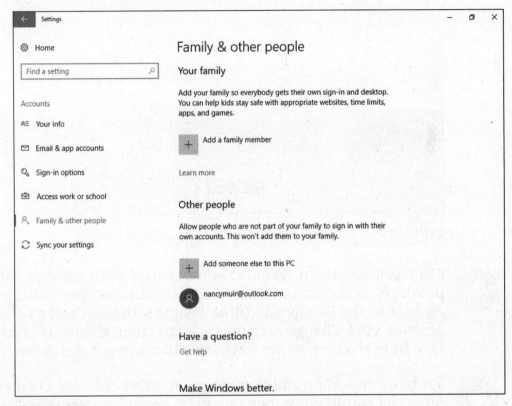

FIGURE 2-5

TIP

If the new user is a child, click Add a Family Member in Step 3 and then in the Add a Child or Adult window select Add a Child. This turns on Family Safety features and allows you to make safety settings.

4. In the resulting window, shown in Figure 2-6, enter a Microsoft email address. Note that if you don't know the person's email address, you can click the I Don't Have This Person's Sign-in Information link to create a new account. Click Next.

5. In the Good to Go dialog box, click Finish.

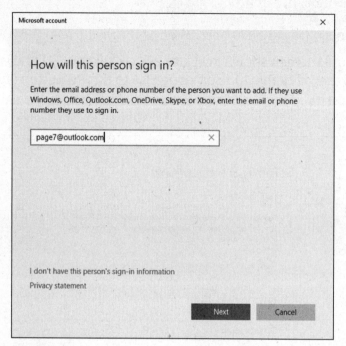

Microsoft account   ✕

How will this person sign in?

Enter the email address or phone number of the person you want to add. If they use Windows, Office, Outlook.com, OneDrive, Skype, or Xbox, enter the email or phone number they use to sign in.

page7@outlook.com   ✕

I don't have this person's sign-in information

Privacy statement

Next   Cancel

FIGURE 2-6

After you create an account, when a user with administrative privileges is logged in, he or she can make changes to the user account in the Family and Other People settings. Click on a user Account, click Change Account Type, and then choose an account type from the drop-down list in the Edit Account dialog box.

TIP

For more on adding and changing user passwords, see Chapter 22. After you set up more than one user, before you get to the password screen, you have to click the icon for the user you wish to log on as.

TIP

If you prefer, you can log in with a four-digit PIN in place of a traditional password. This makes it quicker to sign in. When you've logged in as the user for which you want to set a PIN, go to the Accounts settings shown in Figure 2-5 and click Sign-in Options; then, in the PIN section, click the Add button.

TIP

You can set up several user accounts for your computer, which helps you save and access specific user settings and provides privacy for each user's files with passwords.

Switch User Accounts

1. To change to another user account after you've logged in, you can press Win+L to go to the Windows lock screen.

2. Click anywhere to display the sign-in screen.

3. Click the username you want to log in as, type the password or PIN, and you're taken to the Windows desktop.

Shut Down Your Laptop

1. With a Windows 10 laptop, you can simply close the lid to put the computer to sleep, saving power and returning you to where you left off when you open the lid and sign in again. To turn off your laptop completely, you need to initiate a shutdown sequence in your operating system instead of simply turning off the power with the power button on your computer. Click the Start button.

2. Click the Power button (see Figure 2-7). If you prefer to stop your computer running but not turn the power off, click Sleep (or simply close the lid of your laptop). If you want to reboot (turn off and turn back on) your computer, choose Restart. To shut off the power, click Shut Down.

If your laptop freezes up for some reason, you can try resetting it by turning it off and then back on after a minute or so. To shut down a frozen laptop press the power button on your laptop and hold it until the computer powers off.

Power button

FIGURE 2-7

Chapter **3**

Getting Around Windows 10

Windows 10 was released a few years ago, and since then it has experienced two major upgrades: Windows Anniversary Update and Windows Creator Update. With Windows 10, you get sophisticated tools for searching, organizing apps, and making settings. The Anniversary Update modified the interface with a reorganized Start menu and the Creators Update provided some useful graphics tools such as Paint 3-D.

In this chapter, you discover the basics of getting around Windows 10, using such features as the Start menu, desktop shortcuts, and the taskbar. This chapter shows you how to find and open apps with File Explorer and how to interact with a touchscreen computer. I'll also provide an overview of some very practical features, such as the Action Center for receiving notifications and accessing settings; and Cortana, a personal assistant and search feature that you can use to find information, open apps, or even identify music.

Get an Overview of Windows 10

One cool feature of Windows 10 is how it's been enhanced for those who have touchscreen-enabled laptops. In fact, you could use a laptop without a mouse and keyboard for the most part, if you have a touchscreen machine (though you can still use a mouse and keyboard to get anything done).

Windows 10 focuses on a desktop as its home base (see Figure 3-1). This is where windows will appear when you open apps or settings and where you can place desktop shortcuts to frequently used apps.

In addition, the desktop contains a taskbar along the bottom that offers several tools for working with Windows settings and apps. Three items on the taskbar are noteworthy as new to Windows 10:

> » **Cortana:** This personal assistant is a sophisticated search feature that can return results from a web search, a search of your laptop contents, and even apps, such as Calendar or Maps. You can also ask Cortana to take actions, such as sending an email, setting an appointment, or texting somebody. You can interact with Cortana by entering text or using spoken commands.

Desktop shortcuts   **Open app window**

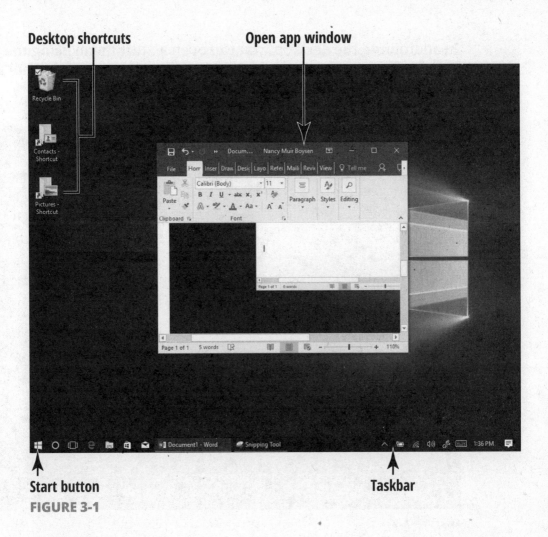

Start button   **Taskbar**

FIGURE 3-1

» **Task View:** This view shows you all open apps on your desktop
and switches between them. It even allows you to create and
view multiple desktops. For example, you might have one desktop with all your work apps open and one with all your games
and entertainment apps displayed.

» **Action Center:** This pane provides a list of notifications about
items, such as new emails or appointment reminders, and buttons for various settings, such as screen brightness and network
connections.

In addition to the desktop, you can open a Start menu using the Start button. This menu, shown in Figure 3-2, provides access to all apps, shut down options, and Settings.

FIGURE 3-2

Work with the Desktop

The desktop is your home base in Windows; from there you can get to everything Windows has to offer, as well as installed applications and the Internet. Figure 3-3 shows the desktop and some of the elements on it, including the following:

» The **taskbar** displays frequently used applications, such as Microsoft Edge (a web browser) and File Explorer (an app used to browse files and folders on your computer). The taskbar displays currently open apps; you can click an icon to switch apps.

» The right end of the taskbar, which is called the **notification area,** contains many commonly used functions, such as the Action Center button, computer date and time settings, the network settings icon, and the icon to control system volume. You can click the Show Hidden Icons button here to display more options.

» The left end of the taskbar contains the Start button, Cortana's search field, and the Task View button.

» The **Recycle Bin,** located on the desktop, holds recently deleted items. It will empty itself when it reaches its maximum size (which you can modify by right-clicking the Recycle Bin and choosing Properties), or you will empty it manually. Check out the task "Empty the Recycle Bin" later in this chapter for more about this.

» **Desktop shortcuts** are icons that reside on the desktop and provide a shortcut to opening a software program or file, functioning much like tiles on the Start menu. Double-click a desktop shortcut to launch the associated program. Your laptop usually comes with some shortcuts, such as the Recycle Bin and a browser shortcut, but you can also add or delete shortcuts. See the "Create a Desktop Shortcut" task later in this chapter.

TIP

Laptop users should pay attention to the Power icon on the taskbar. This icon indicates if your laptop is plugged in or running on battery. If you're running on battery power, the icon shows how much charge you have left. See Chapter 4 for more about power management.

The desktop is always there behind the scenes as you open windows containing apps or settings to get your work done. If you make an app window as big as it can be (maximize it by clicking the Maximize button in the top-right corner, to the left of the Close button), you won't see the desktop, but you can go back to the desktop at any time by shrinking a window (minimizing it by clicking the Minimize button in the top-right corner) or closing the window (clicking the X button in the top-right corner). You can also press Alt+Tab simultaneously to display the desktop and all open apps as icons side-by-side.

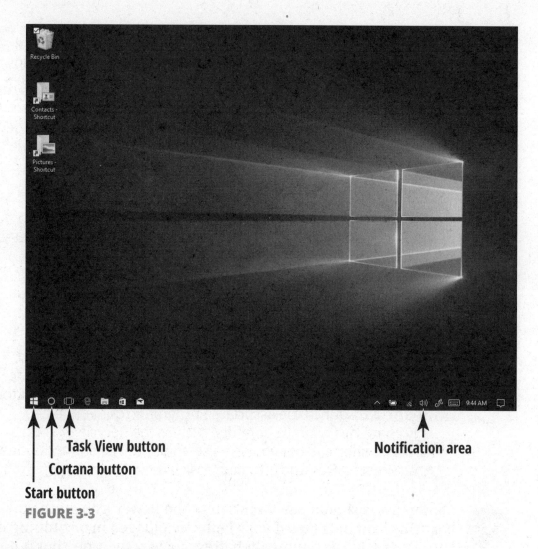

Task View button

Cortana button

Start button

Notification area

FIGURE 3-3

Display the Start Menu

1. The Start menu provides access to all the installed apps and many of the settings for your laptop. Click the Start button in the bottom-left corner of the desktop to display the Start menu (see Figure 3-4).

2. Click on an App, either in the list of Most Used Apps or the alphabetical list of all Apps on the left of the Start menu or by clicking one of the tiles on the right to open an app. The app opens.

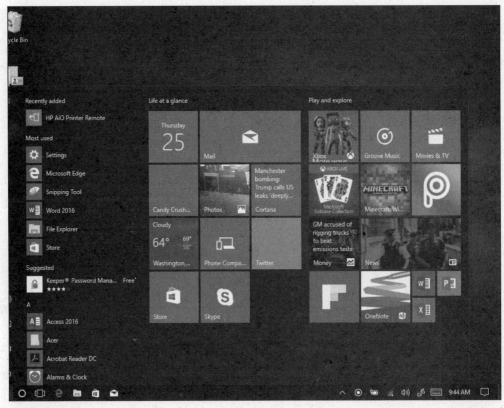

FIGURE 3-4

Use Task View to See Open Apps

1. Task View allows you to move among open apps easily and create multiple desktops. Click the Task View button to open Task View. The resulting view (see Figure 3-5) shows individual desktops on the bottom and all the open apps on the currently selected desktop.

TIP

You can also open Task View by pressing Win+Tab.

2. Click any of the apps shown in Task View to work in that app.

3. When you want to switch to another open app, click the Task View button, then click the app that you want to display on the desktop.

FIGURE 3-5

 TIP You can also switch to another open app from the desktop by holding down the Alt key and pressing Tab repeatedly until the desired app is highlighted. Release the keys to work in the high-lighted app.

Use the Snap Feature to Organize Apps on the Desktop

1. Windows 10 has a feature called Snap used to organize open apps on the desktop. Click on the Task View button and then click on an app you want to work with.

2. Right-click an app window and then select Snap Left or Snap Right. The window snaps to the selected half of the screen and thumbnail images of any other open apps appear on the other half of the screen (see Figure 3-6).

3. Click another open app; the app window snaps to fill the other side of the screen (see Figure 3-7).

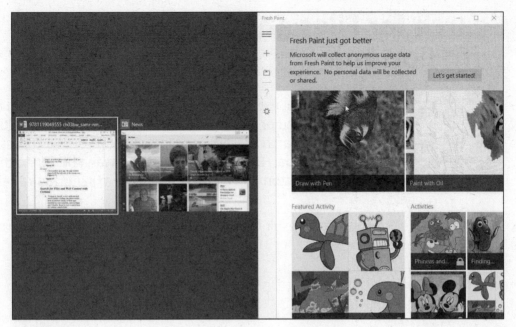

FIGURE 3-6

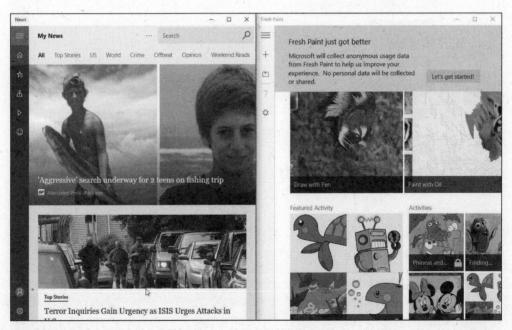

FIGURE 3-7

Search for Files and Web Content with Cortana

1. Cortana is, to a great extent, a very sophisticated search feature that can respond to typed or spoken input. Cortana can return results from an Internet search or from apps installed on your laptop, such as Maps and Calendar. Begin by clicking the Cortana button to the right of the Start button and typing a search term in Cortana's search field.

2. Click a suggested result to view an item related to the search term (see Figure 3-8).

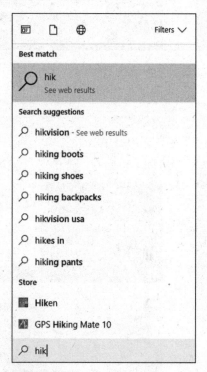

FIGURE 3-8

See Chapter 8 to discover how Cortana can provide help and for more about searching using Cortana, including interacting with the feature using speech.

TIP

Explore the Action Center

1. The Action Center contains notifications of events, such as appointment reminders and required system updates. On the taskbar, click the Action Center button.

2. In the resulting Action Center pane (shown in Figure 3-9) read any notifications near the top of the pane.

3. Click one of the Quick Action buttons near the bottom of the screen. The Quick Action buttons have the following types of functionality:

- *Click a Quick Action button* such as Tablet Mode, Wi-Fi, Bluetooth, Battery Saver, Location, Rotation Lock, or Airplane Mode to turn a feature on or off.

- *Click Brightness* to raise or lower the brightness level.

- *Click a Quick Action button* such as All Settings, Project, or VPN to work with more settings in that category.

FIGURE 3-9

Find a File or Open an Application with File Explorer

1. File Explorer is a program you can use to find a file or folder by navigating through an outline of folders and subfolders. Each folder can contain any number of files. It's a great way to look for files on your laptop. From the desktop, click the File Explorer button on the taskbar (it looks like a set of folders).

2. In the resulting File Explorer window (shown in Figure 3-10), double-click a folder in the main window or in the list along the left side to open the folder.

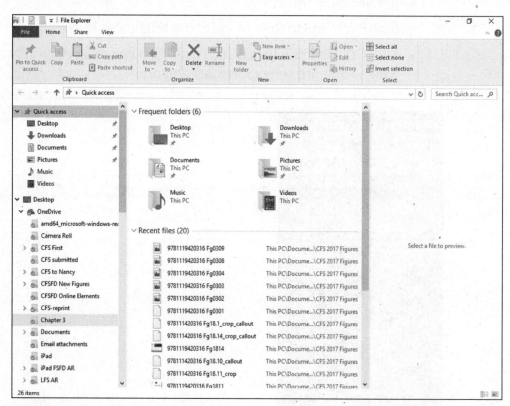

FIGURE 3-10

3. The folder's contents are displayed. If necessary, open a series of folders in this manner until you locate the file you want.

4. When you find the file you want, double-click it to open it.

TIP

To see different perspectives and information about files in File Explorer, click the View tab and choose one of the following options: Extra Large Icons, Large Icons, Medium Icons, or Small Icons for graphical displays, or choose Details to show details such as the last date files were modified.

Work with Windows 10 Using a Touchscreen

If you have a touchscreen device, either a laptop or tablet, you'll be glad to hear that Windows 10 is designed to be used with a touch-screen. Table 3-1 lists several of the ways you can interact with your touchscreen computing device.

TABLE 3-1 **Touchscreen Gestures for Windows 10**

Gesture	Result
Swipe up or down	Move up or down on a web page
Swipe left or right	Move to the right or left to reveal additional content that extends beyond the screen in Windows or an app
Swipe the right edge of the screen	Display the Action Center
Pinch to zoom in or out	Zoom in or out on a page
Tap	Select an item
Right-click	Hold the screen until a small pop-up appears and then lift your finger to reveal the context-specific menu
Swipe the left edge of the screen	Open Task View

TIP

If you are using a 2-in-1 laptop that allows you to remove the monitor from the keyboard, a pop-up message will ask if you want to enter Tablet mode. Click this pop-up, and apps and the Start menu will be displayed full screen to make them more usable on the tablet. If you want to use this mode on a standard laptop, you can click the Tablet Mode Quick Action button in Action Center to do so.

Create Additional Desktops

1. If the work you do on your laptop requires different sets of apps, you'll be glad to hear that you can create different desktops. For example, you might want one desktop containing financial apps and calculators, and another that contains the Music app, an online radio app, and iTunes. To create multiple desktops, click the New Desktop button, which looks like a + symbol in the lower-right corner of the Task View.

2. In the resulting window (see Figure 3-11), you see thumbnails on the bottom of the window representing each Desktop. Click the desktop you just created and then open the apps you want to appear in the new desktop (you can use the list of apps in the Start menu to do this).

FIGURE 3-11

TIP

To return to another Desktop, click the Task View button and then click the desired Desktop button.

TIP

Task View displays a button for each Desktop you create. If there are more than six desktops, you can use right and left arrows, as shown in Figure 3-12, to scroll through the Desktop thumbnails until you find the desktop you want. If you want to close a Desktop, hover over the thumbnail of the Desktop you want to close, and then click the Close button that appears.

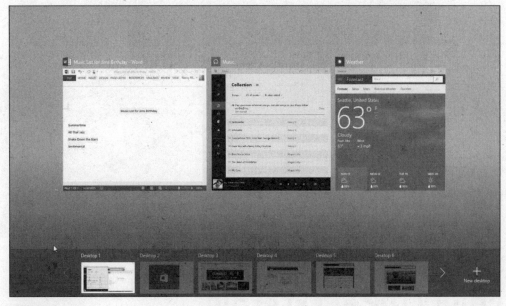

FIGURE 3-12

View All Apps in the Start Menu

1. Click the Start button to open the Start menu (shown in Figure 3-13).

2. Scroll to find an app in the alphabetical list of all apps installed on your laptop shown on the left side of the Start menu.

3. Click an app and click to open it.

TIP

Some items in the Apps list, for example Windows Accessories, have a downward arrow next to them, indicating that there are multiple apps in that category. Click the arrow to view the apps.

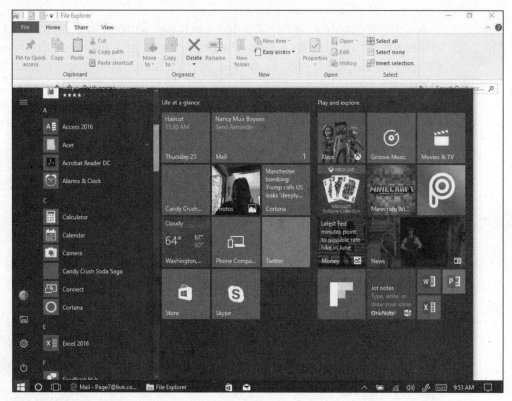

FIGURE 3-13

Empty the Recycle Bin

1. When you throw away junk mail, it's still in the house — it's just in the wastebasket instead of on your desk. That's the idea behind the Windows Recycle Bin. Your old files sit there, and you can retrieve them until you empty it — or until it reaches its size limit and Windows dumps a few files. Right-click the Recycle Bin icon on the Windows desktop and choose Empty Recycle Bin from the menu that appears (see Figure 3-14).

2. In the confirmation dialog box that appears (see Figure 3-15), click Yes. A progress dialog box appears, indicating the contents are being deleted. *Remember:* After you empty the Recycle Bin, all files that were in it are unavailable to you.

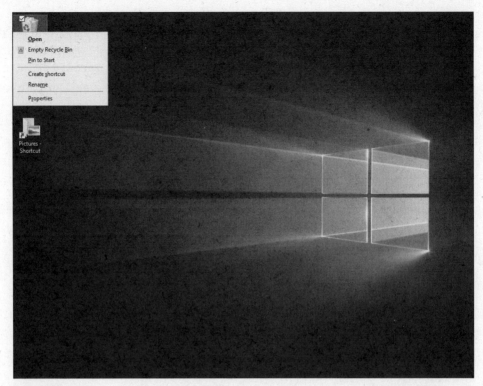

FIGURE 3-14

TIP

Up until the moment you permanently delete items by performing the preceding steps, you can retrieve them from the Recycle Bin by double-clicking the Recycle Bin desktop icon. Select the item you want to retrieve and then click the Restore the Selected Items link on the Manage tab of the Recycle Bin ribbon.

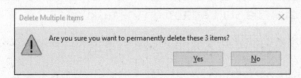

FIGURE 3-15

TIP

You can modify the Recycle Bin properties by right-clicking it and choosing Properties. In the dialog box that appears, you can change the maximum size for the Recycle Bin and whether to immediately delete files you move to the Recycle Bin. You can also deselect the option of having a confirmation dialog box appear when you delete Recycle Bin contents.

Add an App to the Start Menu

1. Click the Start button.

2. Scroll to an app and right-click it.

3. In the menu that appears (see Figure 3-16), click Pin to Start. A tile representing the app appears in the tile region of the Start menu.

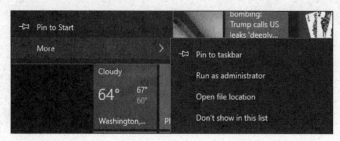

FIGURE 3-16

Create a Desktop Shortcut

1. Shortcuts are handy little icons you can put on the desktop for quick access to items you use on a frequent basis. (See the earlier task, "Work with the Desktop," for an introduction to shortcuts.) To create a new shortcut, first click the Start button on the taskbar.

2. Locate an app and then click and drag it to the desktop, as shown in Figure 3-17.

3. Click and drag the shortcut that appears to the preferred location on the desktop. Double-click the icon to open the app.

TIP

You can create a shortcut for a brand-new item by right-clicking the desktop, clicking New, and then clicking Shortcut. A dialog box opens that allows you to select an item to place there, such as a text document, an image, or a folder. Then double-click the shortcut that appears to open the item.

FIGURE 3-17

Resize Windows

1. When you open an application window, it can be maximized to fill the whole screen, restored down to a smaller window, or minimized to an icon on the taskbar. With an application open and maximized, click the Restore Down button (the icon showing two overlapping windows) in the top-right corner of the program window (see Figure 3-18). The window reduces in size.

Restore Down button

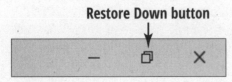

FIGURE 3-18

2. To enlarge a window that has been restored down to fill the screen, click the Maximize button. (**Note:** This button is in the same location as the Restore Down button; this button changes its name to one or the other, depending on whether you have the screen reduced in size or maximized. For many apps, a ScreenTip identifies the button when you rest your mouse pointer on it.)

3. Click the Minimize button (it's to the left of the Restore Down/ Maximize button and looks like a dash or underline) to minimize the window to an icon on the taskbar. To open the window again, just click the taskbar icon.

TIP

With a window maximized, you can't move the window. If you reduce a window in size, you can then click and hold the title bar to drag the window around the desktop, which is one way to view more than one window on your screen at the same time. You can also click and drag the corners of a reduced window to resize it to any size you want.

IN THIS CHAPTER

» **Changing how quickly the computer goes to sleep**

» **Changing how quickly the display is turned off**

» **Changing the display brightness**

» **Adjusting the Battery Saver**

» **Choosing a power plan**

» **Creating a customized power plan**

» **Defining Power button functions**

Chapter **4**

Managing Power

O ne of the big differences between a desktop computer and your laptop is that your laptop can run off of a battery as well as a wall outlet. *Battery life,* or the length of time it takes your laptop battery to run out of juice, is getting better all the time — some recent laptop batteries get as many as 12 hours on one charge. One comparison by *Laptop Magazine* found a few models that stayed the course for as many as 20 hours. (Consider avoiding laptops that get as little as a couple of hours of battery life.)

For that reason, it's important that you understand some tools that Windows 10 provides to help you manage your laptop power so you can take a day trip or survive a power outage, including these:

» Adjusting settings for your display that deal with the screen brightness (a brighter screen uses more power), how frequently your screen automatically dims to save battery charge, and so on.

» Changing how much time lapses before your laptop automatically goes to sleep — a state that uses minimal power but keeps the currently open documents and programs active (and, therefore, quickly available to you).

» Choosing a *power plan,* which has preset timings for actions such as dimming your screen or putting your computer to sleep.

» Creating a customized power plan by choosing settings you want.

» Defining power button functionality gives you some control over what happens when you press the laptop's power button or close the lid.

TIP

If you're happy to accept predetermined power settings, I suggest you just skip the first few tasks in the chapter and go straight to the later task, "Choose a Power Plan."

Change How Quickly the Computer Goes to Sleep

1. After a certain period of inactivity, which you can specify, your computer goes to sleep, turning the screen to black and thereby saving battery power. Click the Start button and then click Settings ➪ System ➪ Power & Sleep. The window shown in Figure 4-1 appears.

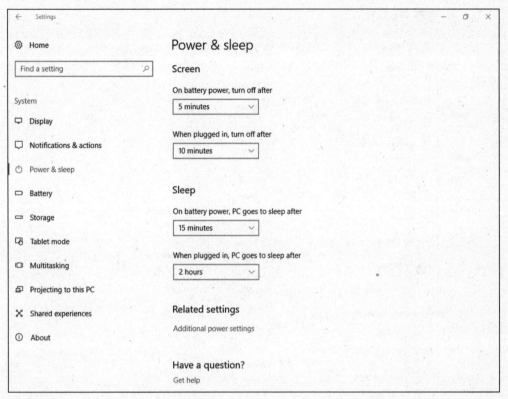

FIGURE 4-1

2. In the Sleep settings, click the arrow in the field labeled On Battery Power, PC Goes to Sleep After.

3. From the drop-down list (see Figure 4-2), select a setting for when the computer automatically puts itself to sleep. A smaller interval saves battery power, but it might disrupt your work. Choose a setting according to your preferences.

4. Click the Close button in the upper-right corner to close the window.

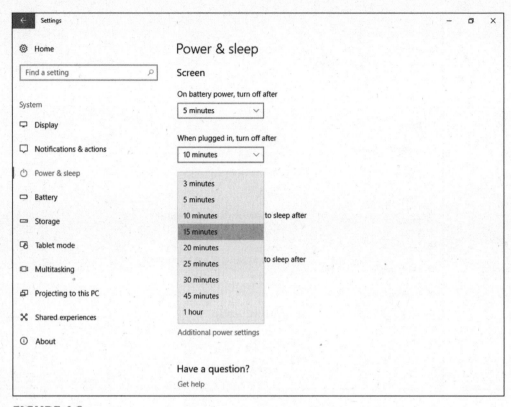

FIGURE 4-2

Change How Quickly the Display is Turned Off

1. You can also set up an interval of inactivity, after which the display is turned off. Click the Start button and then click Settings ⇨ System ⇨ Power & Sleep.

2. Under Screen settings (see Figure 4-3), click the arrow in the On Battery Power, Turn Off After field.

3. From the drop-down list, select a setting for when the computer automatically turns the display off. A smaller interval saves battery power.

4. Click the Close button to close the window.

Click here

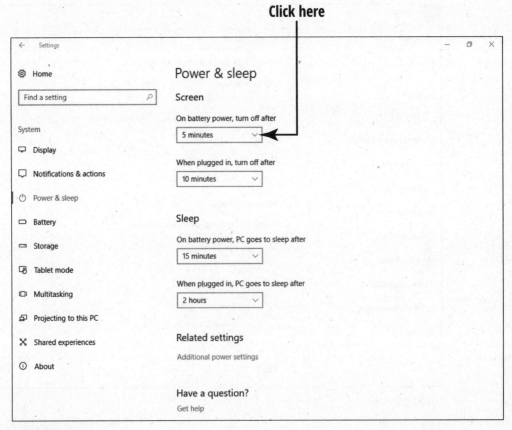

FIGURE 4-3

Change the Display Brightness

1. Click the Start button and then click Settings ⇨ System ⇨ Display.

2. In the resulting window (see Figure 4-4), click and drag the Brightness Level slider to make the screen brighter or dimmer. A dimmer screen saves battery power, but too dim a screen could be hard on your eyes.

3. Click the Close button to close the window.

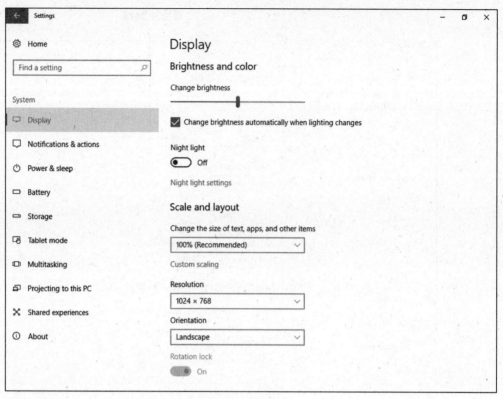

FIGURE 4-4

Adjust the Battery Saver

1. If you know battery charging will not be available for several hours, you can adjust the Battery Saver mode. This setting extends battery life by limiting background activity. In the Start menu, click Settings ➪ System ➪ Battery.

2. In the resulting window (see Figure 4-5), click the Battery Saver slider and move it down to save more battery power (for example, to 20%).

3. Click the Close button to close the window.

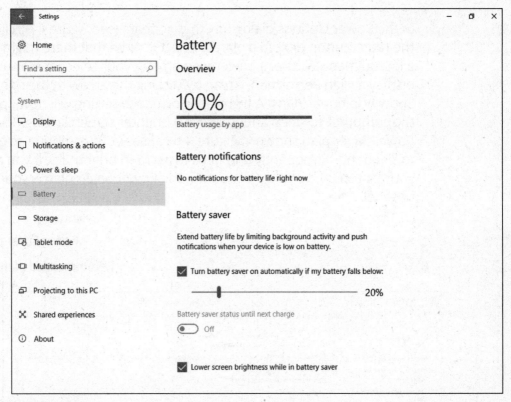

FIGURE 4-5

TIP

A new feature called Power Throttling helps when you're running multiple applications. Power Throttling senses the active app and uses the most efficient power mode to apps running in the background. With its introduction, this feature only works with Intel sixth-generation core processors, but should work with more processors in the future.

Choose a Power Plan

1. From the Start menu, click Settings.

2. In the Settings window that appears, click System ⇨ Power & Sleep ⇨ Additional Power Settings.

3. In the Power Options dialog box that appears (see Figure 4-6), click the radio button next to a plan to select it. Note that there might be a laptop manufacturer's power plan among your selections. You can display a High Performance plan by clicking the arrow to the right of Show Additional Plans. A higher-performance setting will never put the computer to sleep and will have a brighter screen setting. The Power Saver plan shown in Figure 4-6 causes your computer to go to sleep more frequently and dims the screen brightness. If you run your laptop on a battery frequently, the Power Saver plan is your best bet.

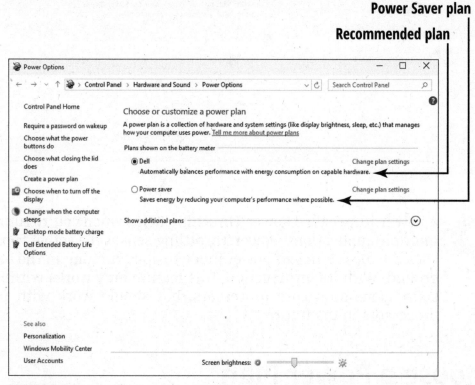

Power Saver plan

Recommended plan

FIGURE 4-6

4. Click the Close button to close the dialog box.

Create a Customized Power Plan

1. If the preset power plans don't appeal to you, you can modify one and save it as your own customized power plan. In the Start menu, click Settings ➪ System ➪ Power & Sleep ➪ Additional Power Settings.

2. In the Power Options dialog box that appears, click the Create a Power Plan link on the left side.

3. In the Create a Power Plan dialog box that appears (shown in Figure 4-7), select the preset plan that is closest to what you want to create.

Select a power plan to customize...

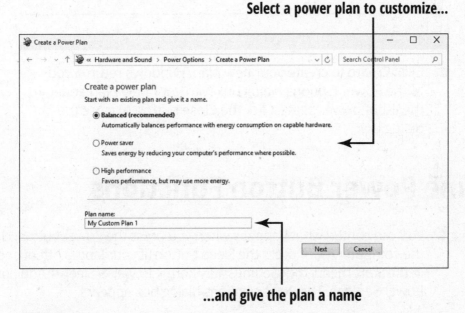

...and give the plan a name

FIGURE 4-7

4. Enter a name for the plan in the Plan Name text box and click Next.

5. In the Edit Plan Settings dialog box that appears (see Figure 4-8), make settings for how the laptop power functions when plugged in or running off the battery. (See the earlier tasks in this chapter for information about changing display settings and changing how quickly the computer goes to sleep.)

Make your plan settings here

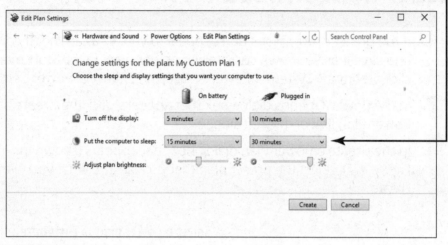

FIGURE 4-8

6. Click Create to create your new plan. Windows returns you to the Power Options dialog box with your new plan added to the list of power plans. Click the Close button to close the dialog box.

Define Power Button Functions

1. You can control what happens when you press the Power button, close the computer lid, or press the Sleep button (if your laptop offers one). In the Start menu, click Settings ⇨ System ⇨ Power & Sleep ⇨ Additional Power Settings. The Power Options dialog box appears.

2. In the Power Options dialog box, click the Choose What the Power Buttons Do link.

3. In the System Settings dialog box that appears (see Figure 4-9), click the When I Press the Power Button or When I Close the Lid drop-down lists in the On Battery column. The options that appear include

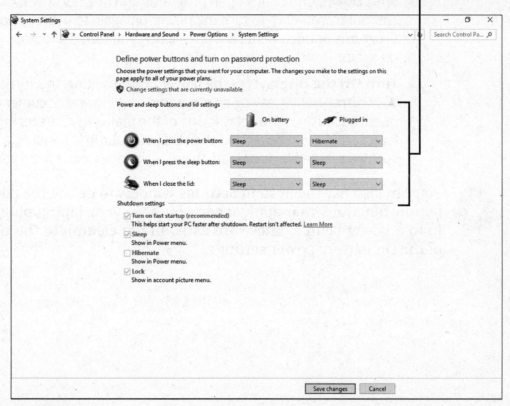

FIGURE 4-9

- **Do Nothing:** Does nothing. You guessed that, right?

- **Sleep:** Essentially pauses your computer, leaving your open programs and documents intact, held in your computer memory. When you awaken your computer, it comes back almost immediately, ready for you to work. Sleep draws a small amount of power.

- **Hibernate:** Saves open programs and documents on your computer hard drive and then turns off your computer so you're not using any power. If you'll be away from your computer for a while but want to return to the items you had opened before quickly, Hibernate is a good choice. Hibernate is usually the default action when you close a laptop lid. Hibernate requires you to log on again when you revive your computer by pressing Enter, clicking the power button, or using your mouse.

- **Shut Down:** Closes any open programs and powers down your computer. You have to turn the power on again to use it — no programs or documents are open when you turn the laptop on again.

- **Turn Off the Display:** For the power button setting, this turns off your display while leaving all programs running and documents open. Because your display is one of the main power users in your laptop, this could be a good choice if your laptop is handling a task, such as a large file download, that doesn't need input from you.

TIP

You can also use the System Settings window to define the power button functions that apply when you have your laptop plugged in to a power source. These are listed in the column to the right of the On Battery power settings.

Chapter **5**

Setting Up Your Display

You chose your silver picture frame, paper clip holder, and solid maple inbox for your real-world desktop, right? Why shouldn't the Windows desktop give you the same flexibility to make things look the way you like? After all, this is the main work area of Windows, space that you traverse many, many times in a typical day. Take it from somebody who spends many hours in front of a computer: Customizing your laptop interface pays off in increased productivity as well as decreased eyestrain.

You can modify tiles in the Start menu to rearrange them, resize them, or create tile groups. In addition, the desktop offers several customization options. To customize the desktop, you can do the following:

» Set up the desktop and lock screen to display background images.

» Use screen saver settings to switch to a pretty animation when you've stopped working for a time.

» Change the background color and choose a Light or Dark mode to help you more easily view things onscreen.

» Modify your *screen resolution* setting, which controls the visual crispness of the images your screen displays. (See Chapter 6 for more about resolution settings that help those with visual challenges.)

Customize the Appearance of Windows

When you take your laptop out of the box, Windows comes with certain preset, or default, settings such as the appearance of the desktop and a color scheme for items you see on your screen. Here are some of the things you can change about the Windows environment and why you might want to change them:

» **Desktop and lock screen backgrounds:** As you work with your laptop, you might find that changing the appearance of various elements on your screen not only makes them more pleasant to look at, but also helps you see the text and images more easily. You can change the graphic that's shown as the desktop background, even displaying your own picture there, and choose from a collection of background images for your lock screen.

» **Screen resolution:** You can adjust your screen resolution to not only affect the crispness of images on your screen but also cause the items on your screen to appear larger, which could help you if you have visual challenges. (See Chapter 6 for more about Windows features that help people with visual, hearing, or dexterity challenges.)

» **Themes:** Windows has built-in desktop *themes* that you can apply quickly. Themes save sets of elements that include menu appearance, background colors or patterns, screen savers, and even mouse cursors and system sounds. If you choose a theme and then modify the way your laptop looks in some way — for example, by changing the color scheme — that change overrides the setting in the theme you last applied.

» **Screen savers:** These animations appear after your laptop remains inactive for a specified time. In the early days of personal computers, screen savers helped to keep monitors from burning out from constant use. Today, people use screen savers to automatically conceal what they're doing from passersby or just to enjoy the pretty picture when they take a break.

Set Your Screen's Resolution

1. Changing screen resolution can make items onscreen easier to see. Right-click the desktop.

2. In the menu that appears, click Display Settings.

3. In the resulting window, click Display on the left side.

4. In the resulting Display settings, click the Resolution drop-down list (as shown in Figure 5-1) and select a higher or lower resolution.

5. Click Apply to accept the new screen resolution. In the message that appears, click Keep Changes to accept the new screen resolution, and then click the Close button to close the window.

Higher resolutions, such as 1400 x 1250, produce smaller, crisper images. Lower resolutions, such as 800 x 600, produce larger, somewhat jagged images. The upside of higher resolution is that more fits on your screen; the downside is that words and graphics are smaller and can therefore be hard to see.

TIP

Remember that you can also use your View settings in most software programs to get a larger or smaller view of your documents without having to change your screen's resolution.

TIP

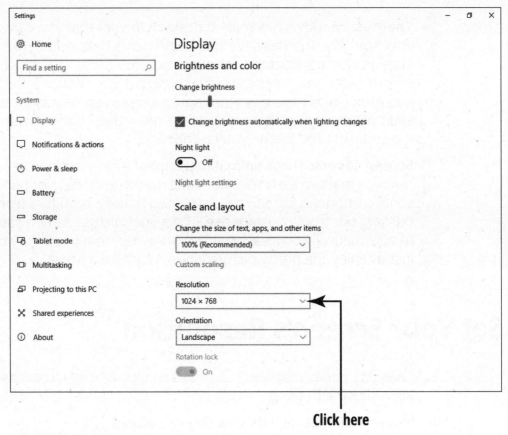

Click here

FIGURE 5-1

Change the Desktop Background and Color

1. Windows 10 offers several preset background patterns and color sets you can choose from the PC Settings. Right-click the desktop and then click Personalize in the menu that appears.

2. In the resulting Personalization window, shown in Figure 5-2, click Background in the left pane.

3. Click the Background drop-down list in the right pane (refer to Figure 5-2) and then click a category: Picture or Solid Color. If you want several images to run as a slideshow, choose Slideshow in this list.

4. Click a background image, picture, or solid color.

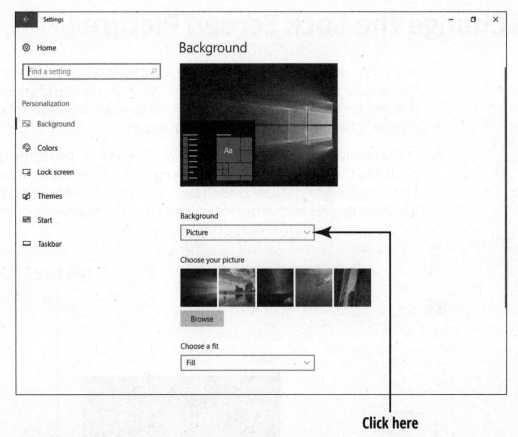

Click here

FIGURE 5-2

5. Click Colors on the left and then click an accent color for elements such as the Start menu, Action Center, or taskbar.

6. Scroll down and under Choose Your Default App Mode, click the Light or Dark setting. Light displays a white background with dark text, while Dark displays a black background with white text.

7. Click the Close button to close the window.

TIP

Some colors are easier on the eyes than others. For example, green is more restful to look at than purple. Choose a color scheme that's pleasant to look at and easy on the eyes!

TIP

You can also click the High Contrast Settings link under the Light/ Dark mode settings to choose high-contrast themes. These give you a few more choices for light and dark combinations.

Change the Lock Screen Picture

1. You can choose a Windows 10 picture for your lock screen (the screen that appears when your laptop goes to sleep) or use one of your own pictures for the lock screen background. Right-click the desktop and then click Personalize in the menu that appears.

2. In the resulting Personalization window, click Lock Screen in the left pane and then click the Background drop-down list in the right pane. Choose a category of background such as Picture (to choose from Windows images or choose one of your own) or Windows Spotlight for the preset Windows image (see Figure 5-3).

Click here...

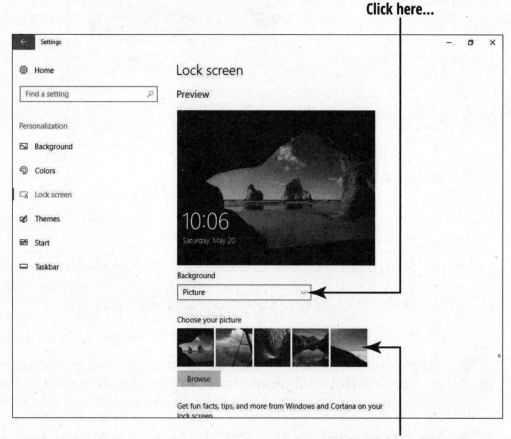

Then click on an image

FIGURE 5-3

3. Click one of the pictures displayed, or click Browse to choose another picture.

4. If you chose to browse for one of your own pictures, from the Pictures folder that's displayed click a picture to use. If the picture is located in another folder, click the Up To link to browse other folders.

5. Click the Choose Picture button.

TIP

You can also choose a few apps that you want to keep running when your lock screen appears. On the Lock Screen tab, scroll down to the Choose an App to Show Detailed Status section and then click the button displayed there. Click one of the apps in the list to display the apps that are available to display, such as Weather or Facebook.

Change Your Account Picture

Windows 10 allows you to assign a unique picture to each user account you create. When you perform these steps, you should be logged in as the user for whom you want to change the account picture; see Chapter 2 for more about this procedure.

1. Press the Start button and then click Settings.

2. Click Accounts. The accounts settings appear (see Figure 5-4).

    With your info selected in the left panel, at this point, you can do one of two things:

    • **Click the Browse for One button** under Create Your Picture and choose a picture from the files that appear (see Figure 5-5). Click the picture and then click the Choose Picture button to apply it to the active account.

    • **Click the Camera button** under Create Your Picture and in the Camera app that opens (see Figure 5-6) snap a picture of a person or object near your laptop's *webcam* (a built-in camera device). Click the Camera button to take the picture, and then click the Done button (shaped like a check mark) to apply it to the active account.

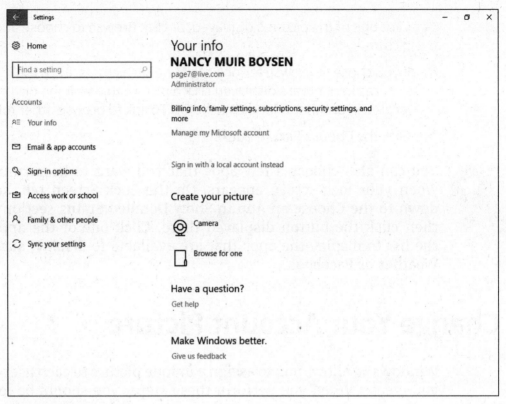

FIGURE 5-4

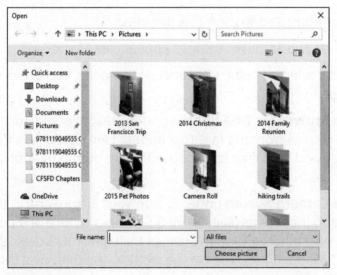

FIGURE 5-5

FIGURE 5-6

TIP

Many computers allow you to switch between a front- and a rear-facing camera to give you more options for taking pictures of objects around you. While in the Camera app, just click the Change Camera button to do this — if your laptop has two cameras.

Choose a Desktop Theme

1. Themes apply several color and image settings at once. Right-click the desktop and choose Personalize.

2. Click Themes in the left panel, as shown in Figure 5-7, and then click an item under Apply a Theme to select a theme.

3. You can also click an item such as Background or Color in the Current theme and use settings that appear to modify the current theme.

4. Click the Close button to close the dialog box.

Select a theme

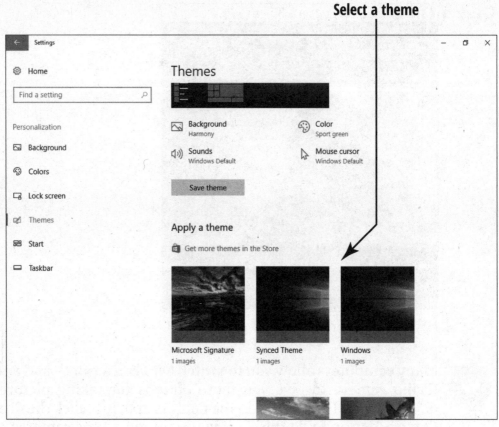

FIGURE 5-7

TIP

Themes save sets of elements including menu appearance, background colors or patterns, screen savers, and even mouse cursors and sounds. If you modify any of these individually — for example, by changing the screen saver to another one — that change overrides the setting in the theme you last applied.

TIP

You can get additional themes in the Windows Store. Click the Get More Themes in the Store link under the Apply a Theme heading to explore available themes, most of which are free.

Set Up a Screen Saver

1. If you want an animated sequence to appear when your laptop isn't in use for a period of time, set up a screen saver. Right-click the desktop and choose Personalize. In the resulting Personalization window, click Lock Screen in the left pane.

2. In the resulting settings, scroll down and click the Screen Saver Settings link to display the Screen Saver Settings dialog box, as shown in Figure 5-8.

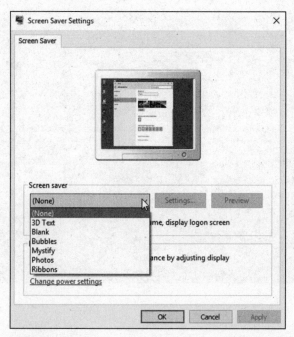

FIGURE 5-8

3. From the Screen Saver drop-down list, choose a screen saver.

4. Use the arrows in the Wait *xx* Minutes text box to set the number of inactivity minutes that Windows 10 waits before displaying the screen saver.

5. Click the Preview button to take a peek at your screen saver of choice. Click the Esc button on your keyboard to leave Preview. When you're happy with your settings, click OK.

Name Tile Groups

1. In the Start menu, tiles represent apps. These tiles are organized in groups such as Life at a Glance or Play and Explore. If you like, you can rename the group. Click the Start button to display the Start menu.

2. Click a group title; it opens for editing (see Figure 5-9).

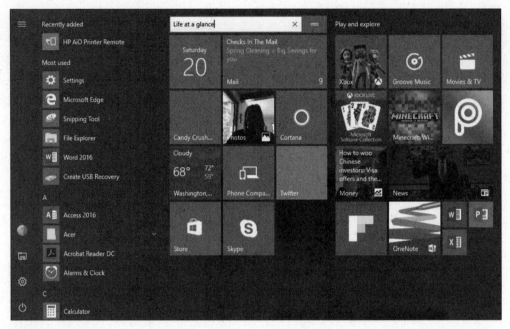

FIGURE 5-9

3. Press the Backspace button on your keyboard to delete the current title and then type a new title.

4. Click anywhere outside the title to save the new name.

TIP

If you want to use the Start menu full screen, right-click the desktop and choose Personalize. In the resulting Personalization window, click Start in the left panel and then click the Use Start Full Screen switch to turn it on. When you click the Start button, the Start menu will open in full screen. You can click the Start button again to return to the desktop.

Rearrange Tiles in the Start Menu

1. If you want the apps you use most often near the top of the Start menu, you can rearrange tiles. Click the Start button to open the Start menu.

2. Click, hold, and drag a tile to a new location.

3. Release the tile and it moves to its new spot in the Start menu.

TIP If you want to move a whole group of tiles, click the title just above the tiles, such as Life at a Glance. Click the button labelled with two stripes on the right side of the group title bar and drag the group to a new location. Release the mouse to finish the move.

Resize Tiles

1. Tiles come in different sizes by default. You may want to resize them to be smaller to fit more in the Start menu or larger to make a more frequently used app easier to find. Click the Start button to open the Start menu.

2. Right-click a tile. In the pop-up menu that appears (see Figure 5-10) hover your mouse over Resize.

3. From the side menu that appears, choose Small, Medium, Wide, or Large.

TIP If you don't need a tile that Windows has displayed by default, it's simple to remove it from the Start menu. Right-click a tile and in the menu shown in Figure 5-10, click Unpin from Start.

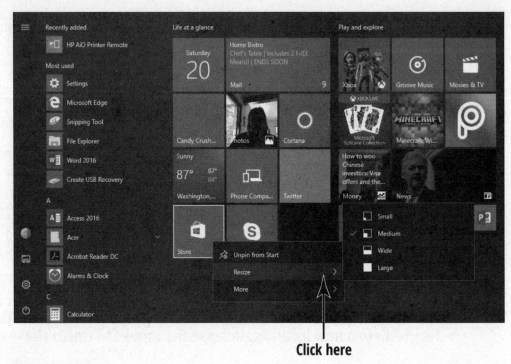

Click here

FIGURE 5-10

IN THIS CHAPTER

» **Using tools for the visually challenged**

» **Replacing sounds with visual cues**

» **Making text larger or smaller**

» **Setting up speech recognition**

» **Modifying how your keyboard works**

» **Using the onscreen keyboard feature**

» **Setting up keyboard repeat rates**

» **Customizing mouse behavior**

» **Changing the cursor**

» **Making your touch visible**

Chapter **6**

Getting Help with Vision, Hearing, and Dexterity Challenges

People face a variety of physical challenges. Windows has to be taught how to support individual users' needs. For example, Windows doesn't know that you might have a vision challenge that requires special help, or that another user finds a certain mouse cursor easier to track, or that your grandchild has difficulty using a keyboard.

You can customize settings for the way that you interact with Windows. This is good news for you because the ability to customize Windows gives you a lot of flexibility in how you get things done.

Here's how you can customize Windows to work with physical challenges:

>> Control features that help visually challenged users to work with a laptop, such as setting a higher contrast, using Narrator to read the onscreen text aloud, or increasing the size of text onscreen.

>> Work with the Speech Recognition feature, which allows you to input data into a document using speech rather than a keyboard or mouse.

>> Modify the mouse functionality for left-handed use, change the cursor to sport a certain look, or make viewing the cursor as it moves around your screen easier.

>> Work with keyboard settings that make input easier for those who are challenged by physical conditions, such as carpal tunnel syndrome or arthritis.

Use Tools for the Visually Challenged

1. You can set up Windows to use higher screen contrast to make things easier to see, speak descriptions to you rather than make you read text, and more. To begin, in the Start menu click Settings; in the Settings window click Ease of Access.

2. In the Ease of Access window (as shown in Figure 6-1), click any of the first three categories on the left to make any of the following settings:

   • **Narrator:** The Narrator reads onscreen text and words you type, as well as announcing actions you take, such as changing the Narrator speed slider. Click Narrator in the left panel and then click the Narrator toggle switch in the right pane to On. Click the Choose a Voice drop-down list to display the available voices and then click to choose one. Click and drag the Speed and Pitch sliders to adjust the voice characteristics. You can use other settings to have Narrator read individual characters you type and/or words, as well as change how Narrator works with the onscreen cursor. The changes you make to these settings are applied immediately.

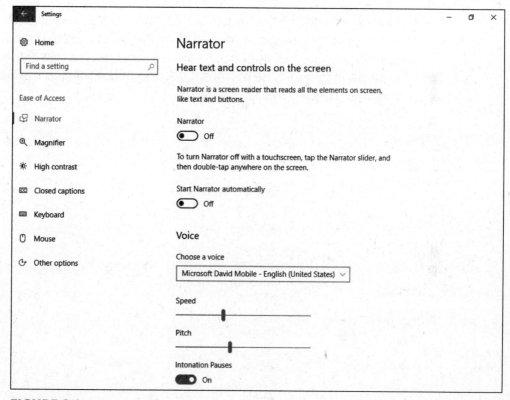

FIGURE 6-1

- **Magnifier:** Magnifier (see Figure 6-2) provides three types of magnified views. Click Magnifier in the left pane and then click the Magnifier toggle switch in the right pane to turn the feature on. Click the Start Magnifier Automatically toggle switch to On if you want the Magnifier to start when you log in to Windows. To choose a view, click the Magnifying Glass icon to open the Magnifier toolbar, and then click Views. In the drop-down list that appears, choose from among the available views:

- *Full Screen:* Makes the Magnifier fill the screen.

- *Lens:* Displays a rectangular magnification lens you can move around the screen.

- *Docked:* Displays a rectangular magnification region that you can dock in one location.

- **High Contrast:** This setting provides four color schemes that can make your screen easier to read. Click High Contrast in the left pane and then click the Choose a Theme drop-down list in the right pane to show the themes. Click one of the themes to select it, and then click Apply.

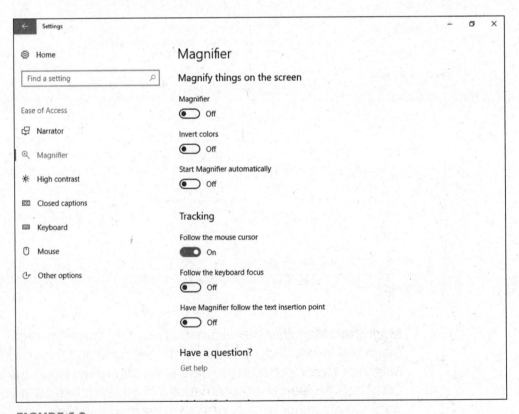

FIGURE 6-2

TIP

Most keyboards include a series of function keys across the top numbered F1 through F12. Though the number of the keys varies, two of them are typically designated for adjusting the brightness of your screen up or down. Locate the keys that show an asterisk-like icon — one larger and one smaller for the brighter or dimmer settings. Press a key to lighten or darken the screen.

3. When you finish making settings, click the Close button to close the dialog box.

TIP

If you bought a laptop with a smaller screen and find text is hard to read, don't run out and buy a new laptop. It's possible to connect your laptop to a standalone monitor using a port on the side of the computer (called an HDMI port). If you mainly use your laptop at home, this may be a less expensive way to upgrade your screen to a larger size. Consult your laptop manual for instructions on how to hook up to a separate monitor.

Replace Sounds with Visual Cues

1. Sometimes, Windows alerts you to events with sounds. If you have hearing challenges, you might prefer to get visual cues. Begin to type **Replace sounds with visual cues** in Cortana's search field, and then press Enter.

2. In the resulting Use Text or Visual Alternatives for Sounds dialog box (see Figure 6-3), make any of the following settings:

   • **Turn On Visual Notifications for Sounds (Sound Sentry).** If you select this check box, Windows will give a visual alert when a sound plays.

   • **Choose Visual Warning.** These warnings essentially flash a portion of your screen to alert you to an event. Choose one option.

   • **Turn On Text Captions for Spoken Dialog (When Available).** Select this check box to control text captions for any spoken words. *Note:* This isn't available with every application you use.

3. To save the new settings, click Apply, and then click the Close button to close the dialog box.

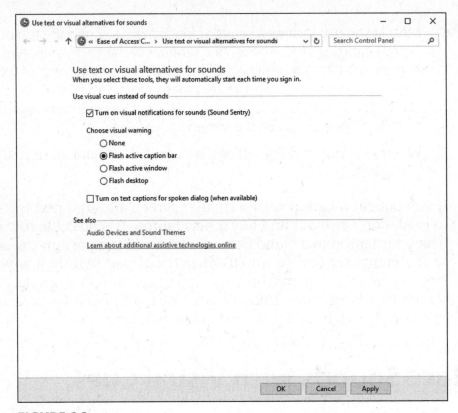

FIGURE 6-3

TIP

Visual cues are useful if you're hard of hearing and don't always pick up system sounds alerting you to error messages or a device disconnect. After the setting is turned on, it's active until you go back to the Use Text or Visual Alternatives for Sounds dialog box and turn it off.

TIP

This may seem obvious, but if you're hard of hearing, you may want to simply increase the volume for your speakers. You can do this by using the volume adjustment in a program such as the Groove Music app (see Chapter 20) or by modifying your system volume by tapping the Volume tool on the taskbar and then using the slider that appears to adjust volume (if you don't see the Volume tool click the Show Hidden Icons button).

Make Text Larger or Smaller

1. In the Start menu, click Settings.

2. In the resulting Settings window click System and then click Display in the left pane (see Figure 6-4).

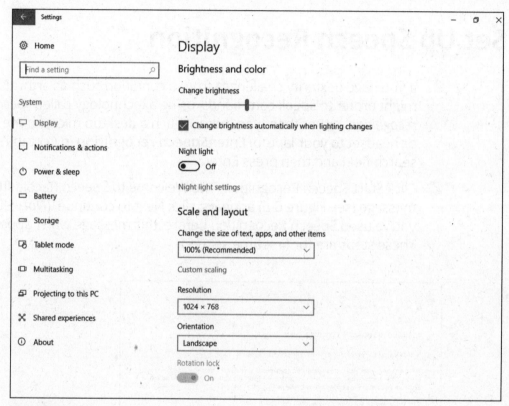

FIGURE 6-4

3. Under Scale and Layout, click the Change the Size of Text, Apps, and Other Items drop-down list and select an option. A message box appears telling you that some apps won't respond to the scaling changes until you sign out of Windows, and offers you a link to sign out now or later. Click Sign Out Now to implement the change.

TIP

You can also change the size of items onscreen by adjusting the screen resolution. In the window shown in Figure 6-4, scroll down and under Custom Scaling, select a different resolution setting from the drop-down list. The smaller the numbers, the larger items will appear onscreen (for example, 1024 x 768 displays items larger than 2160 x 1440).

Set Up Speech Recognition

1. If you have dexterity challenges from a condition such as arthritis, you might prefer to speak commands, using a technology called *speech recognition,* rather than type them. Attach a desktop microphone or headset to your laptop. Enter **Speech recognition** in Cortana's search field and then press Enter.

2. Click Start Speech Recognition. The Welcome to Speech Recognition message (see Figure 6-5) appears; click Next to continue. (***Note:*** If you've used Speech Recognition before, this message won't appear. These steps are for first time set up.)

FIGURE 6-5

3. In the resulting window (shown in Figure 6-6), select the type of microphone that you're using and then click Next. The next screen tells you how to place and use the microphone for optimum results. Click Next.

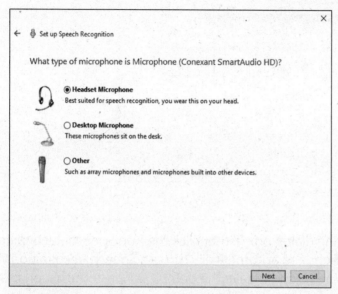

FIGURE 6-6

4. In the following window (see Figure 6-7), read the sample sentence aloud. When you're done, click Next. A dialog box appears telling you that your microphone is now set up. Click Next.

5. In the resulting dialog box, choose whether to enable or disable *document review,* in which Windows examines your documents and email to help it recognize your speech patterns. Click Next.

6. In the resulting dialog box, choose either manual activation mode, where you can use a mouse, pen, or keyboard to turn the feature on, or voice activation, which is useful if you have difficulty manipulating devices because of arthritis or a hand injury. Click Next.

7. In the resulting screen, if you wish to view and/or print a list of Speech Recognition commands, click the View Reference Sheet button to get help with Speech Recognition features. Click Next to proceed.

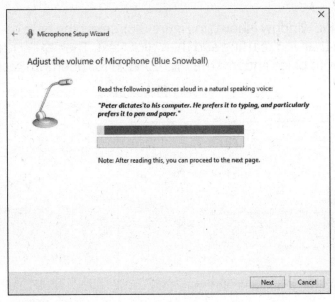

FIGURE 6-7

8. In the resulting dialog box, either click the Run Speech Recognition at Startup check box to automatically turn on Speech Recognition when you start your laptop or leave the default setting to turn it on manually each time you need it. Click Next.

9. The final dialog box informs you that you can now control the laptop by voice, and offers you a Start Tutorial button to help you practice voice commands. Click that button and follow the instructions to move through it, or click Skip Tutorial to skip the tutorial and leave the Speech Recognition setup.

10. When you leave the Speech Recognition setup, the Speech Recognition control panel appears (see Figure 6-8). Say, "Start listening" to activate the feature if you used voice activation in Step 6, or click the Microphone button on the Speech Recognition control panel if you chose manual activation in Step 6. You can now begin using spoken commands to work with your laptop.

FIGURE 6-8

TIP

To stop Speech Recognition, say, "Stop listening" or click the Microphone button on the Speech Recognition control panel. To start the Speech Recognition feature again, click the Microphone button on the Speech Recognition control panel.

Modify How Your Keyboard Works

1. If your hands are a bit stiff or you have carpal tunnel problems, you might look into changing how your keyboard works. Open the Start menu, tap Settings ⇨ Ease of Access ⇨ Keyboard.

2. In the resulting dialog box (see Figure 6-9), make any of these settings:

   • **Sticky Keys:** Enable this setting if you'd like to press keys in keystroke combinations one at a time, rather than in combination. Use additional toggle switches that appear to refine the feature.

   • **Toggle Keys:** You can set up Windows to play a sound when you press Caps Lock, Num Lock, or Scroll Lock (which I do all the time by mistake!). This displays an additional setting to turn on Toggle Keys when you hold the Num Lock key your keyboard, if you have a number pad available.

   • **Filter Keys:** If you sometimes press a key very lightly or press it so hard it activates twice, you can use the Filter Keys setting to change repeat rates to adjust for that. Use the additional toggle switches that appear when you turn on Filter Keys to fine-tune settings if you make this choice.

3. Click the Close button to close the Ease of Access Center.

TIP

You can visit the Types of Assistive Technologies Products page on the Microsoft website (www.microsoft.com/enable/at/types.aspx) to find out more about products that might help you if you have a visual, hearing, or input–related disability.

TIP

Every laptop keyboard has its own unique feel. For example, some take more or less pressure to push down on a key. If your keyboard isn't responsive and you have a condition that makes keyboarding difficult, you might also try connecting a wireless or Bluetooth keyboard to your laptop to see if one works better for you.

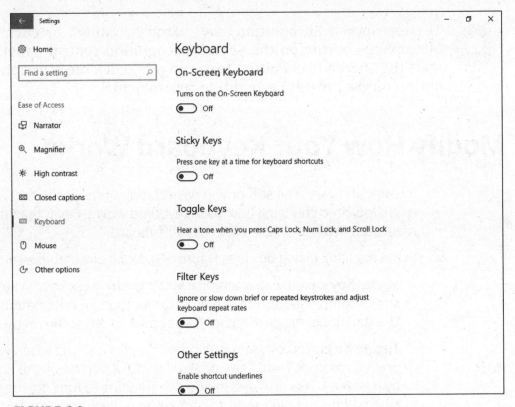

FIGURE 6-9

Use the Onscreen Keyboard Feature

1. Clicking keys with your mouse may be easier than using a regular keyboard. To use the onscreen keyboard, Open the Start menu and click Settings ⇨ Ease of Access.

2. In the Ease of Access dialog box, click Keyboard in the left pane (see Figure 6-10), and then toggle On-Screen Keyboard to On. The onscreen keyboard appears (see Figure 6-11).

TIP

The onscreen keyboard you display using these steps has different features than the standard onscreen keyboard on touch-screen computers in laptop mode. If you have a touch-screen laptop, try both styles of onscreen keyboard to decide which works best for you.

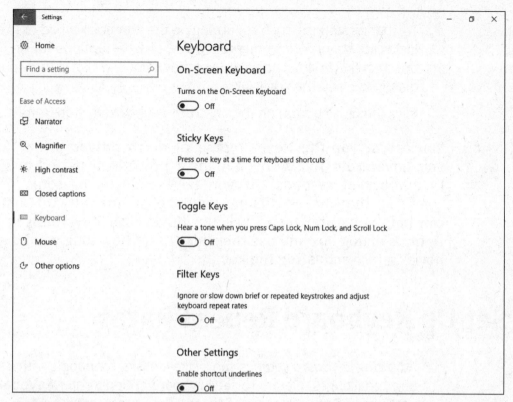

FIGURE 6-10

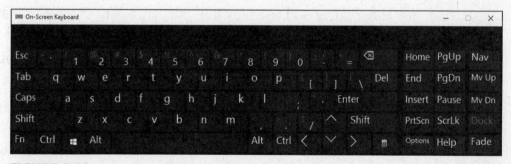

FIGURE 6-11

3. Open a document in any application where you can enter text, and then click or tap the keys on the onscreen keyboard to make entries.

TIP

To use keystroke combinations (such as Ctrl+Z), click the first key (in this case, Ctrl), and then click the second key (Z). You don't have to hold down the first key as you do with a regular keyboard.

4. To change settings, such as turning on the numeric keypad or hearing a click sound when you press a key, click the Options key on the onscreen keyboard, choose one of the options shown in the Options dialog box, and then click OK.

5. Click the Close button on the onscreen keyboard to stop using it.

You can set up the Hover typing mode to activate a key after you hover your mouse over it for a predefined period of time (*x* number of seconds). If you have arthritis or some other condition that makes clicking your mouse difficult, this option can help you enter text. Click the Hover over Keys item in the Options dialog box and use the slider to set how long you have to hover before activating the key.

Set Up Keyboard Repeat Rates

1. Adjusting keyboard settings can make it easier for people with dexterity challenges to type. To see keyboard options, enter **Keyboard settings** in Cortana's search field and then press Enter.

2. In the Keyboard Properties dialog box that appears, click the Speed tab (see Figure 6-12) and drag the sliders to adjust the two Character Repeat settings, which do the following:

   - **Repeat Delay:** Affects the amount of time it takes before a typed character is typed again when you hold down a key.

   - **Repeat Rate:** Adjusts how quickly a character repeats when you hold down a key after the first repeat character appears.

If you want to see how the Character Repeat settings work in action, click in the text box below the two settings and hold down a key to see a demonstration.

3. Drag the slider in the Cursor Blink Rate section. This affects cursors, such as the insertion line that appears in text.

4. Click OK to save and apply changes and close the dialog box.

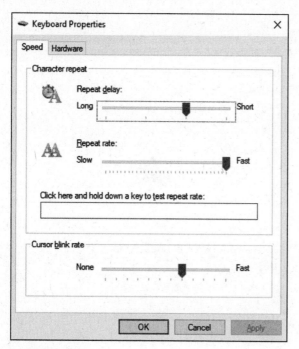

FIGURE 6-12

TIP

If you have trouble with motion (for example, because of arthritis or carpal tunnel syndrome), you might find that you can adjust these settings to make it easier for you to get your work done. For example, if you can't pick up your finger quickly from a key, a slower repeat rate might save you from typing more instances of a character than you'd intended.

Customize Mouse Behavior

1. Instead of manipulating your mouse (in the case of your laptop you might be using your built-in touchpad or a wireless mouse) with your hand, you can use your keyboard to move the cursor. In the Start menu, click Settings ⇨ Ease of Access and then click Mouse in the left pane. The dialog box shown in Figure 6-13 opens.

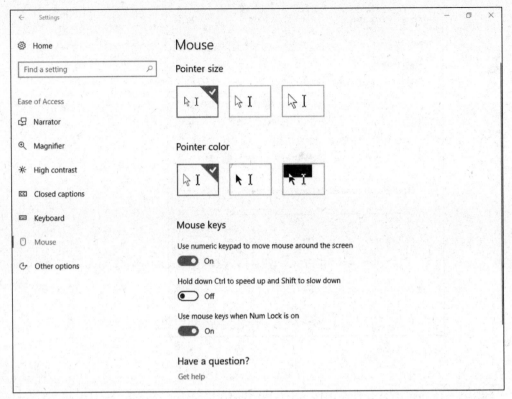

FIGURE 6-13

2. To use the numeric keypad to move your mouse cursor on your screen, click to turn On the toggle setting labeled Use Numeric Keypad to Move Mouse Around the Screen.

TIP

To understand how to use the numeric keypad to move the mouse, visit the Microsoft Accessibility Tutorial web page at `www.microsoft.com/enable/training/windows10/use-numeric-keypad.aspx`. At the bottom of the web page under Guides, click Mobility to download the Mobility Guide.

3. To control the speed at which the cursor moves on the screen, turn on the Hold Down Ctrl to Speed Up and Shift to Slow Down toggle settings.

4. Click the Close button.

TIP

If you're left-handed, in the Start menu click Settings⇨Devices⇨Mouse. In the resulting dialog box, click the Select Your Primary Button drop-down menu and then click to select Right. This setting makes the right mouse button handle all the usual left-button functions, such as clicking and dragging, and the left button handle the typical right-hand functions, such as displaying shortcut menus. This helps left-handed people use the mouse more easily.

TIP

If you want to modify the behavior of the mouse pointer, in the Start menu click Settings⇨Devices⇨Mouse and then scroll down and click Additional Mouse Options. In the resulting Mouse Properties dialog box, click the Pointer Options tab to set the *pointer speed* (how quickly you can drag the mouse pointer around your screen), click the Pointer Options tab to activate the Snap To feature that automatically moves the mouse cursor to the default choice in a dialog box, or modify the little trails that appear when you drag the pointer.

TIP

Although some laptop keyboards have a separate numeric keypad, many have the number keys embedded in the regular keyboard to save space. Using these embedded keys requires that you press the Fn key on the keyboard and then the letter key where the number you want is embedded. (The numbers are usually noted on the keys in a different color, such as red or blue.)

TIP

If your touchpad isn't working well for you, consider buying a wireless mouse, similar to the one you use with your desktop computer. You simply plug a receiver into a USB port on your laptop, and the mouse is activated. When using a standard mouse you might want to invest in a mouse pad with a wrist rest to reduce strain that can lead to carpal tunnel syndrome.

Change the Cursor

1. Having trouble finding the mouse cursor on your screen? You might want to enlarge it or change its shape. Open the Start menu, click Settings ⇨ Ease of Access ⇨ Mouse.

2. In the resulting dialog box, as shown in Figure 6-14, click one of the Pointer Size icons to set the size of the cursor. The size of the cursor changes.

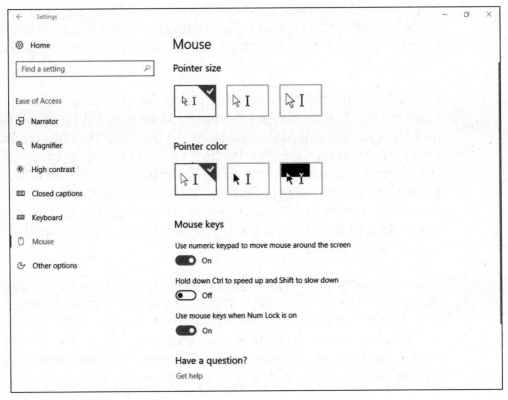

FIGURE 6-14

3. Click one of the Pointer Color icons to set the cursor color. The cursor changes immediately.

4. Click the Close button to close the Mouse dialog box.

Make Your Touch Visible

1. Are you having trouble touching the correct check box on your touch-screen monitor? You can enable a visual feedback feature that shows where you touched the screen. Open the Start menu, click Settings, click Ease of Access, and then click Other Options in the left pane.

2. In the resulting dialog box, as shown in Figure 6-15, click the Show Visual Feedback When I Touch the Screen toggle switch to On. The Touch Feedback feature is turned on.

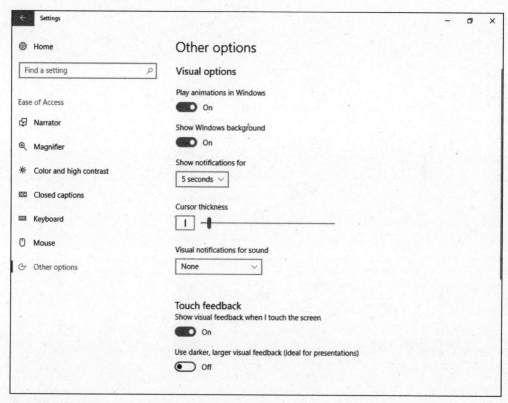

FIGURE 6-15

3. To make the visual feedback darker and larger so you more easily spot it, click the Use Darker, Larger Visual Feedback toggle switch to On.

4. Click the Close button to close the dialog box.

Chapter **7**

Setting Up Printers and Scanners

A laptop is a great storehouse for data, images, and other digital information, but sometimes you need ways to turn printed documents into electronic files you can work with on your laptop by scanning them, and sometimes you need to print *hard copies* (a fancy term for paper printouts) of electronic documents and images. Here's how to do just that:

> » **Printers** allow you to create hard copies of your files on paper, transparencies, or whatever materials your printer can accommodate. To use a printer, you have to install software called a *printer driver* and use certain settings to tell your laptop how to identify your printer and what to print.

» You use a **scanner** to create electronic files — picture files, essentially — from hard copies such as newspaper clippings, your birth certificate or driver's license, photos, or whatever will fit in your scanner. You can then work with the electronic files, send them to others as an email attachment, and modify and print them. Scanners also require that you install a driver, which is typically provided by your scanner's manufacturer. Note that several all-in-one models feature both a printer and a scanner in one.

Install a Printer

1. Read the instructions that came with the printer. Some printers require that you install software before connecting them, but others can be connected right away and use drivers (programs that make them run) stored in Windows.

2. Turn on your laptop and then follow the option that fits your needs:

   - If your printer is a plug-and-play device (most are these days), you can connect it and power it on; Windows installs any required drivers automatically. If your laptop connects via a cable, plug it in.

   - If you have a printer that can connect to your laptop using a wireless signal over a network (no wires required), be sure your wireless printer is turned on and available.

   - If you have one, insert the disc that came with the device, and follow the onscreen instructions.

3. If your printer doesn't connect automatically, you can try adding a printer. Begin by choosing Settings from the Start menu.

4. Click Devices ⇨ Printers & Scanners ⇨ Add a Printer or Scanner and let Windows 10 search for any available devices (see Figure 7-1).

5. When your laptop discovers your printer, select it, click Next, and follow the instructions that appear on your screen.

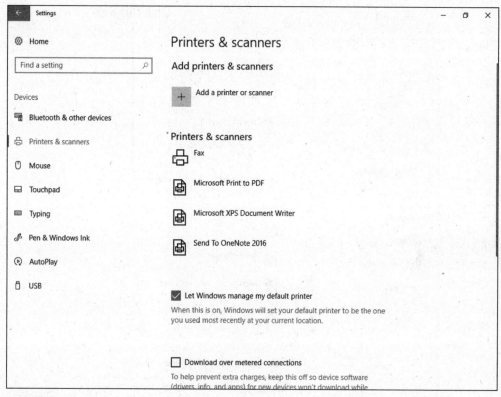

FIGURE 7-1

Add a Printer Manually

1. If the previous procedure doesn't work, go to the Start menu and click Settings ⇨ Devices. In the left panel of the window that appears, click Printer & Scanners and then click the Add a Printer or Scanner link near the top.

2. In the resulting Add Printer Wizard, shown in Figure 7-2, if Windows 10 again doesn't find your printer, click the The Printer That I Want Isn't Listed link.

3. In the following window, click the Add a Local Printer or Network Printer with Manual Settings option and then click Next.

4. In the following window, shown in Figure 7-3, select a port (a slot on your computer into which you plug your printer cord). Click the down arrow on the Use an Existing Port field and select a port, or just use the recommended port setting that Windows selects for you. Click Next.

Click this link

Settings

⚙ Home

Find a setting 🔍

Devices

▤ Bluetooth & other devices

🖨 Printers & scanners

🖱 Mouse

⌨ Touchpad

⌨ Typing

🖊 Pen & Windows Ink

▶ AutoPlay

📱 USB

Printers & scanners

Add printers & scanners

🔄 Refresh

Searching for printers and scanners

The printer that I want isn't listed ◀

Printers & scanners

🖨 Fax

▣ Microsoft Print to PDF

▣ Microsoft XPS Document Writer

▣ Send To OneNote 2016

☑ Let Windows manage my default printer

When this is on, Windows will set your default printer to be the one you used most recently at your current location.

FIGURE 7-2

Select a printer port

🖨 Add Printer

Choose a printer port

A printer port is a type of connection that allows your computer to exchange information with a printer.

◉ Use an existing port: LPT1: (Printer Port) ▼ ◀

○ Create a new port:

Type of port: Local Port

Next   Cancel

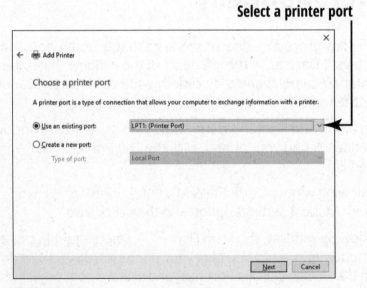

FIGURE 7-3

5. In the next wizard window, choose a manufacturer in the list on the left and then choose a printer model in the list on the right. You then have two options:

- If you have the manufacturer's disc, insert it in the appropriate CD/DVD drive now and click the Have Disk button. Click Next.

- If you don't have the manufacturer's disc, click the Windows Update button to see a list of printer drivers that you can download from the Microsoft website. Click Next.

6. In the resulting dialog box titled Type a Printer Name (see Figure 7-4), enter a printer name or accept the default name that's already been entered. Click Next.

Enter a name for your printer

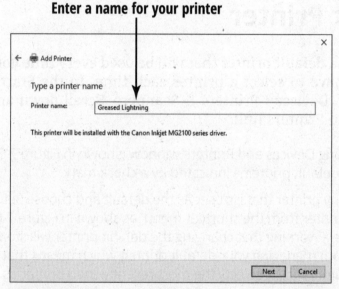

FIGURE 7-4

7. In the resulting dialog box, click the Print a Test Page button and, if the test works, click Finish to complete the Add Printer Wizard.

TIP

If your laptop is on a network, after Step 6, you get additional dialog boxes in the wizard, including one that allows you to share the printer on your network. Select the Do Not Share This Printer option to stop others from using the printer, or select the Share Name option and enter a printer name to share the printer on your network. This means that others can see, select, and use this printer.

TIP

If you need to print on the go, consider a portable printer (also called a mobile printer). These lightweight (five pounds or less) units don't offer the best print quality, but for quick, on-the-fly printing, they can be useful.

Set a Default Printer

You can set up a default printer that will be used every time you print, so you don't have to select a printer each time. In the Start menu, click Settings ⇨ Devices ⇨ Printers & Scanners. Scroll down and click the Devices and Printers link.

1. In the resulting Devices and Printers window (shown in Figure 7-5), the current default printer is indicated by a check mark.

2. Right-click any printer that isn't set as the default and choose Set as Default Printer from the shortcut menu, as shown in Figure 7-6. You may see a warning that changing the default printer will stop Windows from managing your default printer, which means that Windows automatically selects the most recently used printer as the default. If you get this message, click OK.

3. Click the Close button in the Devices and Printers window.

The default printer is checked

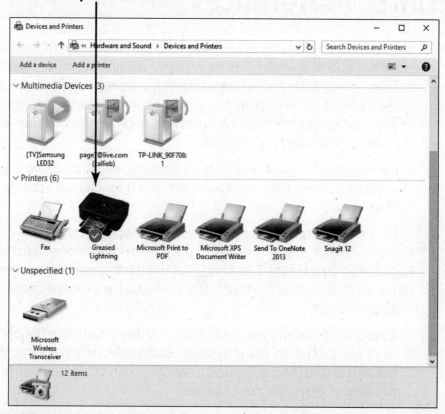

FIGURE 7-5

Choose this option

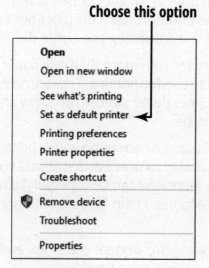

FIGURE 7-6

Set Printer Preferences

1. Your printer might have capabilities, such as being able to print in color or black and white or print in draft quality (which uses less ink) or high quality (which produces a darker, crisper image). To modify these settings for all documents you print, in the Start menu click Settings ⇨ Devices ⇨ Printers & Scanners, and then scroll down and click the Devices and Printers link.

2. In the resulting Devices and Printers window, any printers you've installed are listed. Right-click a printer and then choose Printing Preferences.

3. In the Printing Preferences dialog box that appears (shown in Figure 7-7), click any of the tabs to display various settings, such as Page Setup (see Figure 7-8). Note that different printers might display different choices and different tabs in this dialog box, but common settings include

   - **Color/Grayscale:** If you have a color printer, you have the option of printing in color. The grayscale option uses only black ink. When printing a draft of a color document, you can save colored ink by printing in grayscale, for example.

   - **Quality:** If you want, you can print in fast or draft quality (these settings may have different names depending on your printer's manufacturer) to save ink, or you can print in a higher or best quality for your finished documents. Some printers offer a dpi (dots-per-inch) setting for quality — the higher the dpi setting, the better the quality.

   - **Paper Source:** If you have a printer with more than one paper tray, you can select which tray to use for printing. For example, you might have 8½-x-11-inch paper (letter sized) in one tray and 8½-x-14-inch (legal sized) in another.

   - **Paper Size:** Choose the size of paper or envelope you're printing to. In many cases, this option displays a preview that shows you which way to insert the paper. A preview can be especially handy if you're printing to envelopes and need help figuring out how to insert them in your printer.

4. Click the OK button to close the dialog box and save settings, and then click the Close button to close other open windows.

Click a tab to see different settings

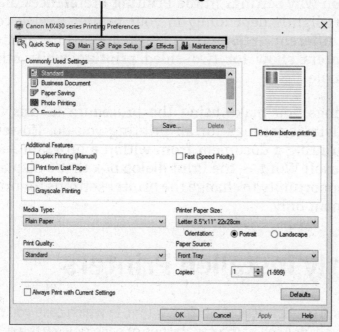

FIGURE 7-7

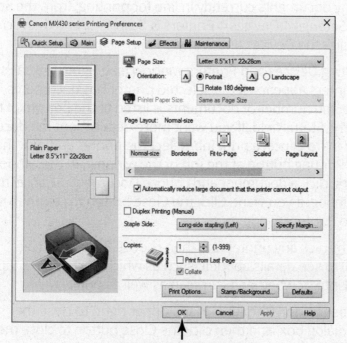

Click OK to save settings

FIGURE 7-8

TIP

There's a reason why settings in the Printing Preferences dialog box may differ slightly depending on your printer model; color printers offer different options than black-and-white printers, and some printers allow for two-sided printing while others don't, for example.

TIP

Whatever settings you make using the procedure in this task become your default settings for all printing you do. However, when you're printing a document from within a program — for instance, Microsoft Word — the Print dialog box that's displayed gives you the opportunity to change the printer settings for printing that document only.

View Currently Installed Printers

1. Over time, you might install multiple printers, in which case you may want to remind yourself of the capabilities of each or view the documents you've sent to be printed. To view the printers you've installed and view any documents currently in line for printing, from the Start menu click Settings ⇨ Devices ⇨ Printers & Scanners, and then scroll down and click the Devices and Printers link.

2. In the resulting Devices and Printers window (see Figure 7-9), a list of installed printers appears. If the selected printer has documents in its print queue, the number of documents is listed at the bottom of the window in the Status field. If you want more detail about the documents or want to cancel a print job, select the printer and click the See What's Printing button at the top of the window. In the window that appears, click a document and choose Document ⇨ Cancel to stop the printing, if you want. Click the Close button to return to the Devices and Printers window.

3. You can right-click any printer and then choose Properties (see Figure 7-10) to see details about it, such as which port on your laptop it's plugged into or whether it can scan as well as print.

4. Click the Close button (the red X in the upper right) to close the Properties dialog box, and then click the Close button to close the Devices and Printers window.

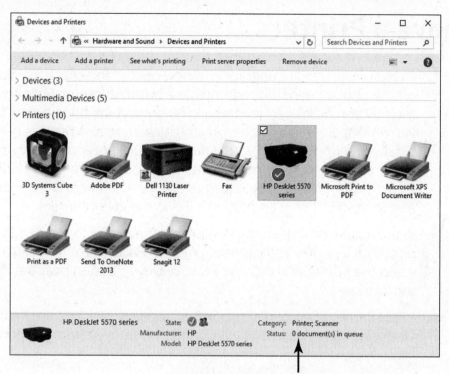

Number of documents in queue to print

FIGURE 7-9

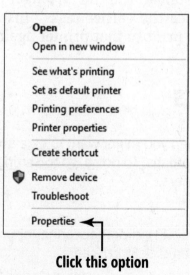

Click this option

FIGURE 7-10

Remove a Printer

1. Over time, you might upgrade to a new printer and chuck the old one, or you've been using a printer in a business center while on a trip that you no longer need when you bring your laptop home. When you no longer need a printer, you might want to also remove the older printer driver from your laptop so your Printers window isn't cluttered with printers you don't need anymore. To remove a printer, from the Start menu click Settings ⇨ Devices ⇨ Printers & Scanners, and then scroll down and click the Devices and Printers link.

2. In the resulting Devices and Printers window (refer to Figure 7-9), right-click a printer and choose Remove Device. (**Note:** You can also select the printer and click the Remove Device button near the top of the window.)

3. In the Remove Device dialog box that appears, click Yes; the Remove Device window closes, and your printer is removed from the printer list.

TIP

If you remove a printer, it's removed from the list of installed printers, and if it was the default printer, Windows assigns default status to another printer you've installed. You can no longer print to it unless you install it again. See the earlier task, "Install a Printer," if you decide you want to print to that printer again.

Modify Scanner Settings

1. After you've set up a printer/scanner, you might want to take a look at or change the scanner default settings. To do so, go to Settings and click Devices. Click Printers & Scanners.

2. Click Devices & Printers.

3. In the resulting window (see Figure 7-11), click the scanner or printer/scanner you have installed, and then click Start Scan.

Click Start Scan

Click Scan

FIGURE 7-11

4. In the dialog box that appears, click drop-down lists for options such as Source, File Type, Color Format (to fine tune the way color is scanned), or Resolution (the higher the resolution, the crisper and cleaner your electronic document, but the more time it may take to scan) to view the available choices.

TIP

When you're ready to run a scan, place the item to be scanned in your scanner. Depending on your model, the item may be placed on a flat bed with a hinged cover or fed through a tray. Click All Apps in the Start menu, scroll down, and then click Scan. In the New Scan window, click the Scan button. After you begin the scan, your laptop displays a dialog box showing you the scan progress and allowing you to view and save the scanned item.

2
Getting Things Done with Software

IN THIS CHAPTER

» Getting an overview of Cortana

» Setting up Cortana

» Setting up Cortana's Notebook

» Interacting with Cortana

» Setting reminders

» Searching with Cortana

» Identifying music with Cortana

Chapter **8**

Connecting with Cortana

ortana is a personal assistant feature that's part of Windows 10. Cortana resembles apps on smartphones, such as Siri on the iPhone, that reply to your voice requests for directions, a list of nearby restaurants, current weather conditions, and more.

Cortana is also your central search feature in Windows 10, which can give you requested information verbally or take you to online search results. You can also use Cortana to set up reminders and even send emails. You can access Cortana from the Windows desktop or lock screen.

Where Cortana goes beyond smartphone apps is in integrating your daily activities and interests to anticipate the type of information you might need. You can set up your preferences in Cortana, help her learn your voice, and have her integrate with apps such as Calendar, Mail, Music, and more.

Get an Overview of Cortana

When you open Cortana, you see information in the Cortana panel that might be useful (see Figure 8-1) depending on settings you've made, such as information about your local weather or traffic conditions or sports teams.

Home   **Notebook**

FIGURE 8-1

Beyond that, Cortana is kind of like the computer in a Star Trek movie that you can command to do various tasks. Although Cortana can't fire a photon torpedo or transport you to a nearby planet, it can make your life easier. Here are just some of the things Cortana can do, from either a voice command or text that you enter in her search box:

» Set appointments and reminders

» Search for information online

» Open apps

» Play and identify music

» Search for files on your laptop

» Get directions using the Maps app

» Send an email

Set Up Cortana

1. When you first open Cortana, you will be asked questions used to set up Cortana such as what you want Cortana to call you (your nickname). You can access Cortana's settings at a later date if you want to change how Cortana is working. Click in Cortana's search box to open Cortana. When the panel appears, click the Notebook button and, in the resulting Notebook panel (see Figure 8-2), click About Me.

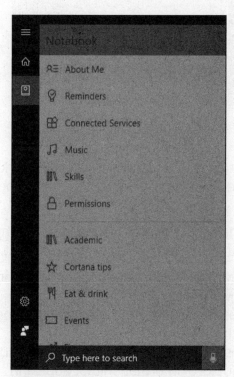

FIGURE 8-2

2. In the resulting About Me panel (see Figure 8-3), you can change your name or your favorite places. Click Edit Favorites and then in the Places panel click the Add button (the + shaped button in the lower-right corner) to add a Favorite.

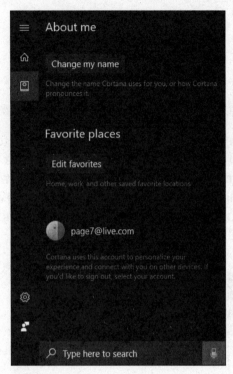

FIGURE 8-3

3. In the resulting panel, begin to type a location, such as your work-place, in the Add a Favorite text box. Click to select the correct location from the search results.

4. In the resulting panel, click the Set as Work or Set as Home setting to On, if appropriate, and click the Save button near the lower right.

5. Click the Settings button to the left. The Settings options shown in Figure 8-4 open. Settings allows you to control whether Cortana responds to the spoken phrase "Hey Cortana", responds to anyone's voice or just yours, finds tracking information in your email and other messages, can be accessed from the lock screen, and enables Taskbar Tidbits (occasional tidbits of information that appear in Cortana's search box) and more.

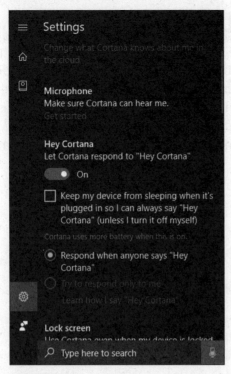

FIGURE 8-4

6. If the Let Cortana Respond to "Hey Cortana" switch is set to Off, click to turn it On. If you are the only one who uses the laptop, click the Learn How I Say "Hey Cortana" button, and then repeat the six phrases that Cortana supplies.

7. To enable access to Cortana on the lock screen, click the Use Cortana Even When My Device Is Locked switch to On.

8. To allow Cortana to access various apps from the lock screen, click the Let Cortana Access My Calendar, Email, Messages, and Other Content Data When My Device Is Locked check box.

TIP

To modify the safety of Cortana searches, scroll down to the SafeSearch settings and choose Strict, Moderate, or Off to control your level of risk when Cortana searches online.

TIP

After you open the Cortana panel, you can close it by clicking the Escape button on your keyboard or by clicking anywhere outside of the Cortana panel.

Set Up Cortana's Notebook

1. You can access Cortana's Notebook to customize how Cortana deals with different topics. For example, you can make settings for Events, Finance, News, Getting Around, and more. To explore any of these categories, click in Cortana's search box to open Cortana's panel, click the Notebook button, and then click a category, in this example, Sports (see Figure 8-5).

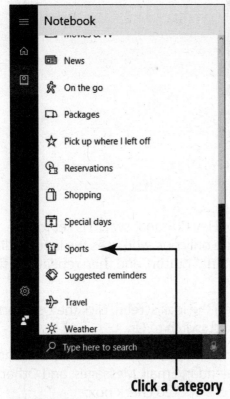

Click a Category

FIGURE 8-5

2. In the resulting Notebook panel if you want to add a team to track, click Add a Team under the Teams You're Tracking heading, and then type a team name in the Search For a Team text box.

3. Select a team from the search results.

4. By default, Score Updates for your Teams and Show Upcoming Games and Matches are set to On. If you want to change this click a switch to Off, and then click Add.

TIP

You can control the pieces of information that appear in Cortana's Home panel when you first open it by choosing to display Cards. To control cards, click the Notebook button, click a topic such as Sports or Eat & Drink, and then turn the Cards & Notifications setting for that topic on or off.

Interact with Cortana

You can interact with Cortana through speech or text. You can speak to Cortana, starting with the phrase "Hey Cortana" or by clicking the microphone button in her search box. With the speech feature active, you can then state a request such as, "Open the Music App" or "What is the Diameter of the Earth?" You can also type a request in the Cortana search box.

Results will vary based on how you ask the question and the request. If you use speech, she may respond verbally or may display search results in the Cortana panel or in Bing. If you type a question, she won't respond verbally, but may show you her response in the panel or in Bing. If you have requested an action, such as sending an email, she may display a form in her panel (see Figure 8-6) that you can use to provide additional information.

TIP

Over time, Cortana should learn more about you and respond more appropriately to your requests. You can also go through a procedure to help her learn your voice, which is discussed in "Set Up Cortana" earlier in this chapter. Bottom line: play around with Cortana using both speech and text and see what results she provides.

FIGURE 8-6

Set Reminders

1. Click the Cortana button in the taskbar to open Cortana and then click the Notebook button. Click Reminders and the Reminders panel opens. (Note that you can also enter **Create a Reminder** in the Cortana search box, or click the Microphone button and say, "Hey Cortana, create a reminder.")

2. Click the Add button (the + shaped button in the bottom-right of the panel, as shown in Figure 8-7) and then in the resulting panel fill in the details of what you want to be reminded to do, which might include a name for the event and the place and time. When you click a field such as Person you might be taken to an app to make a choice. Note that available entry options may appear depending on your selections. When you finish making entries, click the Remind button.

Click to add a reminder

FIGURE 8-7

3. At the time you set to display a reminder, it appears in the bottom-right corner of the desktop. Click either the Snooze or Complete button to allow the reminder to appear a bit later or to indicate the reminder is no longer needed because the task is complete.

You can also display the Notebook panel and click Reminders to view upcoming reminders.

TIP

Search with Cortana

1. You can ask Cortana to look up facts; for example, say, "Hey Cortana, how big is Mars?" The result displays a specific answer at the top, as shown in Figure 8-8.

FIGURE 8-8

2. You can also type or speak to ask Cortana to provide a list of results using the Bing search engine. Say or enter the phrase "Find information about the Hubble space telescope." Cortana will search using Bing and return a list of matches to your request, as shown in Figure 8-9.

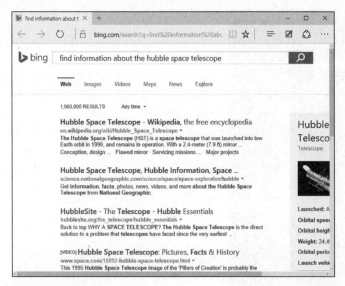

FIGURE 8-9

TIP

Cortana's results aren't limited to facts and figures. Try asking her to find the best nearby pizza restaurant as you travel with your laptop, or to tell you a joke. You can also ask for help with using Windows 10 features. See Chapter 3 for more about searching using Cortana.

Identify Music with Cortana

1. As you're roaming around with your laptop, if you hear a song playing that you don't recognize Cortana can identify it for you. Say, "Hey Cortana, what music is playing?" and Cortana will open in a "Listening for Music" mode. After a few moments, if she recognizes the song, Cortana provides the name of the song, album, and artist.

2. Click on the song title and the Store opens so that you can buy the song or album if you wish, as shown in Figure 8-10. See Chapter 20 for more about buying and playing music.

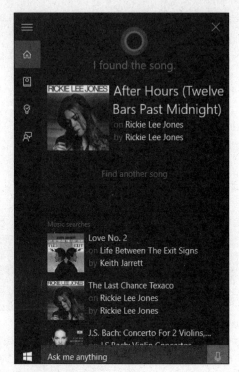

FIGURE 8-10

IN THIS CHAPTER

» **Launching software**

» **Viewing open applications in Task View**

» **Closing software**

» **Moving information between applications**

» **Setting application defaults**

» **Uninstalling an application**

Chapter **9**

Working with Software

You may think of Windows 10 as a set of useful accessories, such as games, music players, and a paint accessory for playing around with images, but Windows 10 is first and foremost an operating system. Windows 10's main purpose is to enable you to run and manage other software, from applications that manage your finances to a great animated game of bingo. By using the best methods for accessing and running software with Windows 10, you save time; setting up Windows 10 in the way that works best for you can make your life easier.

In this chapter, you explore several simple and very handy techniques for launching and moving information between software. You go through step-by-step procedures ranging from setting defaults for which applications to use with various document formats to uninstalling programs when you no longer need them.

TIP

You'll hear software referred to as *programs* or *applications* (*apps* for short). Some apps, such as Paint, come with Windows and are traditionally known as *Windows Accessories*. Apps that you can purchase such as Microsoft Word or Quicken have very robust functionality. Other apps provide simple functions such as a pedometer on your mobile phone or a calendar. Bottom line: You work with these software products in pretty similar ways and don't need to trouble your brain too much with the terminology.

Launch Software

1. Launch software by using any of the following methods:

- Click a tile in the Start menu. (For more about pinning apps to the Start menu, see Chapter 3.)

- Open the Start menu and scroll through the alphabetical list of apps (as shown in Figure 9-1). Click an app to open it.

FIGURE 9-1

- Double-click a shortcut icon on the desktop (see Figure 9-2).

FIGURE 9-2

- Click an item on the desktop taskbar to display a currently open app. The taskbar should display by default. If it doesn't, press the Windows key (on your keyboard) to display it, and then click an icon on the taskbar. See Chapter 3 for more about working with the taskbar.

2. When the software opens, if it's a game, play it; if it's a spreadsheet, enter numbers into it; if it's your email, start deleting junk mail . . . you get the idea.

TIP

See Chapter 11 for more about working with apps in Windows 10.

View Open Apps in Task View

1. Task View shows you all open apps and helps you to switch among them. With two or more apps open, click the Task View button to the right of Cortana's Ask Me About Anything button.

2. Click on a running app to make it active (see Figure 9-3). It will open to the size at which it was last displayed (full screen, minimized, etc.).

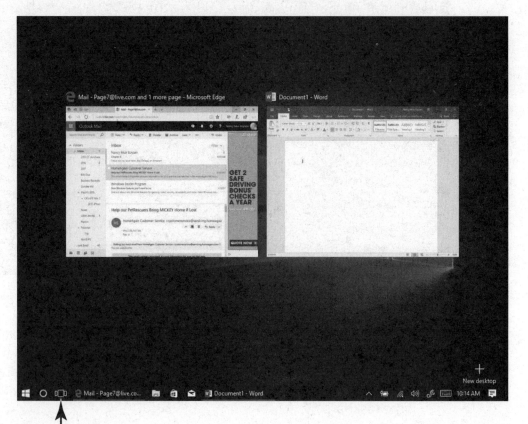

Task View button

FIGURE 9-3

3. Click the Maximize button near the top-right corner to expand a minimized app to full screen.

Close Software

Most mainstream software such as Microsoft Word and Quicken offer a few ways to close the app. On a Windows computer, there is a Close button shaped like an X in the upper-right corner of the app window, as shown in Figure 9-4. Click this button; if you have an unsaved document open you may be asked if you want to save it before closing the app, which is a good idea. If you have already saved the document, the app simply closes. You can also use the File menu command Close or Exit to close the app.

Close

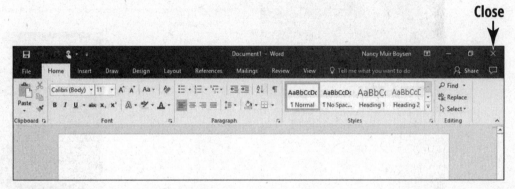

FIGURE 9-4

In most apps, such as games or music players, there may or may not be a Close button. If there isn't, look for a main menu and choose a command such as Exit from the choices that appear.

Move Information between Apps

1. Apps are often designed to allow you to move or copy content from one to the other. For example, you might copy an image on a PowerPoint slide and paste it into a Word document. Click the Start button, click the All Apps button, and open two apps.

2. Browse and open documents in the two apps (see the earlier section for more about opening apps). Right-click the taskbar (see Figure 9-5) and choose Show Windows Side by Side or Show Windows Stacked.

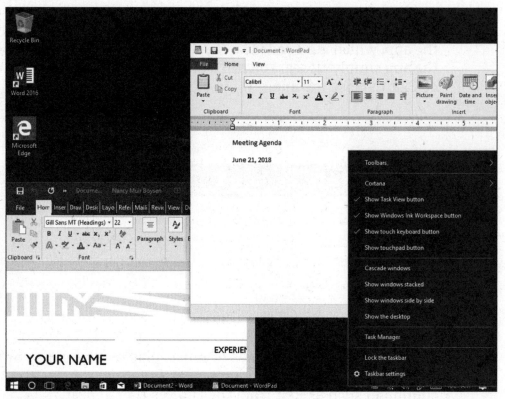

FIGURE 9-5

3. Select the information that you want to move (for example click and drag your mouse to highlight text or numbers, or click on a picture in a document). Drag the selection to the other document window (see Figure 9-6).

4. Release your mouse, and the information is copied to the document in the destination window.

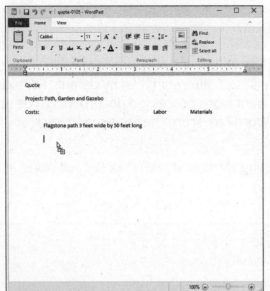
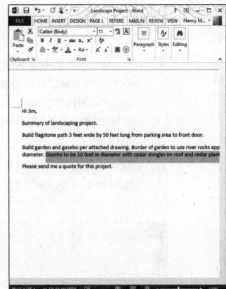

FIGURE 9-6

TIP

You can also use simple cut-and-paste or copy-and-paste keystroke shortcuts to take information from one app and move it or place a copy of it into a document in another app. To do this, first click and drag over the information in a document, and then press Ctrl+X to cut or Ctrl+C to copy the item. Click in the destination document where you want to place the item and press Ctrl+V. Alternately, you can right-click selected content and choose Cut, Copy, or Paste commands from the menu that appears.

TIP

Remember, dragging content won't work between every type of app. For example, you can't click and drag an open picture in Paint into the Calendar app. It will most dependably work when dragging text or objects from one Office or other standard word-processing, presentation, database, or spreadsheet app to another.

Set App Defaults

1. To make working with files easier, you may want to control which apps are used to open files of different types by default. For example, you might always want word processed documents to be opened by Microsoft Word or WordPad. From the Start menu, click Settings.

2. Click Apps. In the resulting window shown click Default Apps, as shown in Figure 9-7.

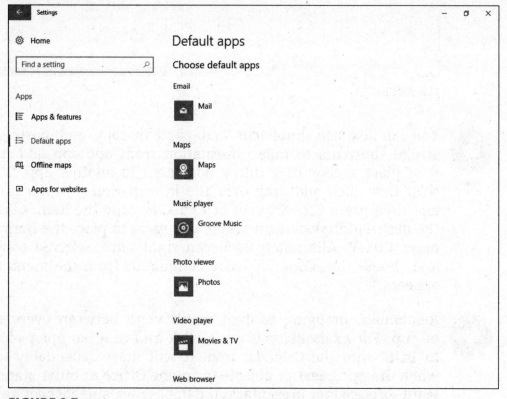

FIGURE 9-7

3. Click an app in the list on the right (see Figure 9-8) and then click another program in the list to set it as the default option. You can also click Look for an App in the Store to locate other apps.

4. Click the Close button.

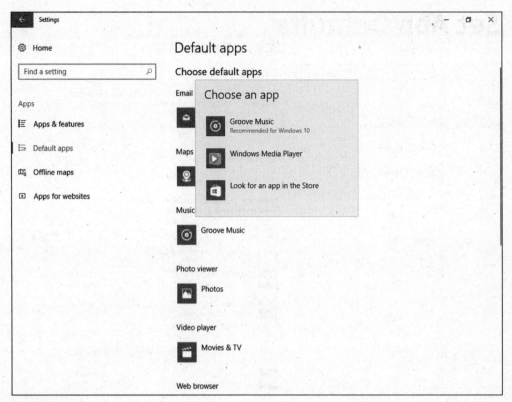

FIGURE 9-8

TIP
You can also view app features such as the date installed or amount of space it takes up by clicking the Apps & Features item in the Apps window.

Uninstall an App

1. If you don't need an app, removing it may help your laptop's performance, which can get bogged down when your hard drive is too cluttered. From the Start menu, click Settings ⇨ Apps.

2. In the resulting window, shown in Figure 9-9, click an app and then click the Uninstall button that appears. Although some apps will display their own uninstall screen, in most cases, a confirmation dialog box appears (see Figure 9-10).

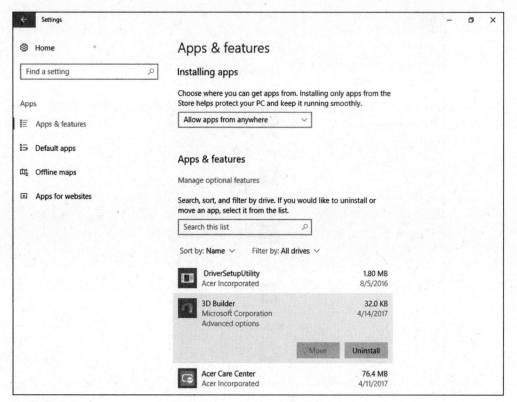

FIGURE 9-9

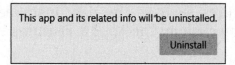

FIGURE 9-10

3. If you're sure that you want to remove the software, click Uninstall in the confirmation dialog box. A progress bar shows the status of the procedure; it disappears when the software has been removed.

4. Click the Close button to close the window.

TIP

With some software suites that include multiple apps, such as Microsoft Office, you get both an Uninstall and a Change option in Step 2. That's because you might want to remove only one app, not the entire suite of apps. For example, you might decide that you have no earthly use for Access but can't let a day go by without using Excel and Word — so why not free up some hard drive space and send Access packing? If you want to modify a software suite in this way, select the suite and then click the Change button rather than the Uninstall button in Step 2 of this task. The dialog box that appears allows you to select the apps that you want to install or uninstall or even open the original installation screen from your software suite.

WARNING

If you click the Change or Uninstall button, some apps will simply be removed with no further input from you. Be really sure that you don't need an app before you remove it, that you have the original software on disc, or that you have a product key for software you downloaded from the Internet so you can reinstall it should you need it again.

Chapter **10**

Working with Files and Folders

J oin me for a moment in the office of yesteryear. Notice all the metal filing cabinets and manila file folders holding paper rather than the sleek computer workstations, ubiquitous laptops and tablets, and cloud storage solutions we use today.

Fast forward: You still organize the work you do every day in files and folders, but today the metal and cardboard have given way to electronic bits and bytes. Files are the individual documents that you save from within applications, such as Word and Excel, and you use folders and subfolders in Windows File Explorer to organize files into groups or categories, such as by project or by year.

In this chapter, you find out how to organize and work with files and folders, including

» **Finding your way around files and folders:** This includes tasks such as locating and opening files and folders using search tools such as Cortana, and using some of the tools on the File Explorer Ribbon.

» **Manipulating files and folders:** These tasks cover moving, renaming, and deleting a file.

» **Squeezing a file's contents:** This involves creating a compressed folder to reduce the size of a large file or set of files to be more manageable when backing up or emailing them.

» **Backing up files and folders:** To avoid losing valuable data, you should know how to make backup copies of your files and folders on a recordable CD/DVD or *flash drive* (a small stick-shaped storage device that fits into a USB port on your laptop).

Understand How Windows Organizes Data

When you work in a software program, such as a word processor, you save your document as a file. Files can be saved to your laptop hard drive, to removable storage media such as USB flash drives (which range in size from a half inch to the size of a stick of gum), or to recordable DVDs (round, flat discs you insert into a disc drive on your laptop). (Note that you can also save files to an online storage site such as OneDrive; this is known as storing content in the cloud. Working with OneDrive and the cloud is covered in detail in Chapter 17.)

You can organize files by placing them in folders that you work with in an app called File Explorer, which is included with Windows. The Windows operating system helps you to organize files and folders in the following ways:

> » **Take advantage of predefined folders.** Windows sets up some folders for you as libraries of content. For example, the first time you start Windows 10 and open File Explorer, you find folders for Documents, Music, Pictures, Downloads, and Videos already set up on your laptop (see Figure 10-1). (See Chapter 3 for an introduction to File Explorer.)

Windows-created folders

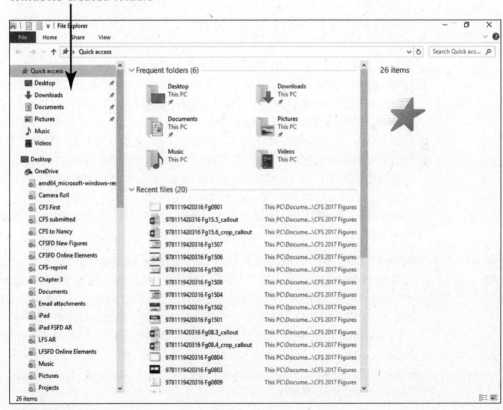

FIGURE 10-1

The Documents folder is a good place to store letters, presentations for your community group, household budgets, and so on. The Pictures folder is where you store picture files, which you may transfer from a digital camera or scanner, receive in an email message from a friend or family member, or download from the Internet. Similarly, the Videos folder is a good place to put files from your camcorder or mobile phone. The Downloads folder is where files you download are stored by default, unless you specify a different location, and the Music folder is where you place tunes you download or transfer from a music player.

» **Create your own folders.** You can create any number of folders and give them a name that identifies the types of files you'll store there. For example, you might create a folder called *Digital Scrapbook* if you use your laptop to create scrapbooks, or a folder called *Taxes* where you save emailed receipts for purchases and electronic tax-filing information.

» **Place folders within folders to further organize files.** A folder you place within another folder is called a *subfolder.* For example, in your Documents folder, you might have a subfolder called *Grandkids* that contains your letters to your grandkids who are away at college. In my Pictures folder, I organize the picture files by creating subfolders that begin with the year and then a description of the event or subject, such as *2018 Home Garden Project, 2017 Christmas, 2018 San Francisco Trip, 20th Family Reunion, Pet Photos,* and so on. In Figure 10-2, you can see subfolders and files stored within the Pictures folder.

» **Move files and folders from one place to another.** Being able to move files and folders helps when you decide it's time to reorganize information on your laptop. For example, when you start using your laptop, you might save all your documents to your Documents folder. That's okay for a while, but in time, you might have dozens of documents saved in that one folder. To make your files easier to locate, you can create subfolders by topic and move files into them.

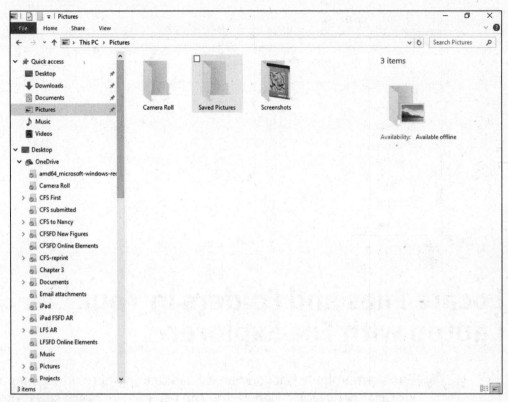

FIGURE 10-2

Access Recently Used Items

1. If you worked on a file recently, File Explorer offers a shortcut to finding and opening it to work on again. Click the File Explorer button in the taskbar.

2. File Explorer opens with Quick Access displayed (see Figure 10-3). Quick Access contains a list of items you've accessed recently, including Recent Files and Frequent Folders.

3. Double-click a file to open it.

FIGURE 10-3

Locate Files and Folders in Your Laptop with File Explorer

1. Can't remember what you named a folder or where on your laptop or storage media you saved it? You can use File Explorer's search feature to find it. First, click the File Explorer button in the taskbar to open File Explorer.

2. In the File Explorer window, click This PC in the list on the left. Click in the Search field at the upper-right corner, and begin typing the name of a file or folder.

3. In the search results that appear (see Figure 10-4), click a file to open it.

TIP

You can narrow your File Explorer search results to folders such as Documents, Downloads, or Pictures by clicking a folder before you type the search term. For instance, if you want to find the file names containing the word "trails" in Documents, click Documents first and then type "trails" in the File Explorer Search field (see Figure 10-5).

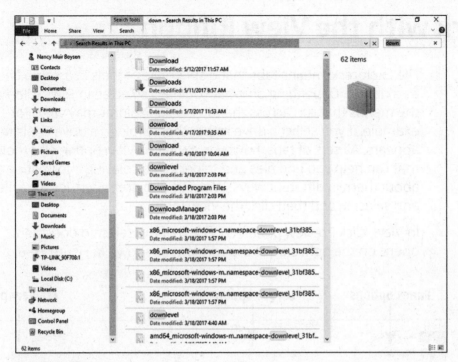

FIGURE 10-4

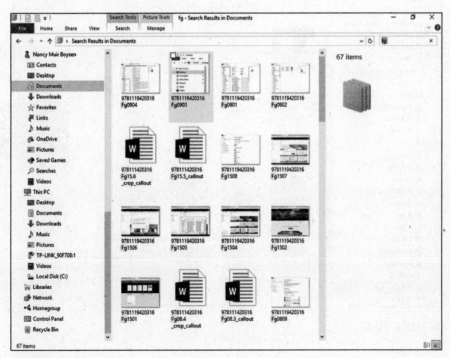

FIGURE 10-5

Work with the View Ribbon

1. File Explorer contains tabs that display sets of tools in an area known as a ribbon. Depending on what you have selected in File Explorer, the menus that run across the top of File Explorer may vary. For example, if you select a drive rather than a folder, a drive Tools tab appears. All sets of tabs, however, contain a View option and tools that can help you find files and folders by displaying information about them in different ways. With File Explorer open, locate a file and select it, and then click the View tab.

2. In View, click Preview pane. A preview of the selected document opens on the right side of the window, as shown in Figure 10-6.

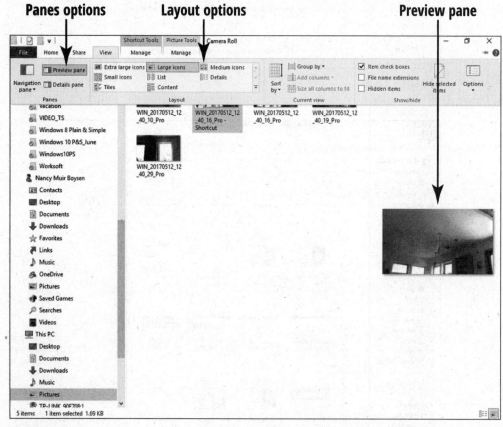

FIGURE 10-6

3. Click the Details pane. Information about the selected file appears in the right pane.

4. Click various options in the Layout section of the ribbon to display information about the file ranging from Details, a simple text list of files with little detail, or Small to Extra Large icons that show a smaller or larger representation of the file's contents.

Search with Cortana

1. If you want to locate files, you can use the Cortana search feature. In the Cortana Search field in the taskbar, begin to type a file name.

2. Possible Search matches appear in categories such as Photos, Documents, or Web (see Figure 10-7). Click a file to open it.

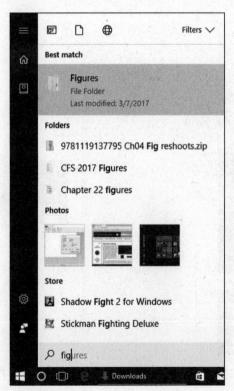

FIGURE 10-7

TIP

If you have typed part of a file name and don't see what you want in the results, keep typing more letters until the file appears in the results.

Move a File or Folder

1. Sometimes you save a file or folder in one place but in reorganizing you decide you want to move the item to another location. To move a file or folder, click the File Explorer button in the taskbar.

2. In File Explorer, click a folder to reveal its contents, or double-click a sub-folder or series of sub-folders to locate the file that you want to move (see Figure 10-8).

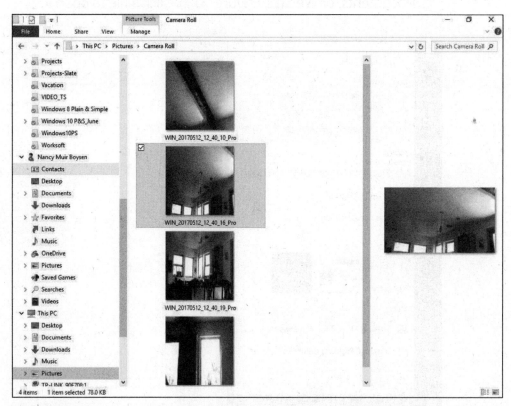

FIGURE 10-8

3. Take one of the following actions:

- **Click and drag** the file to another folder in the Navigation pane on the left side of the window.

- If you **right-click a file or folder,** you're offered options via a shortcut menu: You can move the file, copy it, or create a shortcut to it, for example.

- **Right-click** the file and choose Send To. Then choose from the options shown in the submenu that appears (as shown in Figure 10-9); these options may vary slightly depending on the type of file you choose and your installed software.

4. Click the Close button in the upper-right corner of File Explorer to close it.

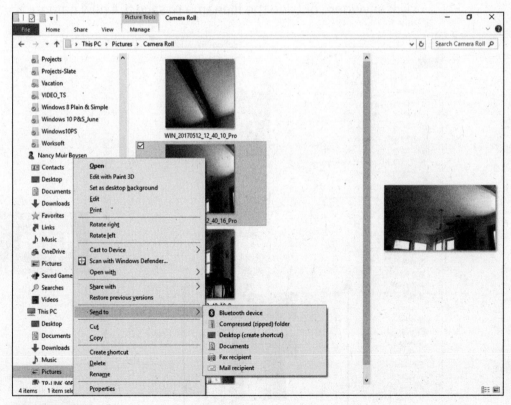

FIGURE 10-9

TIP

If you want to create a copy of a file or folder in another location on your laptop, right-click the item and choose Copy. Use File Explorer to navigate to the location where you want to place a copy, right-click, and choose Paste or press Ctrl+V.

Rename a File or Folder

1. You may want to change the name of a file or folder to update it or differentiate it from other files or folders. Locate the file that you want to rename by using File Explorer.

2. Right-click the file and choose Rename (see Figure 10-10).

3. The filename is now available for editing. Type a new name, and then click anywhere outside the filename to save the new name.

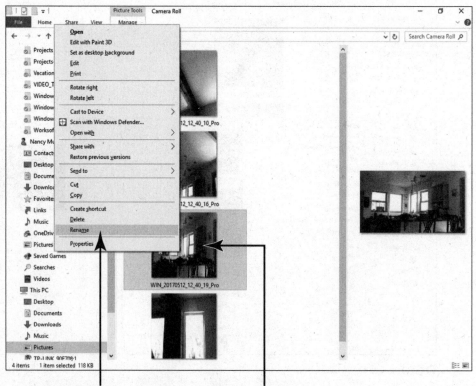

Then choose Rename   **Right-click a file...**

FIGURE 10-10

You can't rename a file to give it the same name as another file located in the same folder. To give a file the same name as another, cut it from its current location, paste it into another folder, and then follow the procedure in this task. Or open the file and save it to a new location with the same name, which creates a copy. Be careful, though: Two files with the same name can cause confusion when you search for files. If at all possible, use unique filenames.

TIP

Create a Shortcut to a File or Folder

1. You can place a shortcut to a file or folder you used recently on the desktop for quick and easy access.

2. In File Explorer, right-click the file or folder that you want and select Send To (as shown in Figure 10-11) and then select Desktop (Create Shortcut).

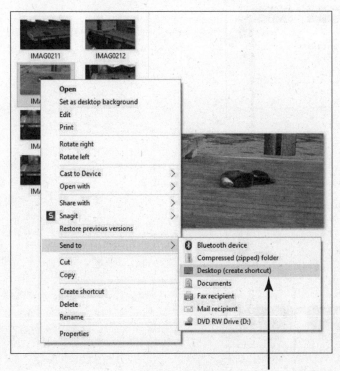

Choose Desktop (create shortcut)

FIGURE 10-11

3. A shortcut appears on the desktop.

TIP

Once you've placed a shortcut on the desktop, to open the file in its originating application or open a folder in File Explorer, simply double-click the desktop shortcut icon.

Delete a File or Folder

1. If you don't need a file or folder anymore, you can clear up clutter on your laptop by deleting it. Locate the file or folder by using File Explorer.

2. Right-click the file or folder that you want to delete and then choose Delete (see Figure 10-12).

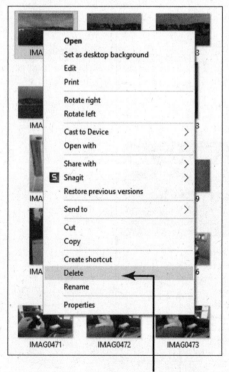

Select this option

FIGURE 10-12

TIP

When you delete a file or folder in Windows, for a time, it's not really gone. It's removed to the Recycle Bin on the desktop. Windows periodically purges older files from this folder, but you may still be able to retrieve recently deleted files and folders from it. To try to restore a deleted file or folder, double-click the Recycle Bin icon on the desktop. Right-click the file or folder and choose Restore. Windows restores the file to wherever it was when you deleted it.

TIP

Instead of right-clicking and choosing Delete from the menu that appears in Step 2 earlier, you can click to select the file and then press the Delete key on your keyboard.

Create a Compressed File or Folder

1. To shrink the size of a file or all the files in a folder, you can compress them. This is often helpful when you're sending an item as an attachment to an email message. Locate the files or folders that you want to compress by using File Explorer. (Click the File Explorer button on the taskbar, and then browse to locate the file[s] or folder[s].)

2. In File Explorer, you can do the following:

- **Select a series of files or folders.** Click a file or folder, press and hold Shift to select a series of items listed consecutively in the folder, and click the final item.

- **Select nonconsecutive items (as shown in Figure 10-13).** Press and hold the Ctrl key and click the items.

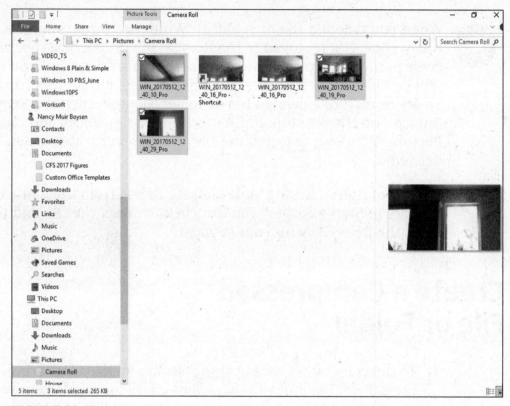

FIGURE 10-13

3. Right-click the selected items. In the resulting shortcut menu (see Figure 10-14), choose Send To and then choose Compressed (Zipped) Folder. A new compressed folder appears below the last selected file in the File Explorer list.

4. The folder icon is named after the last file you selected in the series, but you can rename it. Type a new name or click outside the item to accept the default name.

TIP

You may want to subsequently rename a compressed folder with a name other than the one that Windows automatically assigns to it. See the task "Rename a File or Folder," earlier in this chapter, to find out just how to do that.

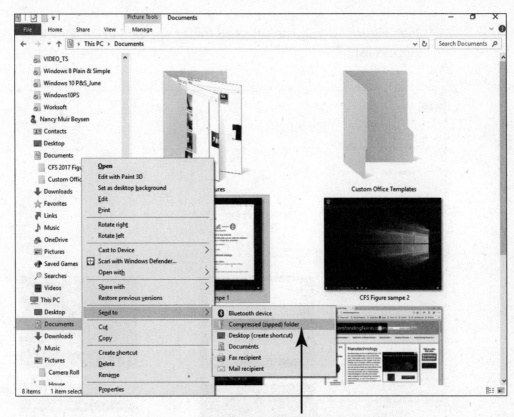

Select Compressed (zipped) folder

FIGURE 10-14

Add a Folder to Your Quick Access List

1. Quick Access offers a fast way to access frequently used folders. Locate the folder that you want to place in Quick Access using File Explorer.

2. In the resulting File Explorer window, right-click the folder. In the short-cut menu that appears, click Pin to Quick Access (see Figure 10-15). The selected folder appears in the Quick Access list.

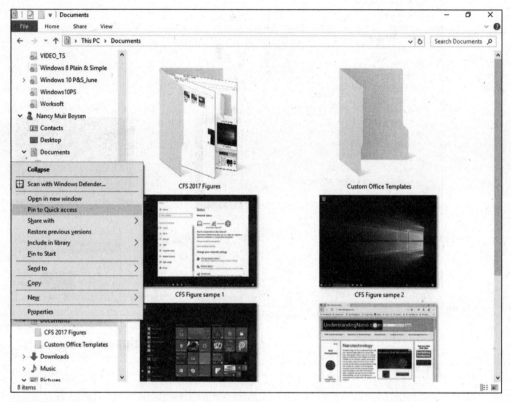

FIGURE 10-15

3. To see a list of folders in Quick Access, as well as recently used files, open File Explorer. File Explorer opens with Quick Access selected.

4. In the Quick Access items, which include folders you have pinned to Quick Access as well as frequently used folders and recently used files (see Figure 10-16), click on an item to open it.

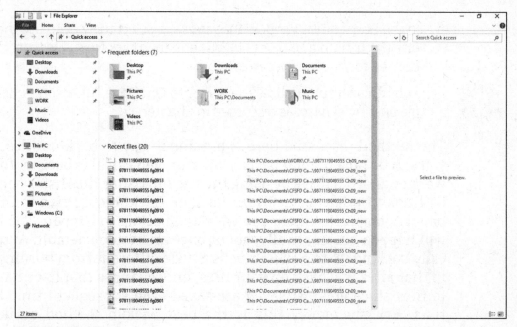

FIGURE 10-16

Back Up Files

1. You've put a lot of work into your files, so don't forget to back them up. If your laptop is damaged or loses data, you'll then have a copy safely tucked away. Place a blank writable DVD-R/RW in your DVD-RW drive and then open File Explorer.

2. Select the files or folders that you want to copy.

3. Click the Share tab on the Ribbon in File Explorer, click Burn to Disc, click the Drive Tools tab that appears, and click Finish Burning

TIP

To save to a drive, instead of burn to disc on the Home tab, click Move To and then select Choose Location from the menu. In the Move Items dialog box, click the drive associated with your USB drive and then click the folder on that drive where you want to save the files. Click the Move button.

4. In the Burn to Disc window that appears, select the way to use the disc (for example USB or CD/DVD) and then click Next. Files are burned to the storage device.

You can also automatically save files to OneDrive, Microsoft's online file sharing service, as discussed in Chapter 17.

TIP

The method discussed here is a manual way to back up files, which you can do on a regular basis. However, you can also back up to a network or another drive by using the Backup Using File History option in Settings⇨Update & Security⇨Backup. Click Add a Drive in the right panel and specify where you want the backup to happen. The backup will happen automatically, about once an hour by default. Automatically backing up to a USB drive is a little different from burning a disc in that after you back up your files, only changes that have happened to files since you last saved are saved each subsequent time backup runs. For my money this is the best backup method available in Windows 10.

Chapter **11**

Working with Windows Apps

Several apps that are preinstalled in Windows 10 can come in handy in planning your activities, connecting with others, and tapping into your creative side. Each app is represented on the Start menu by a tile that you simply click to open.

The News app provides current headlines to keep you informed while the Weather app can tell you whether you need to wear a raincoat or slather on the sunscreen.

The People app is your contact-management resource. You can store contact information and then use information in a contact record to send an email, view a profile, or post a message on that person's Facebook page or other social network.

The Calendar app lets you view your schedule by day, week, or month, and add details about events, such as the date and time, length, and whether it's a recurring event. After you've entered information about an event, you can send yourself a reminder and even invite others to the event.

Finally, the Paint and very cool new Paint 3D apps allow you to manipulate and edit images.

Get Up to Speed with the News App

1. The News app is one of the apps represented by a tile in the Start menu. Click the Start button and then click the News tile (look for the tile with the word News in the bottom-left corner). You may be asked to click the Start button and choose from a list of interests, but for now click Skip to proceed to the News app. The News app opens showing current headlines (see Figure 11-1) and a scrollable list of news categories such as Sports, World, Technology, and Entertainment.

2. Click a news category at the top of the screen such as World, Technology, or Entertainment.

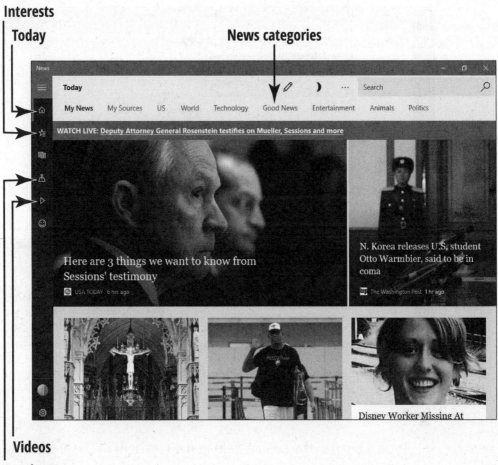

Interests

Today

News categories

Today

My News   My Sources   US   World   Technology   Good News   Entertainment   Animals   Politics

WATCH LIVE: Deputy Attorney General Rosenstein testifies on Mueller, Sessions and more

Here are 3 things we want to know from Sessions' testimony

USA TODAY 6 hrs ago

N. Korea releases U.S. student Otto Warmbier, said to be in coma

The Washington Post 1 hr ago

Disney Worker Missing At

Videos

Local news

FIGURE 11-1

3. Click and drag the vertical scroll bar on the right to scroll down and view the headlines. Click any story that sounds of interest to display it (see Figure 11-2).

4. Use the arrows on the middle of the right and left sides to move to the next or previous page or story, and click the arrow in the top-left corner to go back to the headlines for the news category you selected.

BGR

CEO confirms Apple working on self-driving car system

Chris Smith - BGR - Tuesday, June 13, 2017

Tim Cook has finally confirmed one of the Apple rumors we keep seeing out there: Apple is working on self-driving car technology. The CEO said as much in an interview last week on the same day WWDC 2017 kicked off, but he would not also confirm whether an Apple-brand car is in the works.

"We're focusing on autonomous systems," Cook told *Bloomberg Television*. "It's a core technology that we view as very important. It's probably one of the most difficult A.I.

Provided by BGR

FIGURE 11-2

5. Type a term in the search field at the top right of the News app and click the search icon to see headlines related to that topic (see Figure 11-3). Click a headline to read the story.

6. To add a topic to the news categories shown along the top of the News app, click the Interests button in the toolbar on the left and begin to enter the topic name; the drop-down box shown in Figure 11-4 appears. Click on an interest to add it. Click the Close button to close the Interests window.

TIP

The News app also includes access to Local news and Videos on the toolbar on the left side of the window.

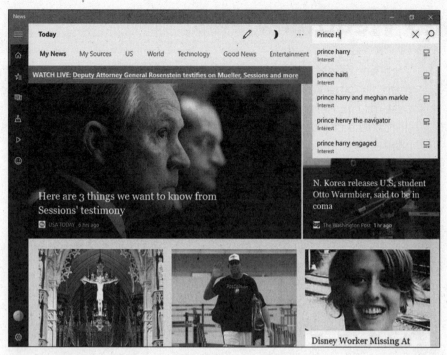

FIGURE 11-3

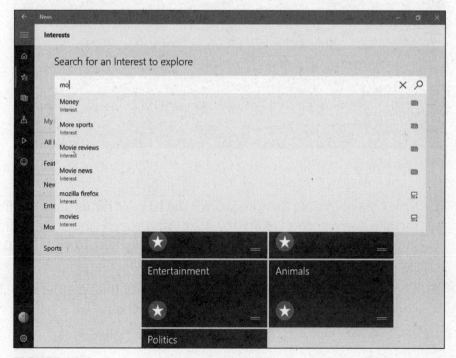

FIGURE 11-4

Display Weather Views

1. Weather offers several sets of information. Click the Start button, and then click the Weather tile to open the Weather app showing the forecast for the next several days (see Figure 11-5). If access to your location and a choice of showing temperatures in Fahrenheit or Celsius are requested, click Start.

FIGURE 11-5

2. Scroll down to view the forecast for the next 24 hours. Day Details include items such as Humidity, Max Wind speed, and Sunrise time, and records for this date such as Record Rain, Record High temperature, and Record Low temperature.

3. Click the Menu button in the top-left corner of the Weather app. The choices shown in the menu in Figure 11-6 appear.

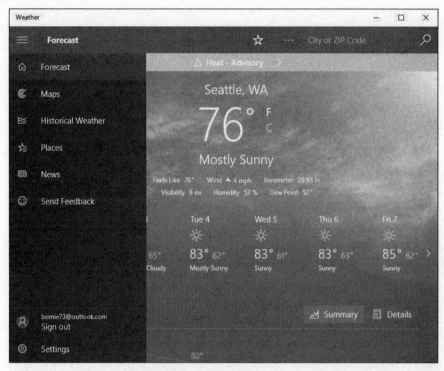

FIGURE 11-6

4. Click Historical Weather; a chart of historical weather trends is displayed.

5. Click Maps; a weather map for your region is shown.

6. Click Settings to set the units (Fahrenheit or Celsius) for temperature or to change your location.

Specify a Location in Weather

1. You can specify one or more favorite places and then display detailed weather information for any of those places easily. To add a place, click the Start button, and then click the Weather tile.

2. Click in the search field at the top-right corner of the Weather app and start typing a city name in the search field. Click the correct city in the search results; the forecast for that city appears in the Weather app.

3. Click the Add to Favorites button (the star shaped icon at the top of the screen) and then click Close.

4. Click the Favorites button (the star in the left toolbar) to display your Favorite Places as shown in Figure 11-7.

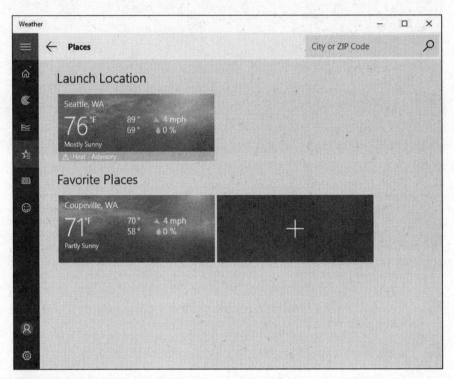

FIGURE 11-7

5. Click one of the Favorite places to display information for it.

You can pin the displayed weather for a particular location to the Start menu. This creates a tile that you can click to retrieve the weather for that location. To pin a location, with it displayed, click the Pin button (the pin shaped button at the top of the window).

To remove a location from your Favorite places, display the Forecast for that location and then click the Remove from Favorites button (the white star at the top of the window).

Add a Contact in the People App

1. After you've entered contacts in the People app, you can look up information about them and send them email, call them using Skype, or post messages to their social network using their contact record. To add a new contact, click People in the Apps list on the Start menu to open the app.

2. Click the add button (the plus symbol) in the left pane of the window shown in Figure 11-8.

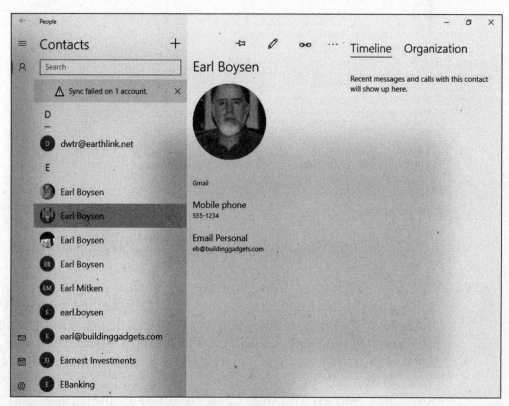

FIGURE 11-8

3. Click the arrow in the Save To box and select an account from the drop-down list, and then enter contact information in the form, as shown in Figure 11-9.

FIGURE 11-9

4. Click the Save button in the lower-left corner of the dialog box.

TIP

When you're logged into Windows 10 with a Microsoft account, contacts from that account are automatically copied into the People app. It's also possible to bring contacts from other accounts into your People app. With the People app open, click the See More button (three lines) in the top of the left pane, and then click Settings in the bottom left of the panel. In the Settings window, click Add an Account. Click an email account type, and sign in to the account you want to add. In the dialog box that appears, scroll down and click Accept (note that this not only allows the People app to import your contacts from your other account, but also allows other Windows apps access to information on calendars, email, and other info in your other account).

TIP

You can find contacts quickly by clicking the search field at the top of the left pane of the People home screen. Type the first letter of the name, which displays a list of contacts whose names start with that letter. Continue to type until the contact's name appears in the list. Then click the contact to see the contact information.

TIP

If you want to get more sophisticated with managing contacts, check out a new feature called My People. Using this feature, you can pin contacts to the taskbar and view a counter for the number of unread messages from those people. You can even drag and drop files onto those contacts to send the files as attachments.

Edit Contact Information

1. Sometimes, you get new information about a contact or find that the information you've already saved to that person's profile changes. To update the information, you can edit the contact. Click the People tile on the Start menu.

2. Click a contact.

3. Click the Edit button (shaped like a pencil) in the upper-right corner of the window.

4. In the Edit Contact screen (see Figure 11-10), edit or add any information in text fields for the contact.

5. For any field with a + symbol next to it, click to display additional options; for example, if you click Phone you can choose from options such as Mobile, Home, or Work.

6. Click the Save button. Click the arrow in the upper-left corner to go back to the People home page.

TIP

Click the Other button to add or edit a job title, significant other, website, or notes for your contact.

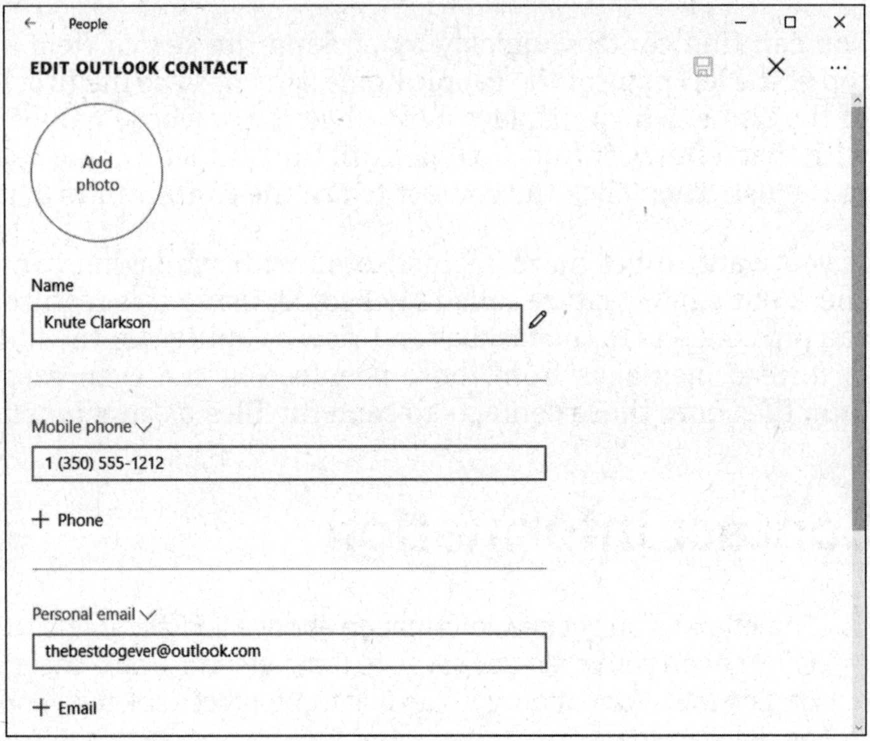

FIGURE 11-10

Send Email to Contacts

1. After you've added contact information, including an email address, you can use the People app to quickly address an email. Click People in the Apps list on the Start menu.

2. Click a contact.

3. Click on the contact's email address in the right panel. In the pop-up menu click Mail and then click OK. If asked which account to use, click the account you've already set up (see Figure 11-11).

4. The Mail app opens with the new message form displayed. Click the Cc & Bcc button to display those fields and then enter any addresses you want to copy on the message, as shown in Figure 11-12.

5. Click in the Subject field and enter a subject for the message.

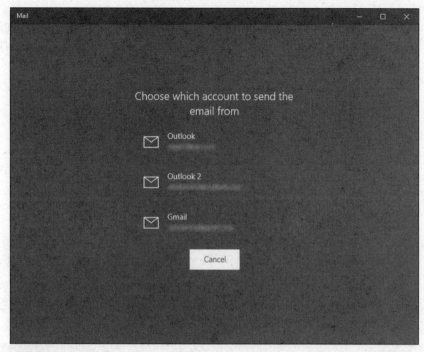

FIGURE 11-11

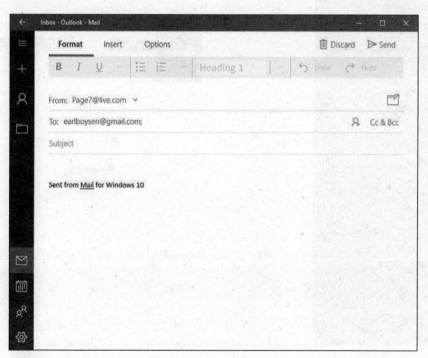

FIGURE 11-12

6. Click in the message area (below the Subject) and enter your message. You can click the Format tab to access some useful text formatting tools.

7. If you want to add attachments click the Insert tab, click the Files button, browse for a file, and then click Open.

8. Click the Send button in the upper-right corner of the window.

Add an Event to Your Calendar

1. The Calendar app is a great way to track your activities. To display and add an event to your Calendar, click the Calendar tile on the Start menu.

2. Click the view you prefer from the list at the top of the window: Today, Day, Week, Month, or Year (see Figure 11-13).

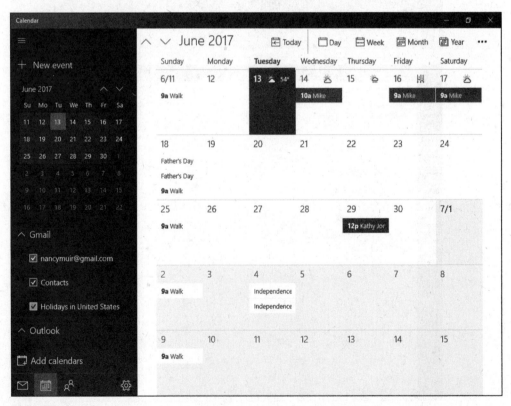

FIGURE 11-13

3. Click the New Event button in the upper-left corner of the window.

4. In the Details dialog box that appears (see Figure 11-14), enter the details of the event in text boxes (such as Event Name or Location) or choose them from drop-down calendars or lists (such as Start or End).

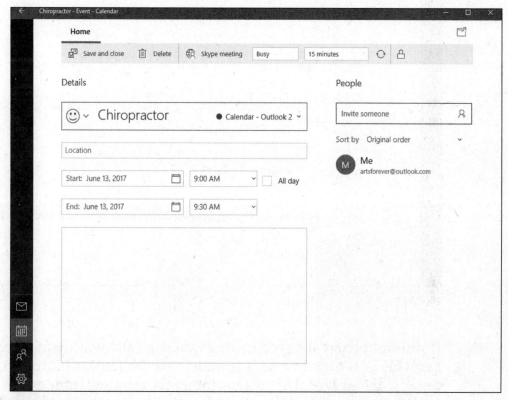

FIGURE 11-14

5. If you have multiple calendar accounts associated with your laptop, click the Calendar field and then select the calendar you want the event to appear in.

6. If you want to be reminded of the event ahead of time, click the Reminder field at the top of the window (see Figure 11-15) and select how long before the event the reminder should occur, such as 15 minutes or 1 week.

7. Click the Save & Close button.

Click here to set a Reminder

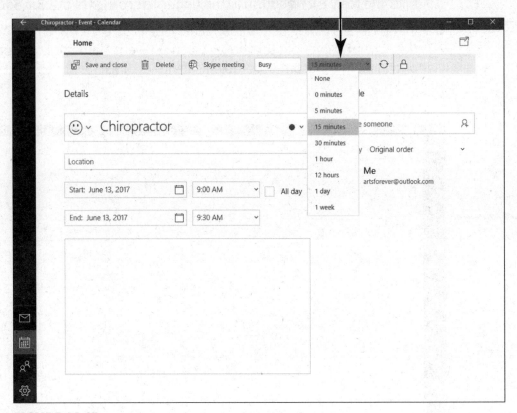

FIGURE 11-15

TIP

If you want to create a recurring event such as a weekly meeting or monthly get-together with friends, use the Repeat button in the Details dialog box. This offers intervals ranging from every day to every year and creates multiple calendar entries accordingly.

TIP

To show events from calendars associated with your laptop, such as a US Holidays calendar or the calendar from an email account, with the Calendar app open click the drop-down list arrow for Outlook or another provider, such as Gmail, in the left pane of the window to open the list of available calendars. Click the check box for any calendar you want to show events from.

TIP

To edit an event after you create it, simply click it in any calendar view. In the resulting Details dialog box modify the details, and then click Save & Close.

Invite People to an Event

1. If you're setting up an event, such as your neighborhood association's meeting or a party, the Calendar app offers a handy way to get the invites out to everybody involved. To create an event and invite others to it, click the New Event button.

2. In the Details dialog box that appears, enter the details of the event in text boxes (such as Event Name and Location) or choose them from drop-down lists (such as Start Time and End Time).

3. Click to indicate that the correct email address is showing in the Event Name box and then click in the Invite Someone field and begin to enter a name. The People app will suggest people and email addresses from your contacts; click one (see Figure 11-16). If you want to invite another person, start to enter the name in the Invite Someone field and click the correct name from the suggested contacts.

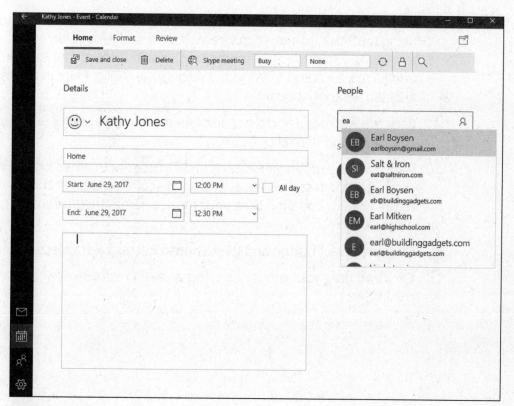

FIGURE 11-16

4. Click the Send button in the upper-left corner of the dialog box. Windows sends an email with details of the event to each invitee.

TIP

If you're browsing through the months or weeks in the Calendar app and want to quickly return to today's events, click Today in the list of time increments at the top of the Calendar home window.

TIP

You can click the Settings button (a sprocket shape) to change Calendar Settings, such as changing the first day of the week, or adding additional accounts that will sync information with the Calendar app.

Work with Paint

1. Paint is a Windows accessory that allows you to work with images using tools that rotate, crop, draw on, and add text, color, and shapes to images. From the Start menu, scroll down through the Apps list and locate and click on Windows Accessories. Click Paint in the list of accessories that appears.

2. Click the File menu and then click Open. Locate an image on your computer and then click Open.

3. With an image open (see Figure 11-17), click the Brushes button and click on a brush style. Click a color in the color palette on the right of the ribbon, and then drag your mouse across the screen to draw a line.

4. Click the Select button and then choose Rectangular Selection.

5. Click and drag your mouse to select a smaller section of the image.

FIGURE 11-17

6. Click the Crop button to crop the image to the selection.
   You can continue to explore Paint tools to draw shapes on
   the image, fill those shapes with color, resize or rotate an object, or
   add a text box (see Figure 11-18).

TIP

If you like working with drawing tools in Paint, check out Windows
Ink. This technology allows you to draw on your screen if you
own a special stylus called a *digital pen*. You tap the Windows Ink
icon in the taskbar to launch the Windows Ink Workspace. Here
you can open Sticky Notes, a Sketchpad, your current screen (for
example, showing a website in a browser), or recently used apps.
When you open one of these, if you have a digital pen, you can
draw directly on your screen and save what you've drawn.

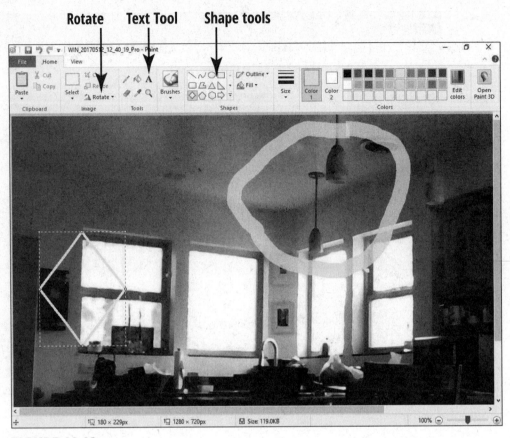

FIGURE 11-18

Discover Paint 3D

1. Paint 3D is a new app that arrived with Windows 10 Creators Update. With Windows Paint open, click the Open Paint 3D button. In the Paint 3D window that appears (see Figure 11-19), click a type of drawing tip in the panel on the right, such as Marker or Pencil.

2. Click and drag the Thickness slider to select how thick the line you draw will be.

3. Click a color in the palette at the bottom of the right panel.

4. Click and drag your mouse across the blank page to draw.

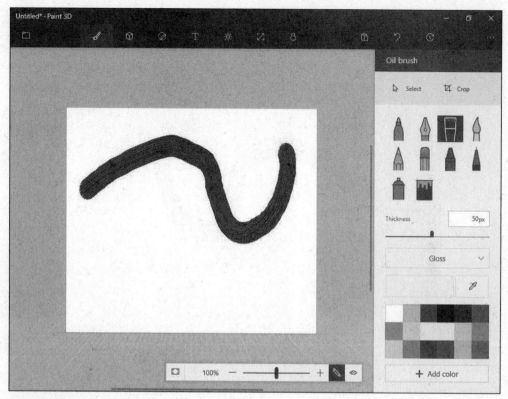

FIGURE 11-19

5. Click the 3D button at the top of the window and select a 3D model, as shown in Figure 11-20.

6. Click the page and draw the 3D object, such as a cat. When you've drawn a 3D object, a new panel appears on the right that allows you to edit the object by grouping objects, cutting, copying, pasting, or deleting the object, or rotating it.

7. Continue to explore buttons along the top of the screen to access tools such as stickers and text, and to add effects.

8. To save what you've created, click the Expand Menu button at the left of the toolbar and select Save.

TIP

You can also open Paint 3D from the list of apps in the Start menu.

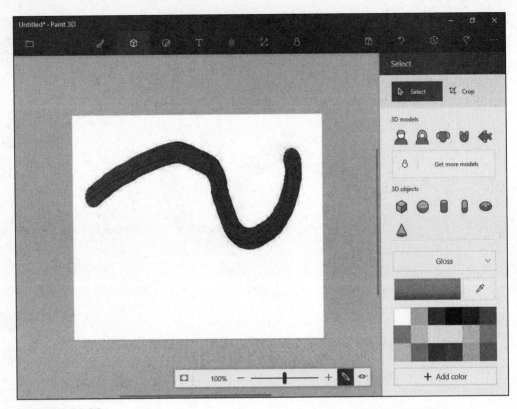

FIGURE 11-20

3 Going Online

Chapter **12**

Hitting the Road with Your Laptop

The preinstalled Maps app in Windows 10 helps you to take full advantage of your laptop's portability. When you want to take a business trip, visit family, or just hit the road for a vacation, you can use the Maps app to help you plan your route. You can also use several popular travel websites to find information about destinations from Paris to Niagara Falls, check on flights and buy tickets, and even find a hotel.

In this chapter, I give you ideas for using the Maps app and the Internet to plan your travel. Don't forget to bring your laptop along for the ride to get updates and more to help you enjoy the journey.

Use the Maps App

Most mapping applications make use of information about your location whenever you're connected to the Internet to provide directions, updates on traffic, and even listings of local businesses such as restaurants and gas stations.

The Maps app is preinstalled with Windows 10. It allows you to keep a record of favorite locations and even get 3-D views of many major cities.

Set Your Location

When you first click the Maps app in the Apps list in the Start menu, you see a message (see Figure 12-1) asking if Maps can use your location. If you click the No button, Maps can only estimate your location, so directions and traffic information may be less exact. If you click the Yes button, Maps can use your location to provide more specific maps, but you are then allowing a remote service to pinpoint your location (though with Maps that affords little risk).

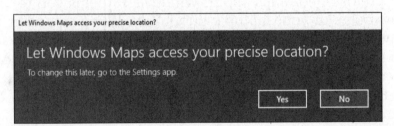

FIGURE 12-1

For example, if children use your laptop, allowing a service to pinpoint your location could also allow very computer savvy people to find them. However, for most folks, allowing use of your location for a service such as Maps is pretty safe, so you can click Yes to continue. The map that appears will be specific to your location.

Show Traffic

1. After you open Maps, toolbars appear along the top and right side of the app (see Figure 12-2). Click the Show My Location button on the right side to zoom in on your location.

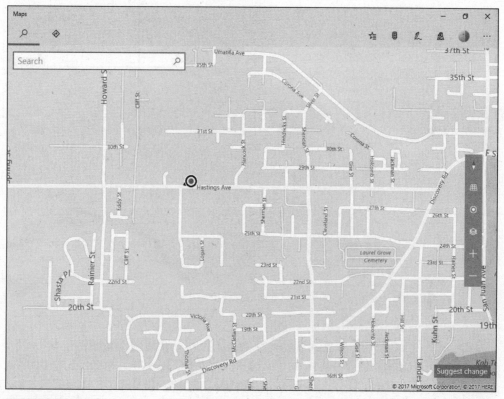

FIGURE 12-2

2. Click the Map Views button (third from the bottom, looking like a stack of papers) on the right and then click the Traffic On/Off switch in the pop-up that appears. Traffic alerts such as those shown in Figure 12-3 appear. (Click Zoom In if needed to get a closer view.)

3. Click an alert to display information about its severity, start time, and estimated end time (refer to Figure 12-3). Click outside the Map Views panel to hide this information.

Traffic incidents　　　　　　　　　　　**Route**　　　　　　　　**Map Views button**

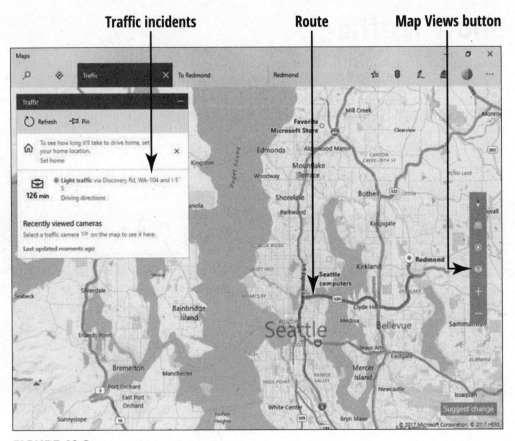

FIGURE 12-3

TIP

You can click the Search tool and enter a location to get a list of categories such as Hotels, Coffee, Restaurants, Shopping, and Museums. Click a category to display a list of nearby locations on the left side. You can then click a location and click a link to access that business's website, get directions, or place a call to them using Skype.

Get Directions

1. With the Maps app open, click the Directions button (a diamond-shaped direction sign near the upper-left corner). A Directions panel appears (see Figure 12-4).

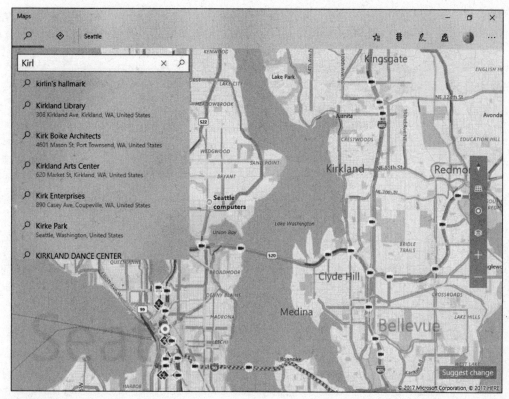

FIGURE 12-4

2. Enter a start point in the field labeled A.

3. Enter a destination address in the field labeled B and click Get Directions on the right side of that field.

4. If you are offered a few choices of start point or destination, click the correct one, and then click one of three icons: Drive (a car), Transit (a bus), or Walking (a person) to get directions for that mode of transportation (see Figure 12-5).

When you open the Directions panel, click the Route Options link (refer to Figure 12-3) to choose to avoid highways, ferries, unpaved roads, tunnels, or tolls.

TIP

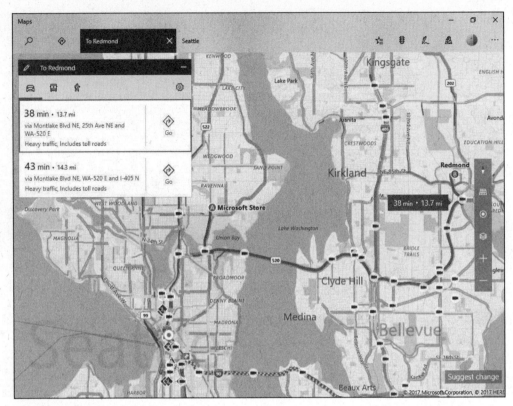

FIGURE 12-5

Plan Travel Online

The Internet is full of services that help you plan and book travel. Some search dozens of other sites for deals; others offer deals from a single source.

There are many online services such as Kayak (www.kayak.com) shown in Figure 12-6 and Expedia (www.expedia.com) that allow you to find airfares, hotels, rental cars, and more travel-related items.

Here are some tips for using these services:

» Look for current deals, which may require you to book a trip on short notice.

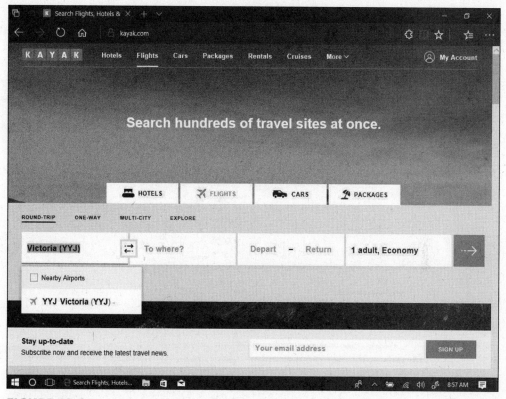

FIGURE 12-6

>> Explore discounts for booking a flight, hotel, or rental car together.

>> Use the search tools in these services to find the best deal from a variety of airlines and hotels and then compare the prices; some offers can be much lower than others.

>> If you're flexible in your travel dates some sites can find you a better deal than if your dates are inflexible.

You can also visit individual sites for hotels, airlines, and rental car agencies online and check out their latest packages and deals. Some offer a discount for booking online. In addition, look for

sites specializing in B&Bs or vacation exchanges, such as www.
HomeExchange.com shown in Figure 12-7.

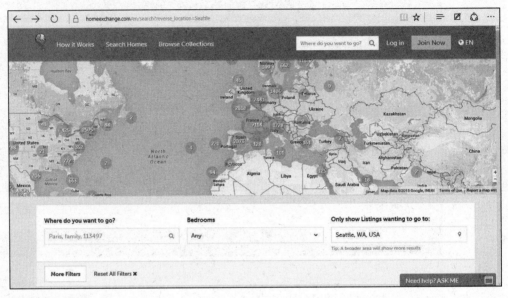

FIGURE 12-7

Get Travel Advice and Information

From travel magazines to travel blogs and currency conversion tools, there's a wealth of information available on the Internet to help you plan your trip.

Check out some of these sites for useful travel information:

» **Travel and Leisure magazine** (www.travelandleisure.com): This site includes articles about various destinations and travel tips (see Figure 12-8).

» **Flight Aware** (www.flightaware.com): This site allows you track any flight in real time to see whether a flight has left the gate, is en route, or has arrived.

FIGURE 12-8

» **Trip Advisor** (`www.tripadvisor.com`): Get reviews from people like you for all kinds of travel destinations and restaurants, hotels, and even vacation rentals. You can also use their booking tools to book a trip.

» **Yahoo Currency Converter** (`http://finance.yahoo.com/currency-converter`): Find out the latest information about how much your buck will get you in foreign countries. Be aware that there are many free currency converter sites out there, but not all are safe.

» **Rick Steves** (`www.ricksteves.com`): This popular television travel show host's site (see Figure 12-9) offers very practical travel tips about everything from packing to using a cell phone when you travel internationally.

TIP

Don't forget to check out AARP Travel (`http://travel.aarp.org`) for travel services and advice, as well as discounts for seniors who are members of AARP. If you use another trip-planning service, remember to indicate that you're an AARP member to get available discounts.

FIGURE 12-9

Chapter **13**

Understanding Internet Basics

For many people, going online might be the major reason to buy a laptop. You can use the Internet to check stock quotes, play interactive games with others, shop, and file your taxes, for example. For seniors especially, the Internet can provide a way to keep in touch with family and friends located around the country or on the other side of the world via email, instant messaging, or video calling. You can share photos of your grandchildren or connect with others who share your hobbies or interests.

But before you begin all those wonderful activities, it helps to understand some basics about the Internet and how it works.

This chapter helps you understand what the Internet and World Wide Web are, as well as some basics about connecting to the Internet and navigating it. I also tell you about the Microsoft Edge app, which is built into Windows 10.

Understand What the Internet Is

The "Internet," "links," the "web". . . . People and the media bounce around many online-related terms these days, and folks sometimes use them incorrectly. Your first step in getting familiar with the Internet is to understand what some of these terms mean.

Here's a list of common Internet-related terms:

» The *Internet* is a large network of computers that contain information and technology tools that anybody with an Internet connection can access. (See the next section for information about Internet connections.)

» Residing on that network of computers is a huge set of documents and services, which form the *World Wide Web,* usually referred to as, simply, the *web.* The www notation at the start of a website address (known as a URL) is an acronym for *World Wide Web.*

» The web includes *websites,* such as shopping and government websites. These sites are made up of collections of *web pages* just as a book is made up of individual pages. Websites have many purposes: For example, a website can be informational, function as a retail store, or host social networking communities where people can exchange ideas and thoughts.

» You can buy, sell, or bid for a wide variety of items in an entire online marketplace referred to as the world of *e-commerce.*

» To get around online, you use a software program called a *browser.* Many browsers are available, and they're free. Microsoft

Edge is Microsoft's latest browser, taking the place of Internet Explorer; others include Mozilla Firefox, Google Chrome, Safari, and Opera. Browsers offer tools to help you navigate from website to website and from one web page to another.

» Each web page has a unique address that you use to reach it, called a Uniform Resource Locator (URL). You enter a URL in a browser's address bar to go to a website or a particular page within a site.

» When you open a website, you might see colored text or graphics that represent *hyperlinks,* also referred to as *links.* You can click links to move from place to place within a web page, within a website, or between websites. Figure 13-1 shows some hyperlinks indicated by colored text or graphics.

Graphical hyperlinks

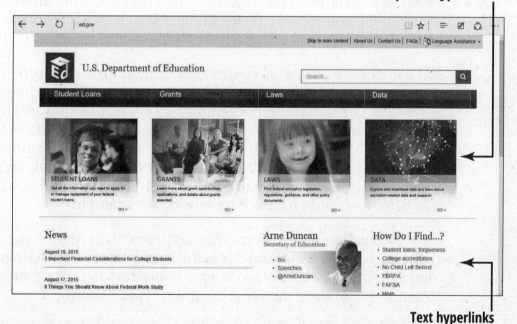

Text hyperlinks

FIGURE 13-1

TIP

A link can be a graphic (such as a company logo or button) or text. A text link often is displayed in a color such as blue. A colored text link typically changes color when you click on it. After you click a link, the link itself usually changes color to indicate that you've followed the link. Some websites also include tabs, drop-down lists, and menus for navigation.

Explore Different Types of Internet Connections

Before you can connect to the Internet for the first time, you have to have certain hardware in place and choose your *Internet service provider* (also referred to as an *ISP* or simply a *provider*). An ISP is a company that owns dedicated computers (called *servers*) that you use to access the Internet. This could be the company that provides your phone or TV connection, for example. ISPs charge a monthly fee for providing an Internet connection.

You can choose a type of connection to go online. The type of connection you want determines which companies you can choose from to provide the service. For example, a DSL connection might come through your phone company, whereas a cable connection is available through your cable-TV company. Not every type of connection is necessarily available in every area, so check first with phone, cable, and local Internet providers to find out your options and costs. Some ISPs offer discounts to AARP members, for example.

Each connection type offers pros and cons in terms of the quality of the signal and potential service interruptions, depending on the company and your locale, so do your homework before signing on the dotted line. Here are the most common types of connections:

» **Digital Subscriber Line (DSL):** This service is delivered through your phone land line, but your phone is available to you to make calls even when you're connected to the Internet. DSL is a form of broadband communication, which may use phone lines and fiber-optic cables for transmission. You have to subscribe to a broadband service (check with your phone company) and pay a monthly fee for access. Some providers also let you purchase DSL service "naked," or without telephone service, if you use a mobile phone.

» **Cable:** You may instead go through your local cable company to get your Internet service via the cable that brings your TV programming. This is another type of broadband service, and it's relatively fast. Check with your cable company for monthly fees. Many cable providers offer plans that bundle TV, phone, and Internet services.

» **Satellite:** Especially in rural areas, satellite Internet providers may be your only option. This requires that you install a satellite dish. HughesNet, dishNET (from Dish Network), and Exede (from ViaSat) are three providers of satellite connections to check into.

» **Wireless hotspots:** If you take a wireless-enabled laptop computer, tablet, or smartphone with you on a trip, you can piggyback on somebody else's connection. You will find wireless hotspots in many public places, such as airports, cafes, and hotels. If you're in range of such a hotspot, your laptop usually finds the connection automatically, making Internet service available to you for free or for a fee. You may need to enter a password to connect your computer. You can also buy your own portable wireless hotspot from a provider such as Verizon or in some cases use your smartphone to connect a laptop or tablet to the Internet via the cellular network. This type of connection also requires a data plan with the mobile carrier.

TIP

Satellite and mobile connections often restrict how much data you can download per month (data includes websites you view and emails you open, for example). Overages with mobile data plans can be expensive, so be sure to monitor your data usage once you get started with a new plan.

» **Dialup:** This is the slowest connection method, but it's relatively inexpensive. With a dialup connection, you use a phone line to connect to the Internet, entering some phone numbers (*local access numbers*) that your ISP provides. Using these local access numbers, you won't incur long distance charges for your connection. However, with this type of connection, you can't use a phone line for phone calls while you're connected to the Internet, so it's no longer a popular way to connect.

Internet connections have different speeds that depend partially on your laptop's capabilities and partially on the connection you get from your provider. Before you choose a provider, it's important to understand how faster connection speeds can benefit you:

» Faster speeds allow you to send data faster, for example to download a photo to your laptop. In addition, web pages and images display faster.

» Dialup connection speeds run at the low end, about 56 kilobits per second, or Kbps. Most broadband connections today start at around 1,000 Kbps (kilobits per second) and range up to 40 Mbps (megabits per second), or more. If you have a slower connection, a file might take minutes to upload. (For example, you might upload a file you're attaching to an email.) This same operation might take only seconds at a higher speed.

» Broadband services typically offer different plans that provide different access speeds. These plans can give you savings if you're economy minded and don't mind the lower speeds, or offer you much better speeds if you're willing to pay for them.

Depending on your type of connection, you'll need different hardware:

» Some laptops come with a built-in modem for dialup connections (though these are being left out more and more as people move to wireless connections) and are enabled for wireless.

» A broadband connection uses an Ethernet cable and a broadband modem, which your provider should make available. For a wired connection, the Ethernet cable connects the modem to your laptop. From there, you will also need a telephone cable to connect the modem to your phone line (for DSL) or a coaxial cable to connect the modem with a cable line or incoming line from a satellite dish.

» If you want to make your broadband connection wireless, your phone or cable company can provide you with a wireless router (for a price), or you can buy one from an office supply or electronics store. Instead of connecting the modem to the laptop, you use the Ethernet cable to connect the broadband modem to the wireless router, which enables two-way wireless communication. A wireless adapter in the laptop enables it to connect with the wireless router. Most new laptop's now offer built-in wireless adapters that enable them to pick up wireless signals. If you have a laptop that doesn't have a built-in wireless modem, you can add this hardware by buying and installing a wireless USB adapter.

If this all sounds like Greek to you, review your laptop's system specifications for information about its networking capabilities, and then visit a computer or major office supply store and ask representatives for their advice about your specific hardware.

TIP

Many providers offer free or low-cost setup when you open a new account. If you're not technical by nature, consider taking advantage of this when you sign up.

TIP

If you fly with your laptop, you may be able to connect to the Internet during the flight. Also, it's important to remember that during takeoff and landing, you'll be asked to turn off electronics so that they don't interfere with air traffic communications. Be alert to the announcement if you intend to use your laptop on the plane. Some tablet computers and smartphones come with an Airplane mode setting that disables any disruptive communications while in flight.

Set Up a Wi-Fi Internet Connection

1. The first step is to set up a connection in Windows so you can access the Internet. Right-click the Network Settings button on the taskbar and then select Open Network and Sharing Center on the menu that appears.

2. In the resulting Network and Sharing Center window (see Figure 13-2), click the Network and Sharing Center link near the bottom and then click Set Up a New Connection or Network.

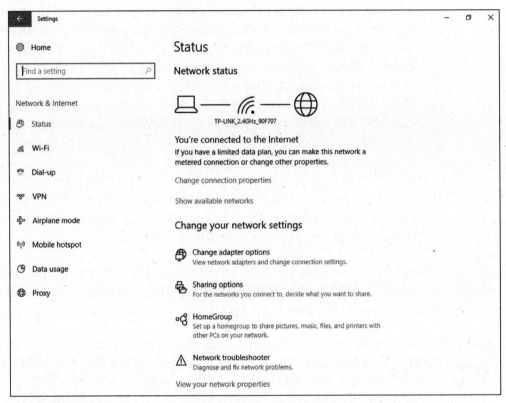

FIGURE 13-2

3. In the Choose a Connection Option window, click Next to accept the default option of creating a new Internet connection. If you're already connected to the Internet, a window appears; click Set Up a New Connection Anyway.

4. In the resulting dialog box, click your connection. (These steps follow the selection of Broadband.)

5. In the resulting dialog box, shown in Figure 13-3, enter your user-name and password, and change the connection name if you wish (this is optional), and then click Connect. Windows automatically detects the connection, and the Network and Sharing Center appears with your connection listed.

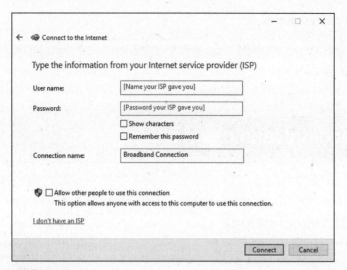

FIGURE 13-3

TIP

In some cases, if you have a disc from your ISP, you don't need to follow the preceding steps. Just pop that DVD into your DVD drive, and in no time, a window appears that gives you the steps to follow to get set up.

Practice Navigation Basics with the Microsoft Edge App

1. A browser is a program that you use to navigate, manage, and use features on the various pages of content on the web. You can practice how to get around the web using a browser such as Microsoft Edge, included with Windows 10. Open Microsoft Edge by clicking the Microsoft Edge button on the taskbar.

2. Click the address bar at the top and enter a website address (as shown in Figure 13-4; www.understandingnano.com is an example website), and then press Enter.

3. On the resulting website, click a link to display another page. Try using navigation tools on the page (such as the What Is Nanotechnology menu on the page in Figure 13-4) or enter a search term in the Search box to find topics within the site.

Enter a web address here

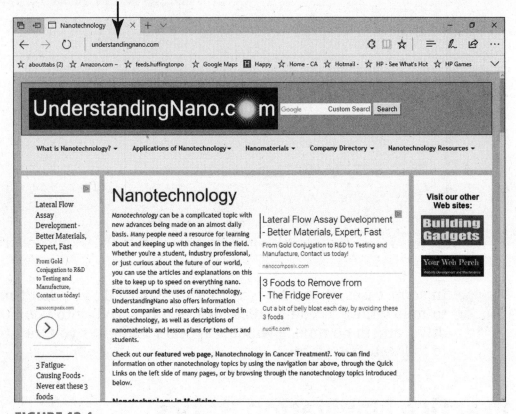

FIGURE 13-4

TIP

A link can be text or graphics (such as an icon or photo). A text link is often blue. After you click a link, it usually changes to another color (such as purple) to show that you've followed it before.

4. Click the Back button to the left of the address bar to move back to the first page that you visited. Click the Forward button just to the right of the Back button to go forward to the second page that you visited.

TIP

The Refresh button (a curved arrow) to the right of the Forward button is useful for navigating sites. Clicking the Refresh button redisplays the current page. This is especially useful if a page, such as on a stock market site, updates information frequently. You can also use the Refresh button if a page doesn't load correctly; it might load correctly when refreshed.

TIP

You can quickly access frequently viewed sites by marking them as Favorites. See Chapter 14 for more info about marking and organizing Favorites.

Use Other Browsers

You aren't restricted to using Microsoft Edge as a web browser. Many other browsers are available, such as Google Chrome (shown in Figure 13-5) and Mozilla Firefox, and they're free for you to download to your computer. Each browser has unique features, but all browsers have certain things in common, so it's not hard to catch on to how they work. If you've used one browser, for the most part, you can use them all.

FIGURE 13-5

Browsers have these features in common:

» **An address bar:** At the top of browsers there's a box where you can enter an address (like www.msn.com) and go directly to that site.

» **A search box:** Every browser allows you to search using a word or phrase to find a website. Search results are displayed, and you can click the closest match to view that site.

» **Navigation tools:** Typically, there will be arrows you use to go back to a previously viewed site and forward to the last site displayed.

» **Favorites, bookmarks, and history:** Most browsers allow you to save your favorite site or bookmark a site or page to make it easy to return to. In addition, browsers maintain a search history to help you find that restaurant menu or Wikipedia entry you viewed in the last week or so.

Browsers offer different features for displaying and managing tabs.

TIP The latest versions of Windows 10 and Microsoft Edge include new Preview and multiple tab features. See Chapter 14 for more about these.

Understand Tabs in Browsers

Most browsers use tabs (Figure 13-6 shows tabs in the Microsoft Edge app), which allow you to keep multiple web pages open at once and easily switch among them by clicking the tabs. A *tab* offers a way to display and navigate among any number of web pages. You don't have to create a new tab to go to another site, but you can more quickly switch between two or more sites without a lot of clicking around or entering URLs.

In Microsoft Edge, for example, tabs across the top of the page look like tabs used to divide index cards into topics. Click on a tab to display that page.

To add a new tab in Microsoft Edge, click the New Tab button to the right of the current far right tab, or press Ctrl+T. Type the URL you want to show in the address bar for the new tab, then press Enter. (See Figure 13-7.) To close a tab, click the Close Tab (X) button on the right end of the tab. Pressing Ctrl+W closes the current tab. To go to another open tab, simply click anywhere on the tab away from the Close Tab button.

Open tab   **Active tab you're on**   **New Tab button**

FIGURE 13-6

Enter web address here   **Close Tab button** **New Tab button**

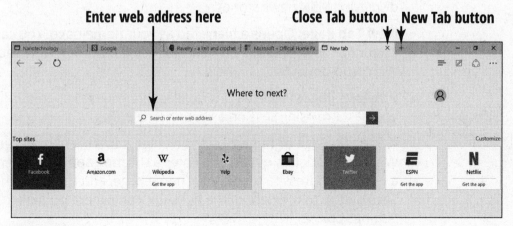

FIGURE 13-7

Understand Start and Home Pages

In most browsers, the first page you see when you open the browser is your home page, which you can specify. In fact, you can even choose to reload the tab(s) you had open during your last browser session as your home page(s).

Your home page(s) appear automatically every time you open Microsoft Edge, so choose a site that you go to often for this setting. For example, if you like to start your day by reading the news from the online version of your local paper, you could set that up as your home page. Or, if you like to check on your finances throughout the day by going to a financial site and checking stock quotes and news, you could make that website your home page. See the next task, where I tell you how to set this up.

Set Up a Home Page in Microsoft Edge

1. Open Microsoft Edge. Near the upper-right corner, click the Settings & More button (it looks like three dots in a horizontal row; see Figure 13-8) and choose Settings from the menu.

2. In the resulting Settings pane, under the Open Microsoft Edge With section, click the option button for the type of home page you want.

   - **Start Page:** Choose this to open with Microsoft's default start page displaying MSN news stories.

   - **New Tab Page:** Opens a blank tab as your home page. You can customize what appears on new tabs using the Open New Tabs With drop-down list.

   - **Previous Pages:** Sets the prior pages that you had open during your last browsing session as your home pages.

   - **A Specific Page or Pages:** Lets you enter a specific home page. When you click this option, the Enter a URL box appears. Enter a website address to use as your home page, and then click the Save button to the right of the field. Click anywhere outside the Settings box.

Settings and More button

FIGURE 13-8

3. After you choose a home page setting, close and restart Microsoft Edge to verify your home page.

TIP

To remove a home page that you've set up, go to the Settings pane mentioned in Step 2 of this task and, under the A Specific Page or Pages option, click the Remove (X) button beside the URL and then click the Save button to the right. Set another home page as needed, and save it. Click anywhere outside the pane to close it.

Chapter **14**

Browsing the Web

A *browser* is a program that you can use to move from one web page to another, but you can also use it to perform searches for information and images. Most browsers, such as Microsoft Edge that debuts with Windows 10, Google Chrome, and Mozilla

Firefox, are available for free. Macintosh computers come with a browser called Safari preinstalled with the operating system.

Chapter 13 introduced browser basics, such as how to go directly to a site when you know the web address, how to use the Back and Forward buttons to move among sites you've visited, and how to set up the home page that opens automatically when you launch your browser.

In this chapter, you discover the ins and outs of using Microsoft Edge — the browser included with Windows 10.

Using Microsoft Edge, you can

» **Navigate all around the web.** Use the Microsoft Edge navigation features to go back to places you've been (via pinned tabs and the Favorites and History features), and use Bing or Cortana to search for new places to visit.

» **Take advantage of reading and note-taking features.** You can create a list of articles you'd like to read later, view them in Reading view for a more natural reading experience, or make your own notes on a page.

» **Print content from web pages.** When you find what you want online, such as an image or article, just use Microsoft Edge's Print feature to generate a hard copy.

» **Customize your web-browsing experience.** You can modify some Microsoft Edge features, such as the default home page, to make your online work easier.

Learn More about Microsoft Edge

With Windows 10, Microsoft introduced a brand new browser: Microsoft Edge.

Microsoft Edge was designed to load web pages more quickly than its predecessor, Internet Explorer. It also features a less-cluttered screen (see Figure 14-1), with just a few simple buttons and an address bar near the top of the screen. You can use tabs to open additional pages. With settings you can manage from the Settings and More menu, you can change what appears when you first open Microsoft Edge, pin a web page to the Start menu, and more.

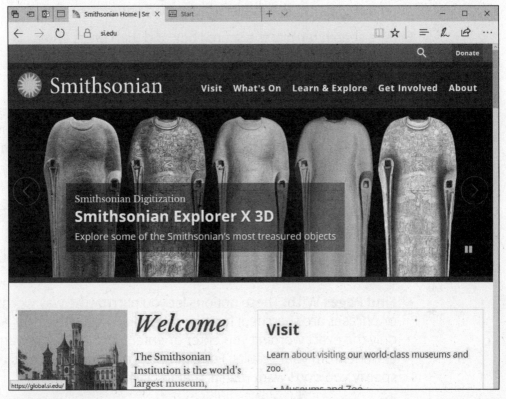

FIGURE 14-1

Internet Explorer will still be available. It will open automatically whenever you try to browse to a page that hasn't been updated to open in Microsoft Edge. Because you probably won't see that happen often, this chapter covers how to handle a variety of tasks in Microsoft Edge.

Search the Web

1. You can use words and phrases to search for information on the web using a search engine no matter which browser you use. In this example, you'll use Microsoft Edge and Google, a popular search engine. Open Microsoft Edge by clicking its button on the taskbar, enter www.google.com in the address bar, and press Enter.

2. Enter a search term in the search box and then press Enter.

TIP

   To start your search in a new tab, click the New Tab button or press Ctrl+T before entering www.google.com in the address bar.

3. In the search results that appear (see Figure 14-2), you can click a link to go to that web page. If you don't see the link that you need, move the mouse pointer over the right edge of the screen to make the scroll bar appear. Then drag the scroll bar to view more results.

4. Click Settings in the links located under the Search box near the upper right (refer to Figure 14-2), and then click Advanced Search from the menu that appears to change Search parameters.

5. In the resulting Advanced Search page, shown in Figure 14-3, you can modify the following parameters:

   - **Find Pages With:** These options let you narrow the way words or phrases are searched; for example, you can find matches for only the exact wording you enter or enter words that you want to exclude from your results. For example, you could search *flu* and specify you don't want results that involve *swine flu*.

   - **Then Narrow Your Results By:** Here you can select language and region. You can also limit results based on when information on the site was last updated, if you're looking for the most current information on the subject you're searching. You can specify a site address and where on the page to search. You can also adjust safety settings for your search by choosing between the options in the SafeSearch drop-down list, or adjust the file type, and *usage rights settings* (in other words, any copyrights that prohibit you from reusing content).

6. When you're done with the settings, scroll down and click the Advanced Search button to run the search again based on the new criteria.

Click a link in the results list

Settings and More button

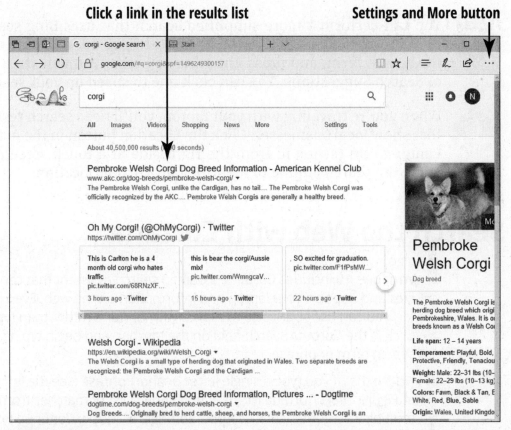

FIGURE 14-2

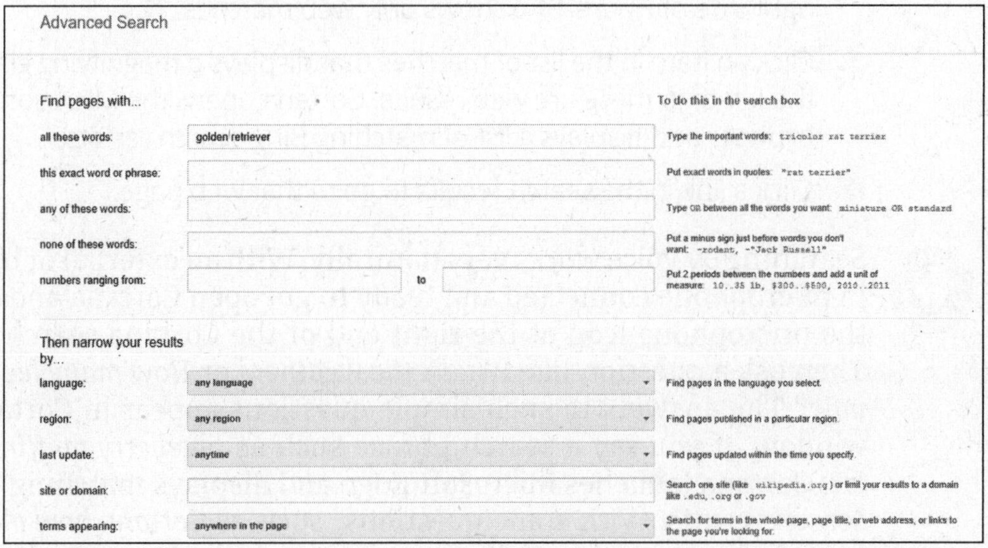

FIGURE 14-3

You can perform a more simplified search that uses Bing search in Microsoft Edge. Click in the Microsoft Edge address bar, type the search term, and press Enter. As you type, you will see a list of Search Suggestions. You can click one to speed up your search.

When you're traveling with your laptop, you'll need search results that show local businesses. Click the Location button in the Action Center to On (swipe in from the right side of a touch screen) to allow the search engine to identify your current location.

Search the Web with Cortana

1. Windows 10 includes Cortana, a built-in search assistant that can find files and apps on your laptop and information on the web. Even better, you can use your voice to search with Cortana rather than typing. Click in the Cortana search field on the taskbar, and begin typing a search term or phrase.

2. Notice that if you type a single letter or short phrase (see the left side of Figure 14-4), Cortana might at first show a list of matches from multiple categories, such as Apps, Settings, or Music. Continue typing a search phrase to make the search more specific (see the right side of Figure 14-4) and narrow it to fewer categories. For example, the right side of Figure 14-4 shows only web matches.

3. Click an item in the list of matches that displays a magnifying glass to the left of it; these are web results. Cortana opens the Microsoft Edge browser and displays a list of matching Bing search results.

4. Click a link in the search results to go to that web page.

Searching by voice works very naturally. With an external or built-in microphone connected and ready to go, open Cortana and click the microphone icon at the right end of the Cortana search box. Then ask a question like *What's the weather?* or *How many feet in a mile?* The answers to such simple questions appear in Cortana's window. If you say a search phrase such as *blueberry muffin recipe*, Cortana launches Microsoft Edge and displays matching Bing search results. With some questions, such as *Cortana how old are you?* she'll respond verbally.

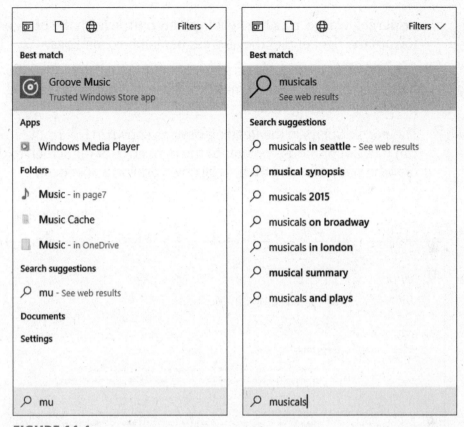

FIGURE 14-4

TIP

If you come across a phrase or term on a web page that you want to learn more about, drag over it with your mouse to select it. Then, right-click the selected term and click Ask Cortana in the shortcut menu that appears. A pane filled with helpful information about the topic appears to the right. After you finish reading the information, click back on the web page to close the pane.

Use Reading View

1. Microsoft Edge's Reading view provides a more comfortable, clean way to view a web page. It reformats page text to be narrower, offers larger font size, and removes distractions such as navigation links and ads. To change to Reading view after starting Microsoft Edge and displaying a page, click the Reading View button (with the book on it) toward the right end of the address bar in Microsoft Edge.

TIP

If the Reading View button is grayed out (disabled), the current page has formatting or other elements that prevent it from displaying properly in Reading view.

2. The page displays in the Reading view, as shown in Figure 14-5. You can move your mouse pointer to the right edge of the screen to display the scroll bar, and then scroll down and up as needed.

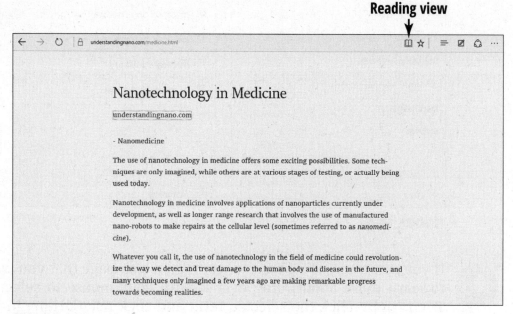

FIGURE 14-5

3. Click the Reading View button to return to the regular view.

Find Content on a Web Page

1. After starting Microsoft Edge, enter a URL in the address bar, and press Enter. Click the Settings and More button (it has a row of three dots on it), and choose Find on Page, as shown in Figure 14-6.

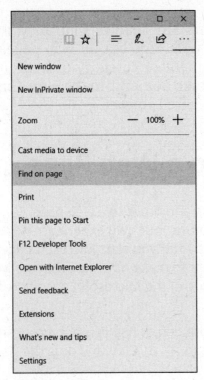

FIGURE 14-6

2. In the resulting Find on Page toolbar that appears below the address bar, enter the word that you want to search for. As you type, all instances of the word on the page are highlighted.

3. Click the Next button (see Figure 14-7) and you move from one highlighted instance of the word to the next. If you want to move to a previous instance, click the Previous button.

FIGURE 14-7

4. When you're done searching on a page, click the Close button at the right end of the Find on Page toolbar.

TIP

Many websites have a Search This Site feature that allows you to search not only the displayed web page but all web pages on a website, or to search by department or category of item in an online store. Look for a Search text box and make sure that it searches the site — and not the entire Internet.

Add Your Own Notes to a Web Page

1. You can add your own highlighting and notes to a web page. For example, you might do this to capture your own experience with a recipe or instructions for a project. After you start Microsoft Edge and display the web page that you want to make notes on, click the Make a Web Note button on the right side of the Microsoft Edge address bar (it looks like a pen).

2. In the toolbar that appears, click the pen or highlighter button, and then click the color to use (see Figure 14-8). Click and drag the size option at the bottom.

3. Drag with the mouse to write or draw on the page. Release the mouse button when you want to stop marking, and press the mouse button again to resume your note taking.

4. Click the Save Web Note button on the toolbar. A dialog box appears. Click One Note, Favorites, or Reading List at the top, and then click the Save button.

5. Click the Close button on the Web Notes toolbar.

TIP

Writing and drawing onscreen with a regular mouse can be awkward. You can get a drawing tablet and stylus that connects to your laptop via USB. After you plug it in and set it up, if needed, you can use the stylus to write and draw just as you would use a pencil. Using one of these tablets makes adding web notes feel the same as doodling on paper. If your laptop has a touchscreen, you can just use it in the same way.

Pick a color

FIGURE 14-8

Add a Web Page to the Reading List

1. You can add a web page to a reading list in Microsoft Edge so that you can come back to it at a later time. Open Microsoft Edge, go to a news or information website, and then click the link to the article that you want to read later.

2. Click the Add to Favorites or Reading List button (with a star on it) on the address bar.

3. In the dialog box that appears (see Figure 14-9), click the Save In drop-down arrow and select Reading List.

4. Edit the Name for the reading list item, if you want.

5. Click the Add button.

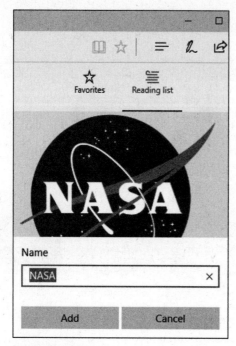

FIGURE 14-9

TIP
Microsoft Edge stores all your reading list items and favorites in the Hub. Other browsers store marked pages in a Favorites list or Bookmarks folder.

Pin a Tab

1. If you have a favorite website that you access all the time, one option is to pin a tab so that the tab appears every time you open your browser. When you pin a tab, it appears to the left side of the tabs display with only an icon, no title or Close button. To pin a tab, first display the site you want to pin.

2. Right-click the tab and then click Pin.

3. To unpin a tab, right click the tab and then select Unpin from the drop-down menu that appears.

Add a Website to Favorites and Create a Folder

1. If there's a site you intend to revisit, you may want to save it to Microsoft Edge's Favorites list in the Hub so you can easily go there again. To use this feature, open Microsoft Edge from the desktop, enter the URL of a website that you want to add to your Favorites list, and then press Enter.

2. Click the Add to Favorites or Reading List button on the address bar. In the Add To window that opens, click Favorites at the top.

3. Modify the name of the Favorite listing to something easily recognizable, as shown in Figure 14-10.

Modify the name here

FIGURE 14-10

4. If you wish, choose another folder from the Save In drop-down list to store the favorite in. Or, to create a new folder, click the Create New Folder link, and then type a name in the Folder Name text box that appears.

5. Click the Add button to add the site.

Use Favorites

1. You can go back to one of your favorites at any time from the Hub. With Microsoft Edge open, click the Hub button (three horizontal lines) on the address bar.

2. In the Hub pane that appears (see Figure 14-11), click the Favorites (star) button.

3. If you saved the favorite in a folder, click the folder in the list. When you see the favorite you want to open, double-click it. The Hub pane closes, and the favorite site appears in the current tab. And the Add to Favorites or Reading List button changes to show a filled yellow star.

Regularly cleaning out your favorites or reading list is a good idea — after all, do you really need the sites that you used to plan last year's vacation? With the Hub displayed, right-click any item and then choose Delete to remove it.

TIP

If you created new folders when adding favorites, you can manually transfer those favorites into a different folder. To do this, just display the Hub and click and drag a favorite listed there onto another folder.

TIP

Favorites button

Hub button

FIGURE 14-11

View Your Browsing History

1. If you went to a site recently and want to return there again but can't remember the name, you might check your browsing history in the Hub to find it. In Microsoft Edge, click the Hub button in the address bar and then click the History button (with the clock face on it) in the Hub pane to display the History list (see Figure 14-12).

2. As the History list accumulates items, it groups them by date, such as Last Hour, Earlier Today, and Last Week. You can click any of the time category labels to expand or collapse the entries in the group (see Figure 14-13).

History button

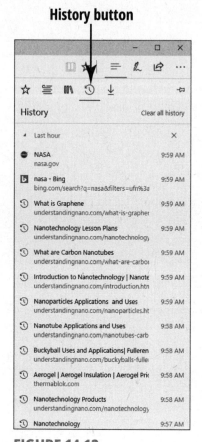

FIGURE 14-12

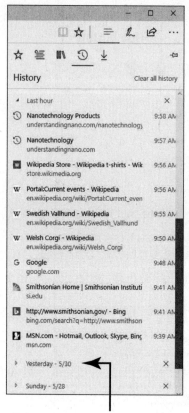

Click a time category to expand it

FIGURE 14-13

3. Once you've expanded the desired time category you can click an item to go to it. The History pane closes.

TIP

To delete a single item from the History list, move the mouse pointer over it, and click the Delete (X) that appears at the right. (Refer to Figure 14-13.) You can also right-click the item and click Delete. To remove all the history items, click the Clear All History link near the upper-right corner of the History pane.

TIP

You can pin the Hub pane open temporarily by clicking the Pin This Pane button (the pushpin icon) in the upper-right corner of the pane. Click the Close (X) button that replaces the pin button when you want to unpin the pane.

View Your Reading List

1. Finding your reading list items works like using favorites and your browsing history. Open Microsoft Edge, click the Hub button on the address bar, and then click the Reading List button (with a stack of papers on it) in the Hub pane.

2. In the list that appears, click the item to read (see Figure 14-14). The Hub pane closes, and the reading list item opens in the current tab.

Reading List button

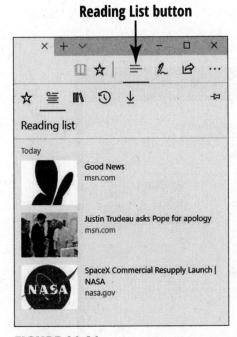

FIGURE 14-14

TIP

PDF is a document format that you can view using a PDF reader, rather than with a program such as Word or Pages. If you often deal with documents online, check out the new Edge PDF Reader. You can use this reader for filling out forms, making notes on PDFs, rotating PDFs, or adding a table of contents to a PDF document. When you open a PDF document, it opens Edge PDF Reader by default.

Print a Web Page

1. If a web page includes a link or button to print or display a print version of a page, click that and follow the instructions.

2. If the page doesn't include a link for printing, click the Settings and More button on the Microsoft Edge address bar, and then click Print in the menu that appears.

3. In the resulting Print window (see Figure 14-15), choose a printer from the Printer drop-down list, if needed. Then click the plus button beside the Number of Copies text box to print multiple copies.

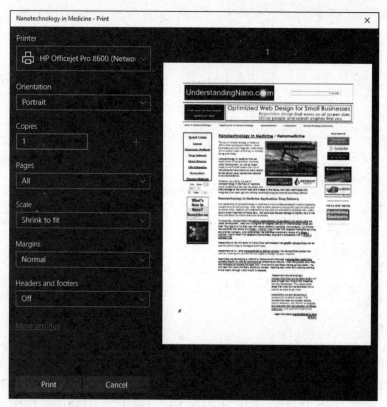

FIGURE 14-15

TIP

Note that clicking the More Settings link at the bottom of the window usually opens another window with more settings for the printer selected in the main Print window. These settings might include different paper sizes, duplex (two-sided) printing, color mode, or resolution. After you chose any settings here, click OK to return to the main Print window.

4. After you adjust any settings, click Print.

Adjust Microsoft Edge Settings

1. You can work with a variety of settings that adjust how Microsoft Edge works. Click the Settings and More button at the far right end of the Microsoft Edge address bar, and then click Settings in the menu that appears.

2. In the Settings pane that appears (see Figure 14-16), make selections for the settings such as these:

- **Choose a Theme:** Choose the Light or Dark theme from this drop-down list.

- **Open Microsoft Edge With:** As described in Chapter 13, the choices here determine what displays when you start Microsoft Edge.

- **Open New Tabs With:** This drop-down list controls the content for new browser tabs. Chapter 15 provides more details about these choices.

- **Show the Favorites Bar:** Use the On/Off slider to control whether an additional favorites bar appears below the address bar.

- **Clear Browsing Data:** Click the Choose What To Clear button here to delete various types of browsing data. Chapter 15 covers this in more detail.

FIGURE 14-16

3. Move the mouse to the right edge of the Settings panel to display the scroll bar, and then scroll down. Clicking the View Advanced Settings button under Advanced Settings displays an additional pane of Microsoft Edge settings.

4. When you finish your changes, click the Settings and More button again or click a blank area of the current web page to close the Settings pane.

Chapter **15**

Staying Safe While Online

Getting active online carries with it certain risks, like most things in life. But just as you know how to drive or walk around town safely when you know the rules of the road, you can stay relatively safe online.

In this chapter, you discover some of the risks and safety nets that you can take advantage of to avoid those risks, including

» **Understand what risks exist.** Some risks are human, in the form of online predators wanting to steal your money or abuse you emotionally; other risks come from technology, such as computer viruses. For the former, you can use the same common sense you use when interacting offline to stay safe. For the latter, there are tools and browser settings to protect you.

» **Be aware of what information you share.** Abuses such as ID theft occur most often when you or somebody you know shares information about you that's nobody's business. Find out how to spot who is exposing information (including you) and what information to keep private, and you'll become much safer online.

» **Avoid scams and undesirable content.** Use various privacy settings in Windows 10 to limit exposure to undesirable information, such as blocking pop-ups. Also, find out how to spot various email scams and fraud so you don't become a victim.

» **Create safe passwords.** Passwords don't have to be hard to remember, just hard to guess. I provide some guidance in this chapter about creating passwords that are hard to crack.

Understand Technology Risks on the Internet

When you buy a car, it has certain safety features built in. Sometimes after you drive it off the lot, you might find that the manufacturer slipped up and either recalls your car or requests that you go to the dealer's service department for replacement of a faulty part.

Your laptop is similar to your car in terms of the need for safety. It comes with an operating system (such as Microsoft Windows) built in, and that operating system has security features. Sometimes that operating system has flaws — or new threats emerge after it's first released — and you need to install an update to keep it secure. And as you use your laptop, you're exposing it to dangerous conditions and situations that you have to guard against.

Threats to your laptop security can come from a file you copy from a disc you insert into your laptop, but most of the time, the danger is from a program that you download from the Internet. These downloads can happen when you click a link, open an attachment in an email, or download a piece of software without realizing that *malware* (malicious software) is attached to it.

You need to be aware of these three main types of dangerous programs:

» A *virus* is a little program that some nasty person thought up to spread around the Internet and infect computers. A virus can do a variety of things but, typically, it attacks your data by deleting files, scrambling data, or making changes to your system settings that cause your laptop to grind to a halt.

» *Spyware* consists of programs responsible for tracking what you do with your laptop. Some spyware simply helps companies you do business with track your activities so that they can figure out how to sell things to you; other spyware is used for more insidious purposes, such as stealing your passwords.

» *Adware* is the computer equivalent of telemarketing phone calls at dinner time. After adware is downloaded onto your laptop, you'll see annoying pop-up windows trying to sell things to you all day long. Beyond the annoyance, adware can quickly clog up your laptop. The laptop's performance slows down, and it's hard to get anything done at all.

To protect your information and your laptop from these various types of malware, you can do several things:

» **You can buy and install an antivirus, antispyware, or antiadware program.** It's critical that you install an antivirus program, such as those from McAfee, Symantec, or Trend Micro, or the freely downloadable AVG Free at www.avg.com (see Figure 15-1).

People come up with new viruses every day, so it's important that you use software that's up to date with the latest virus definitions and that protects your laptop from the latest threats. Many antivirus programs are purchased by yearly subscription, which gives you access to updated virus definitions that the company constantly gathers throughout the year. Be sure to update the definitions of viruses on your laptop regularly using this software, and then run a scan of your laptop on a regular basis. For convenience, you can use settings in the software to activate automatic updates and scans. Consult your program's Help tool for instructions on how to use these features.

FIGURE 15-1

» **Install a program that combines tools for detecting adware and spyware.** Windows 10 has a built-in program, Windows Defender, which includes an antispyware feature. (I cover Windows Defender tools in Chapter 22.) You can also purchase programs such as Spyware Doctor (from PC Tools) or download free tools such as Spybot (from CNET) or Spyware Terminator.

» **Use Windows tools to keep Windows up to date.** Updating Windows ensures that you are current with security features, and fixes to security problems.

» **Turn on a firewall**. This feature stops other people or programs from accessing your laptop over an Internet connection without your permission. (I cover Windows Defender and firewalls in Chapter 22.)

» **Use your browser's privacy and security features,** such as the Suggested Content and InPrivate Browsing features in Microsoft Edge.

Use Suggested Content

1. You can allow Microsoft Edge to suggest sites you might like that are similar to the sites you visit most, and these are typically safe sites. Open Edge, click the More Actions button, and then click Settings in the menu that appears.

2. Click the box below Open New Tabs With, and click Top Sites and Suggested Content, as shown in Figure 15-2. Click outside of the Settings pane to close it.

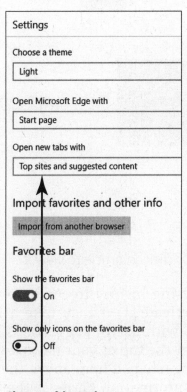

Choose this option

FIGURE 15-2

3. Click the New Tab button or press Ctrl+T. Tiles for top sites appear (see Figure 15-3), as well as a My Feed section with suggested content.

Top site files

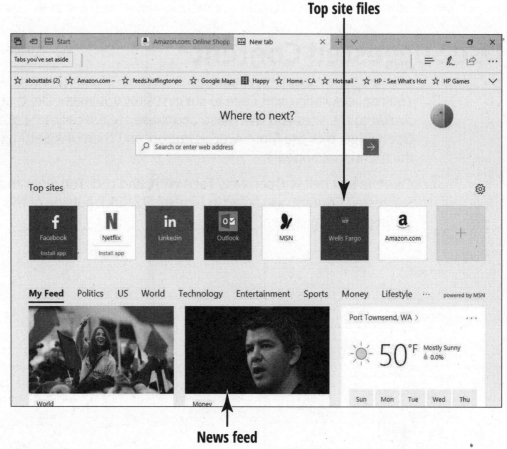

News feed

FIGURE 15-3

4. Click a site tile to open its website or click an article to view it.

TIP

Suggested content uses your browsing history to come up with suggestions, so when you first activate it, it may take a little while before the feature comes up with useful suggestions. You can customize what topics appear at the top of your news feed by clicking the Customize link (the cog-shaped item above the Top Sites tiles), clicking one or more Information Cards at the bottom, and then clicking Save.

Download Files Safely

1. The two tricks to downloading files while staying safe from malware are to only download from sites you trust and to never download file attachments to emails that you aren't completely sure are safe. The most dangerous files to download are executable files that sport an .exe extension at the end of the filename. Clicking on these will run a program of some kind, and could therefore pose an active threat. Open a trusted website that contains downloadable files. Typically, websites offer a Download button or link that initiates a file download.

    If you don't know of a file to download but want to practice these steps, try www.adobe.com. From that site, you can search for and download the free Adobe Acrobat Reader DC a handy and popular utility program.

2. Click the appropriate link or button to proceed. Windows might display a dialog box asking your permission to proceed with the download; click Yes. The download also, in some cases, might open in a separate Microsoft Edge window.

3. By default, a security scan runs before the document download begins. The toolbar that appears along the bottom of the screen, shown in Figure 15-4, displays different choices depending on the type of file downloaded:

FIGURE 15-4

- **For an executable file, click Run to download the file to a temporary folder.** This is the option to choose to download the Adobe software. You can run a software installation program, for example. However, beware: If you run a program you obtained from the Internet, you could be introducing dangerous viruses to your system. You might want to set up an antivirus program to scan files before downloading them.

- **For a document file such as a PDF file, click Open to open the file in another browser tab or the app for that type of document that's installed on your laptop.**

- **For any type of file, you can click View Downloads (for example if you're not sure if you already downloaded the file).**
The Hub opens and shows you recent downloads, as shown in Figure 15-5. You can click the Clear (X) button beside a download to remove it from the list, or click Clear All to clear the list of past downloads. Or, you can click Open Folder to open your Downloads folder to work with downloaded files. Press Esc or click elsewhere on the browser window to close the Hub pane.

FIGURE 15-5

The Downloads folder is one of your default user folders. Open this folder to view all downloads.

If you're worried that a particular file might be unsafe to download (for example, if it's from an unknown source or if you discover that it's an executable file type, which could contain a virus), click the Close button in the download toolbar.

If a particular file will take a long time to download (some can take 20 minutes or more), you may have to babysit it. If your laptop goes into standby mode, it could pause the download. If your laptop automatically downloads Windows updates, it may cause your laptop to restart automatically as well, cancelling or halting your download. Check in periodically to keep things moving along.

TIP

You might want to explore the new Storage Sense feature that allows you to automatically delete files that have been stored in your Downloads folder for more than 30 days. Open the Settings window and select System. Click the Storage option in the left panel and click the Storage Sense On/Off setting to On.

Use InPrivate Browsing

1. InPrivate Browsing is a feature that stops Edge from saving information, such as cookies and your browsing history during your browsing session. InPrivate Browsing allows you to block or allow sites that automatically collect information about your browsing habits. InPrivate Browsing is not active by default when you open an Edge window. To use InPrivate Browsing, open Edge and click the More Actions button.

2. In the menu that appears, click New InPrivate Window and enter a URL address for the site you want to open. As shown in Figure 15-6, the Edge browser window that appears displays InPrivate at the upper-left corner. The tab that appears is titled InPrivate and displays a description of InPrivate browsing.

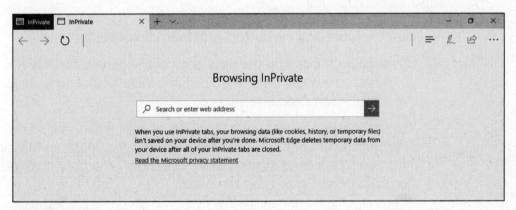

FIGURE 15-6

3. You can now surf the web privately by entering a search phrase or web address in the Search box and pressing Enter, or by clicking in the Address bar, typing a web address, and pressing Enter.

4. To turn off InPrivate Browsing, click the Close button in the upper-right corner of the InPrivate window.

If you don't want to use InPrivate Browsing but would like to periodically clear your browsing history manually, with Edge open, click the Hub button to the right of the Address bar (it looks like three horizontal lines), and then click the History icon at the top of the pane (this looks like a little clock face). Click the triangle icon beside any date to review your history for that date, and click the Delete (X) button if you decide to delete it. Or, you can click Clear All History to delete all history entries. Press Esc to close the Hub when you finish.

Use SmartScreen Filter

When you activate SmartScreen Filter, you allow Microsoft to check its database for information on the websites you visit. Microsoft alerts you if any of those websites are known to generate phishing scams or download malware to visitors' computers. SmartScreen Filter is on by default, but if it gets turned off, to turn it on again, open Edge and follow these steps:

1. Click the More Actions button, and then click Settings.

2. Hover your mouse over the right edge of the pane to display the scroll bar, scroll down, and then click the View Advanced Settings button under Advanced Settings.

3. Use the mouse to display the scroll bar at right again, and scroll down. Click the on/off button below Help Protect Me from Malicious Sites and Downloads with Windows Defender SmartScreen to display On. Then press Esc to close the pane.

Once it's turned on, SmartScreen Filter automatically checks websites and will generate a warning message if you visit one that has reported problems. However, that information is updated only periodically, so if you have concerns about a particular site, avoid browsing to it.

Change Privacy Settings

1. You can modify how Microsoft Edge deals with privacy settings to keep information about your browsing habits or identity safer. In Microsoft Edge, click the Settings and More button, and then click Settings.

2. Move the mouse pointer to the right edge of the Settings pane to display the scroll bar, scroll down, and click View Advanced Settings button under Advanced Settings.

3. In the Advanced Settings pane, scroll down to the Privacy and Services heading. Click the drop-down list under Cookies, then click either Block All Cookies or Block Only Third Party Cookies (refer to Figure 15-7).

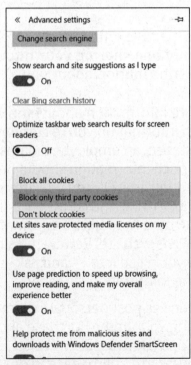

FIGURE 15-7

4. Press Esc or click outside the pane to close it.

TIP

You can also use the Block Pop-Ups setting near the top of the Advanced Settings pane. When this setting is toggled on Microsoft Edge prevents any pop-up windows from loading when you visit a site. While pop-ups generally show harmless or annoying ads, some may be associated with phishing schemes or malware, so your computer is more secure with pop-ups blocked.

TIP

Some sites, such as online news and magazine sites that you subscribe to, must use cookies to store your logon information. If you have cookies disabled, Remember Me or Keep Me Signed In options won't work on those pages, and you'll have to enter your logon information each time you visit the site.

Understand Information Exposure

Many people think that if they aren't active online, their information isn't exposed. But you aren't the only one sharing your information. Consider how others might handle information about you.

» **Employers:** Many employers share information about employees. Consider carefully how much information you're comfortable with sharing through, for instance, an employee bio posted on your company website. How much information should be visible to other employees on your intranet? When you attend a conference, is the attendee list shown in online conference documents? And even if you're retired, there may still be information about you on your former employer's website. Review the site to determine if it reveals more than you'd like it to — and ask your employer to take down or alter the information if needed.

» **Government agencies:** Some agencies post personal information, such as documents concerning your home purchase and property tax (see Figure 15-8), on publicly available websites. Government agencies may also post birth, marriage, and death certificates, and these documents may contain your Social Security number, loan number, copies of your signature, and so on. You should check government records carefully to see if private information is posted and, if it is, demand that it be removed.

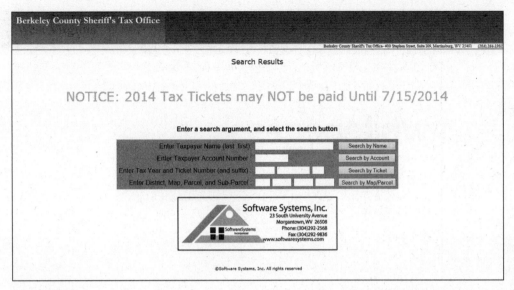

FIGURE 15-8

» **Family members and friends:** They may write about you in their blogs, post photos of you, or mention you on special-interest sites such as those focused on genealogy.

» **Clubs and organizations:** Organizations with whom you volunteer, the church you attend, and professional associations you belong to may reveal facts such as your address, age, income bracket, and how much money you've donated.

» **Newspapers:** If you've been featured in a newspaper article, you may be surprised to find the story, along with a picture of you or information about your work, activities, or family, by doing a simple online search. If you're interviewed, ask for the chance to review the information that the newspaper will include, and be sure that you're comfortable with exposing that information.

» **Online directories:** Services such as www.whitepages.com, shown in Figure 15-9, or www.anywho.com list your home phone number and address, unless you specifically request that these be removed. You may be charged a small fee associated with removing your information — a so-called privacy tax — but you may find the cost worthwhile.

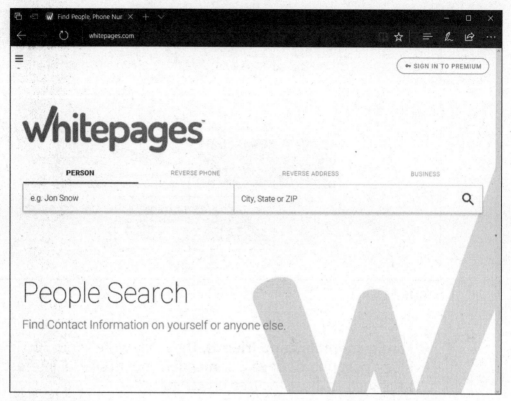

FIGURE 15-9

Online directories often include the names of members of your family, your email address, the value of your home, your neighbors' names and the values of their homes, an online mapping tool to provide a view of your home, driving directions to your home, and your age. The record may also include previous addresses, schools you've attended, and links for people to run background checks on you. (Background check services generally charge a fee.) A smart con person can use all that information to convince you that he's a friend of a friend or even a relative in distress who needs money.

WARNING

Because services get new information from many sources, you'll need to check back periodically to see if your information has again been put online — if it has, contact the company or go through its removal process again.

TIP

Try entering your home phone number in any browser's address line; chances are you'll get an online directory listing with your address and phone number (although this doesn't work for cell-phone numbers).

TIP

Many web browsers not only track browsing data, but also save the personal data you enter into online forms so that information can be reused later to fill forms automatically. In Microsoft Edge, you can stop the browser from saving form entries. Click the More Actions button under Settings/Privacy and Services and then click View Advanced Settings. Click the Save Form Entries switch to turn the setting off.

Keep Your Information Private

Sharing personal information with friends and family enriches your relationships and helps you build new ones. The key is to avoid sharing information online with the wrong people and shady companies because, just as in the real world, exposing your personal information is one of your biggest risks.

Criminals come in all flavors, but the more savvy ones collect information in a very systematic way. Each piece of information is like a series of brushstrokes that, over time, form a very clear picture of your life. And after criminals collect and organize the information, they never throw it away because they may be able to use it many times over.

Fortunately, information exposure is a risk you have a great deal of control over. Before sharing information, such as your date of birth, make sure that you're comfortable with how the recipient will use the information.

>> **Address and phone number:** Abuse of this information results in you receiving increased telemarketing calls and junk mail. Although less common, this information may also increase a scammer's ability to steal your identity and make your home a more interesting target for break-ins.

» **Names of husband/wife, father, and mother (including mother's maiden name), siblings, children, and grandchildren:** This information is very interesting to criminals, who can use it to gain your confidence and then scam you, or use it to guess your passwords or secret-question answers, which often include family members' names. This information may also expose your family members to ID theft, fraud, and personal harm.

» **Information about your car:** Limit access to license plate numbers; VINs (vehicle identification numbers); registration information; make, model, and title number of your car; your insurance carrier's name and coverage limits; loan information; and driver's license number. The key criminal abuse of this information includes car theft (or theft of parts of the car) and insurance fraud. The type of car you drive may also indicate your financial status, and that adds one more piece of information to the pool of data criminals collect about you.

» **Information about work history:** In the hands of criminals, your work history can be very useful for "authenticating" the fraudster and convincing people and organizations to provide him or her with more about your financial records or identity.

» **Information about your credit status:** This information can be abused in so many ways that any time you're asked to provide this online, your answer should be "No." Don't fall for the temptation to check your credit scores for free through sites that aren't guaranteed as being reputable. Another frequent abuse of credit information is found in free mortgage calculators that ask you to put in all kinds of personal information in order for them to determine what credit you may qualify for.

TIP

Many people set automatic responders in their email, letting people know when they'll be away from their offices. This is really helpful for colleagues, but exercise caution and limit whom you provide the information to. Leaving a message that says, "Gone 11/2–11/12. I'm taking the family to Hawaii for ten days," may make your house a prime target for burglary. And you'll probably never make the connection between the information you exposed and the offline crime.

WARNING

You may need to show your work history, particularly on resumes you post on Internet job or business-networking sites. Be selective about where you post this information, create a separate email account to list on the resume, and tell what kinds of work you've done rather than give specifics about which companies and what dates. Interested, legitimate employers can then contact you privately, and you won't have given away your life history to the world. After you've landed the job, take down your resume. Think of it as risk management — when you need a job, the risk of information exposure is less than the need to get a job.

Spot Phishing Scams and Other Email Fraud

As in the offline world, the Internet has a criminal element. These cybercriminals use Internet tools to commit the same crimes they've always committed, from robbing you to misusing your good name and financial information. Know how to spot the types of scams that occur online and you'll go a long way toward steering clear of Internet crime.

Before you click a link that comes in a forwarded email message or forward a message to others, ask yourself:

» **Is the information legitimate?** Sites such as www.truthorfiction. com, www.snopes.com (see Figure 15-10), or http://urbanlegends online.com can help you discover if an email is a scam.

» **Does a message ask you to click links in email or instant messages?** If you're unsure whether a message is genuinely from a company or bank that you use, call them, using the number from a past statement or the phone book. *Remember:* Don't call a phone number listed in the email; it could be a fake. To visit a company's or bank's website, type the address in yourself if you know it or use your own bookmark rather than clicking a link. If the website is new to you, search for the company online and use that link to visit its site. Don't click the link in an email, or you may land on a site that looks right — but is in reality a good fake.

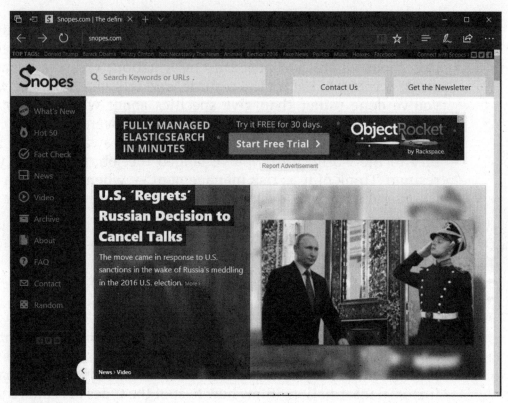

FIGURE 15-10

» **Does the email have a photo or video to download?** If so, exercise caution. If you know the person and he told you he would be sending the photo or video, it's probably fine to download, but if the photo or video has been forwarded several times and you don't know the person who sent it originally, be careful. It may deliver a virus or other type of malware to your laptop.

In addition to asking yourself these questions, also remember the following:

» **If you decide to forward (or send) email to a group, always put their email addresses on the Bcc: (or Blind Carbon Copy) line.** This keeps everyone's email safe from fraud and scams.

» **Think *before* you click.** Doing so will save you and others from scams, fraud, hoaxes, and malware.

Create Strong Passwords

A strong password can be one of your best friends in protecting your information in online accounts and sites. Never give your password to others, and change passwords on particularly sensitive accounts, such as bank and investment accounts, regularly.

Table 15-1 outlines five principles for creating strong passwords.

TABLE 15-1 **Principles for Strong Passwords**

Principle	How to Do It
Length	Use at least ten characters.
Strength	Mix it up with upper- and lowercase letters, characters, and numbers.
Obscurity	Use nothing that's associated with you, your family, your company, and so on.
Protection	Don't place paper reminders near your laptop.
Change	The more sensitive the information, the more frequently you should change your password.

Look at Table 15-2 for examples of password patterns that are safe but also easy to remember.

TIP

Edge includes a feature that can remember passwords for you. Click the More Actions button, and then click Settings. Scroll down, and click View Advanced Settings. Under Privacy and Services, click the On/Off switch below Offer To Save Passwords to turn it On. You can then use the Manage Passwords choice to remove saved passwords, if needed.

TABLE 15-2 **Examples of Strong Passwords**

Logic	Password
Use a familiar phrase typed with a variation of capitalization and numbers instead of words (text message shorthand).	L8r_L8rNot2day = Later, later, not today 2BorNot2B_ThatIsThe? = To be or not to be, that is the question.
Incorporate shortcut codes or acronyms.	CSThnknAU2day = Can't Stop Thinking About You today 2Hot2Hndle = Too hot to handle
Create a password from an easy-to-remember phrase that describes what you're doing, with key letters replaced by numbers or symbols.	1mlook1ngatyahoo = I'm looking at Yahoo (I replaced the Is with 1s.) MyWork@HomeNeverEnds
Spell a word backward with at least one letter representing a character or number.	$lidoffaD = Daffodils (The $ replaces the s.) y1frettuB = Butterfly (The 1 replaces the l.) QWERTY7654321 = This is the 6 letters from left to right in the top row of your keyboard, plus the numbers from right to left across the top going backward.
Use patterns from your keyboard. (See Figure 15-11.) Make your keyboard a palette and make any shape you want.	1QAZSEDCFT6 is really just making a W on your keyboard. (Refer to Figure 15-11.)

FIGURE 15-11

Chapter **16**

Keeping in Touch with Mail

An email app is a tool you can use to send messages to others. These messages are delivered to the recipient's email inbox, usually within seconds. You can attach files to email messages and even put images within the message body. You can get an email account through your Internet provider or through sites such as Yahoo! and Microsoft Outlook.com. These accounts are typically free.

When you have one or more email accounts, you can set them up in the Mail app in Windows 10, and then use that app to send and receive email for all of your Outlook.com, Gmail, and other accounts in one place. Mail uses the information you store in the People app for addressing your emails, and it can sync contacts from your individual accounts to the People app if you choose.

TIP

With Windows 10, setting up Yahoo!, AOL, and many other types of email accounts is possible in addition to Outlook and Google. These programs provide tools for working with email, including more sophisticated tools to format message text or add a signature (for example your company name and phone number) to every message you send.

To make your emailing life easy, this chapter takes a look at these tasks:

» **Choose an email provider.** Find out how to locate email providers and what types of features they offer.

» **Set up your email accounts in the Mail app.** Make settings to access your existing accounts from within the Mail app so you can check all your messages in one place. This is useful if you use both work and home email accounts, for example. If you do access work email from home you can use the Microsoft Exchange type of account to do so (check with your work network administrator about how to do this).

» **Receive, send, and forward messages.** Deal with the ins and outs of receiving and sending email.

» **Make settings for each account.** Set up how often content is downloaded, and whether to synchronize your email, contacts, and calendar information from each account.

Sign Up for an Internet-Based Email Account

Your Internet service provider (ISP) — whether that's your cable or Phone Company or a local provider — probably offers you a free email account along with your service. You can also get free accounts from many online sources, such as Yahoo!, AOL, Gmail, and Outlook. com. The Mail app in Windows 10 can work with these types of online accounts — as well as Microsoft Exchange accounts, which are typically business accounts such as the one that a company provides. By default, the email address that's part of the Microsoft account you use to sign in to Windows is already set up for you in the Mail app. You're free to set up more email accounts in Mail, for example if you want to have one email address you use when buying items online and one that's more private.

Here are some tips for getting your own email account:

» **Using email accounts provided by an ISP:** Check with your ISP to see whether an email account comes with your connection service. If it does, your ISP should provide instructions on how to choose an *email alias* (that's the name on your account, such as SusieXYZ@aol.com) and password, and instructions on how to sign into the account.

» **Searching for an email provider:** If your ISP doesn't offer email, or you prefer to use another service because of the features it offers, use your browser's search engine to look for what's available. Don't use the search term *free email* because results for any search with the word *free* included are much more likely to return sites that will download bad programs like viruses and spyware onto your laptop. Besides, just about all email accounts today are free! Alternatively, you can go directly to services such as Yahoo, Outlook, AOL, or Gmail (Google's email) by entering their addresses in your browser's address field (for example, www.gmail.com).

» **Finding out about features:** Email accounts come with certain features. For example, each account includes a certain amount of storage for your saved messages. (Look for one that provides 15 gigabytes or more. Some providers charge extra for anything beyond a minimal amount of storage space.) The account should also include an easy-to-use address book feature to save your contacts' information. Some services provide better formatting tools for text, as well as calendar and to-do list features.

Whatever service you use, make sure it has good junk-mail filtering to protect you from unwanted emails. You should be able to modify junk-mail filter settings so that the service places messages from certain senders or with certain content in a junk-mail folder, where you can review the messages and exercise caution when choosing to open or delete them.

» **Signing up for an email account:** When you find an email account you want to use, sign up (usually there will be a Sign Up or Get an Account button or link to click) by providing your name and other contact information and selecting a username and password. The username is your email address, in the form of UserName@*service*.com, where the *service* is, for example, Yahoo!, Outlook, or AOL. Some usernames might be taken, so have a few options in mind.

» **Making sure your username is a safe one:** If possible, don't use your full name, your location, age, or other identifiers. Such personal identifiers might help scam artists or predators find out more about you than you want them to know.

Set Up an Email Account

1. You can set up the Windows 10 Mail app to manage Outlook and other accounts so that you can receive all your email messages in one place. Click the Start button on the taskbar, and then click Settings.

2. Click the Email & App Accounts link shown in Figure 16-1.

3. Click Add an Account.

4. Click a provider option as shown in Figure 16-2.

Click here

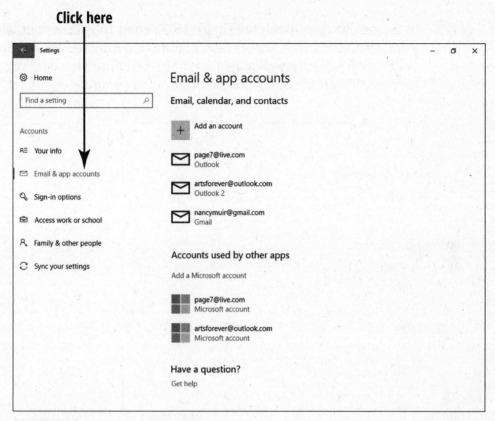

FIGURE 16-1

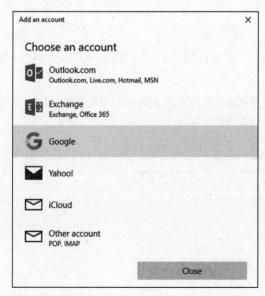

FIGURE 16-2

5. In the resulting window (see Figure 16-3), enter the account email address. Click Sign In. For some accounts, you may see an additional verification screen (see Figure 16-4) or be prompted to select account recovery information. Follow the prompts to continue.

Add your Microsoft account

Sign in with your Microsoft account to access your documents, settings, and purchases on all your devices. Learn more

Email, phone, or Skype

Password

Forgot my password

No account? Create one!

Microsoft privacy statement

Sign in

FIGURE 16-3

6. In the next window, titled Connecting to a Service, scroll down and click the Allow button.

7. Mail takes a moment to set up the account, and then displays the All Done! window. Click the Done button.

Click the account in the Manage Accounts panel on the right to sign in, open the inbox, and view your messages.

FIGURE 16-4

Get to Know Mail

The Mail app (see Figure 16-5) may look a bit different from other email programs that use menus and tools to take actions such as deleting an email, creating a new email, and so on. Mail has a sparser, cleaner interface in line with the whole Windows 10 approach. You have a list of emails in the inbox for the selected account on the left. You can click the Folder icon along the left side of the window to display folders included in that inbox. Some typical folders are your Inbox, where most incoming mail appears; your Drafts folder, where drafts of emails are saved, ready to be sent; and your Sent Mail folder, where copies of sent emails are stored. You can set up any other folders by signing in at the email provider's website, such as www.outlook.com, mail.yahoo.com, or www.gmail.com because you can't set these up in Mail.

With the Folders panel displayed, when you click Inbox or another folder, the right portion of the screen shows the list of messages in the folder.

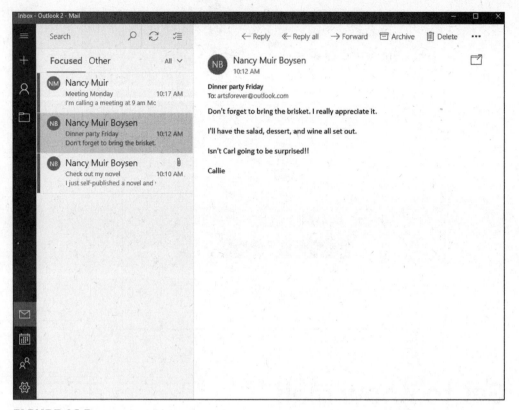

FIGURE 16-5

TIP To move a message to another folder, right-click it and then click the Move command in the shortcut menu that appears. Click a folder, and the message is moved there.

TIP When you access Outlook and many of the other online email services using your browser, you're using a program that's hosted online, rather than software installed on your laptop. That makes it easy to access your mail from any computer because your messages and folders are stored online. If you use what's called an email client such as Mail to access various email accounts in one place, the client software and your downloaded messages are stored on your laptop.

Open Mail and Receive Messages

1. Click the Start button, and then click the Mail tile.

   TIP The first time you start the Mail app, a Welcome screen appears. Click the Get Started button to see the Accounts screen. There, you can click Add Account to add another account or click Ready to Go to skip this step.

2. Click All Accounts at the left (it looks like a head and shoulders), and then click the account you want to read mail from. The contents of the Inbox are displayed, as shown in Figure 16-6.

Click to create new message   **Inbox contents**

FIGURE 16-6

3. Click a message, and its contents appear in the Mail window. Use the scroll bar to move through the message contents.

4. If the message has an attachment, you'll see a paper clip symbol (see Figure 16-6) next to it in the list of received files. When you open the message, a preview of the attachment appears in the message (see Figure 16-7). Right-click the thumbnail and choose one of the following options from the menu that appears:

- **Open:** The file opens in the app that Windows 10 associates it with. You may be prompted to choose an application to use to open the attachment.

- **Save:** Windows 10 opens the Documents folder, where you can enter a name and click Save to save the file in that folder.

5. If you open the document, to return to the list of messages from the window that appears click the Close button in the document window.

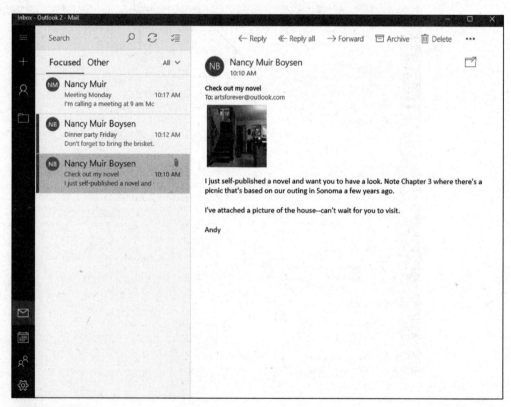

FIGURE 16-7

TIP

If your mail doesn't come through, it's probably because your email provider's servers are experiencing technical problems. Just wait a little while, and try clicking the Sync This View button, the double arrows above the inbox (refer to Figure 16-6), to check for the latest mail on the servers. If you still can't get mail, make sure your connection to the Internet is active. Mail will show in your Inbox, but if you've lost your connection, Mail can't receive new messages.

TIP

If you move your mouse over a message in the Inbox message list, little trashcan and flag icons appear at the right. Click the trashcan icon to delete the message. Click the flag icon to display a red flag on the message at all times, marking it as a priority message you may want to review again later. Click the Archive button to store a copy in the Archives folder.

Create and Send Email

1. Creating email is as simple as filling out a few fields in a form. Open Mail, and if you have more than one email account, click All Accounts at the left, and click the account from which you want to send the email.

2. Click the New Mail button on the left (refer to Figure 16-6).

3. Type the email address of the recipient(s) in the To field, using a semicolon to separate addresses. If you want to send a courtesy copy of the message to other people, click the Cc & Bcc link. Enter addresses in the Cc field or, to send a blind copy, enter addresses in the Bcc field.

4. Click in the Subject field (see Figure 16-8) and type a concise, yet descriptive subject.

5. Click in the message pane beneath the subject and type your message (see Figure 16-9).

TIP

Don't press Enter at the end of a line when typing a message. Mail and most email programs have an automatic text-wrap feature that does this for you. Do be concise. If you have lots to say, consider sending a letter by snail mail or overnight delivery. Most people tire of reading text onscreen after a short while.

Subject field

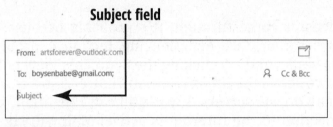

FIGURE 16-8

FIGURE 16-9

TIP

Keep email etiquette in mind as you type. For example, don't type in ALL CAPITAL LETTERS. This is called shouting, which is considered rude. Do be polite even if you're really, really angry. Your message could be forwarded to just about anybody, just about anywhere, and you don't want to get a reputation as a hothead.

6. If you want, you can use the buttons on the Format tab to change the appearance of the text. Drag over the text to select it and then click a button to apply formatting. For example, you might click the Bold button or the Font Color button to make the text stand out. You can use the Bullet and Numbering buttons to define lists. You can also choose a priority for the message if you want to, by clicking the Options tab and clicking either the High Importance or Low Importance button.

7. When you finish typing your message, click the Send button. The message goes on its way!

If you're sending an email to many recipients, consider putting their addresses in the Bcc field. This not only prevents each recipient from receiving a lengthy list of email addresses, but also protects the identity of everybody on the list from hackers. If you're forwarding an email from somebody else, consider whether you should delete the email of the original sender and recipients to protect people's privacy.

Remember that when you're creating an email, you can address it to a stored contact in the People app. (The trick is that when you add the contact in People, you have to choose the right account type—Outlook, Gmail, and so on.) Begin to type a stored contact in an address field (To, Bcc, or Cc), and Mail provides a list of likely matches from your contacts. Just click the correct name or email address when it appears in the list to enter it.

Send an Attachment

1. It's very convenient to be able to attach a document or image file to an email that the recipient can open and view on his end. To do this, open Mail and click New Mail to create a new email message, address it, and enter a subject.

2. Click the Insert tab and click Files (see Figure 16-10).

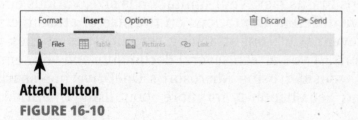

Attach button

FIGURE 16-10

3. The Open dialog box appears. Locate the file or files that you want and click it (or them).

4. Click the Open button. A thumbnail of the attached file appears in the message body (see Figure 16-11) indicating that it's uploaded. If you have other attachments from other folders on your laptop, you can click the Files button again and repeat the previous steps as many times as you like to add more attachments. You can also click Table or Pictures to attach those.

FIGURE 16-11

5. Click the Send button to send the message and attachment.

TIP

You can attach as many files as you like to a single email by repeating steps in this task. Your limitation is size. Various email providers have different limitations on the size of attachments, and some prevent you from attaching certain types of files for security reasons. If you attach several documents and your email fails to send, consider using Microsoft's OneDrive file-sharing service instead. See Chapter 17 for more about using OneDrive.

TIP

If you change your mind about sending a message while you're creating it, just click the Discard button (it's near the top-right corner sporting a trash can icon). To remove an attachment before sending a message, click the X button in the attachment thumbnail.

Read a Message

1. When you receive an email, your next step is to read it. Choose either the Focused or Other tab. The Focused inbox contains messages Mail considers you likely to want to read; the Other inbox contains all other messages.

2. Click an email message in your Inbox. Unread messages have a blue line to the left and messages you've read have no line.

TIP

You can click the Sync This View (double-arrow circle) button above your Inbox to check for new messages.

3. Click in the message body and use the scroll bar in the message window to scroll down through the message and read it (see Figure 16-12).

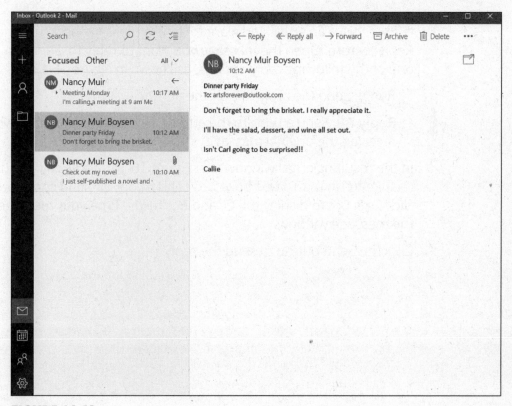

FIGURE 16-12

4. If you want to delete the message, simply click the Delete button in the toolbar.

If you'd like to save an attachment to a local storage drive (your laptop's hard drive or a USB stick, for example), right-click the thumbnail of the attachment in the message, click Save, choose the location to save the file to, and then click Save.

When you're travelling around with a laptop and reading emails, remember that people can look over your shoulder. If you're reading or writing sensitive information, consider displaying it when you get to the privacy of your home or hotel.

Reply to a Message

1. If you receive an email and want to send a message back, use the Reply feature. Open the message you want to reply to, and then click one of the following reply options, as shown in Figure 16-13:

   • **Reply:** Send the reply to only the author.

   • **Reply All:** Send a reply to the author as well as to everyone who received the original message.

2. In the resulting email window (see Figure 16-14), enter any additional recipient(s) in the To text boxes; to send a copy or blind copy you can click Cc & Bcc to display the Cc and Bcc fields. Type your message in the message window.

3. Click the Send button to send the reply.

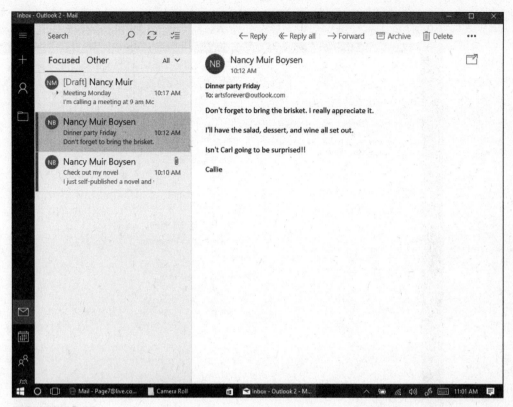

FIGURE 16-13

TIP

Replying to a message creates a conversation or message thread; a small triangle appears to the left of the message in the Inbox.

TIP

If you start creating a message or reply and have it open for a few moments, Mail automatically saves it as a draft. If you click the Back button without sending the message, Mail adds a copy of the message in the Drafts folder with [Draft] added in the message listing. You can open the message later from there to finish and send it.

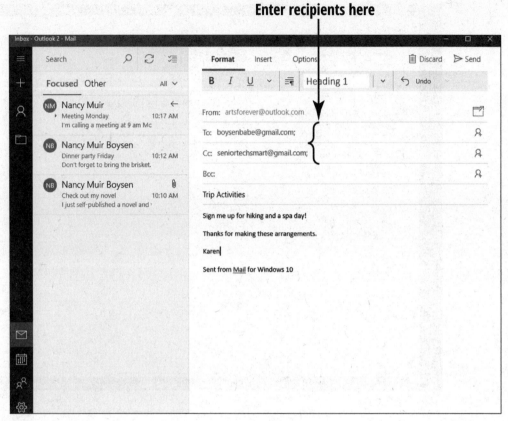

Enter recipients here

FIGURE 16-14

Forward Email

1. To share an email you receive with others, use the Forward feature. Open the email message that you want to forward in Mail.

2. Click the Forward button.

3. In the message that appears with FW: added to the beginning of the subject line, enter a new recipient(s) in the To and/or Cc and Bcc fields, and then enter any message that you want to include in the message window, as shown in the example in Figure 16-15.

Message text

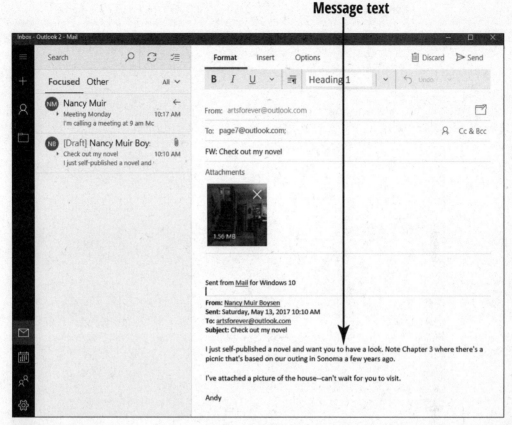

FIGURE 16-15

4. Click Send to forward the message.

Make Account Settings in Mail

1. Each account that you set up in Mail has its own settings. Click the Mail tile on the Start menu.

2. From within Mail click the Settings icon in the lower-left corner, and then click Manage Accounts in the Settings pane (see Figure 16-16).

Click this option

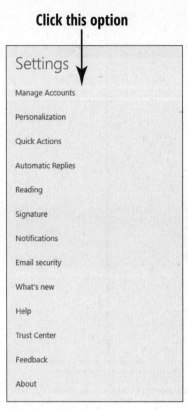

Settings

Manage Accounts

Personalization

Quick Actions

Automatic Replies

Reading

Signature

Notifications

Email security

What's new

Help

Trust Center

Feedback

About

FIGURE 16-16

3. Click the account for which you want to change settings.

4. Edit the Account Name if you want.

5. Click Change Mailbox Sync Settings in the Account Settings window. In the panel displayed in Figure 16-17, you can make the following changes:

- **Download New Content.** You can click this box and, from the drop-down list that appears, choose to download content when a message arrives or every 15 or 30 or 60 minutes. If you prefer, you can choose to download items only when you click the button beside the account by clicking the Manually option here.

- **Download Email From.** This is a handy setting if you're away from Mail for a while and have been checking messages in your browser. If so, you may not want to download a month's worth of messages you've already read, so choose another setting from this drop-down list, such as The Last 7 Days.

Outlook sync settings

Download new content

based on my usage ⌄

If you get a lot of mail one day or don't check your account for a few days, we'll change your sync settings accordingly to save you data and battery.

Currently syncing: **as items arrive**

☑ Always download full message and Internet images

Download email from

the last 7 days ⌄

Server

col402-m.hotmail.com

☑ Server requires encrypted (SSL) connection

Sync options

Email

[Done] [Cancel]

FIGURE 16-17

- **Sync Email Contacts or Calendars.** Syncing involves having certain actions and content delivery or deletions coordinated among different accounts or services, such as downloading your email to your phone or computer. Click the Email sync option to On or Off depending on whether you want to sync online email with your computer.

6. Click the Done button to go back to the Account Settings window.

7. Click the Save button to finish and close the window.

The steps above work for an Outlook account. Note that other email clients, such as Google, may offer different settings options.

TIP

CONTROLLING NOTIFICATIONS IN WINDOWS 10

Some people like to get a notification when new email arrives. To change notification settings for new email, press Win+I, click System, and then click Notifications & Actions at left. Scroll down to see the Mail option and make sure it is set to On (see Figure 16-18).

FIGURE 16-18

TIP

To remove an account from Mail, click Delete Account in the Account Settings window in Step 5 above. For the account you use to sign in to Windows, you'll have to perform this procedure through Settings (press Win+I) and then click Accounts. Click the account name and then click the Manage button.

IN THIS CHAPTER

» **Using applications online**

» **Understanding how OneDrive works with the cloud**

» **Adding files to OneDrive online**

» **Sharing a file or folder using OneDrive**

» **Creating a new OneDrive folder**

» **Turning on the Sync feature**

» **Choosing which settings you want to sync**

Chapter **17**

Working in the Cloud

Y ou may have heard the term *cloud* bandied about. The term comes from the world of computer networks, where certain functionality isn't installed on computers but resides on the network itself, in the so-called cloud.

Today, the definition of the term has broadened to include functionality that resides on the Internet. If you can get work done without using an installed piece of software — or if you store and share content online — you're working in the cloud. The cloud is especially useful to you if you travel with your laptop as you can store content online and access it wherever you are (if you have an Internet connection) without having to carry it on a USB stick, or store it on your hard drive.

In this chapter, you discover the types of applications you might use in the cloud, saving you the cost and effort of buying and installing software. In addition, I explore two Windows 10 features that help you access your own data in the cloud: OneDrive and Sync. OneDrive is a file-sharing service that has been around for a while, but with Windows 10, sharing files from your laptop with others or with yourself on another computer is more tightly integrated. Sync allows you to share the settings you've made in Windows 10 on one computer with other Windows 10 computers.

Use Applications Online

Certain apps, such as Maps and People, are built into Windows 10. You may purchase or download and install other apps, such as drawing apps or television viewing apps like Netflix, or more robust applications, such as Microsoft Word or Excel. Although these apps and applications may connect to the Internet to get information — such as the latest traffic info, or software help files — the software itself is installed on your laptop.

Today, you have the option of using software in the cloud, meaning that you never have to install the software on your laptop; instead, you simply make use of it online. Here are some examples you can explore:

» **Online office suites:** For example, the Google Docs suite of online software (available at http://docs.google.com/; see Figure 17-1) includes word processor, spreadsheet, and presentation software products you can use by logging into your Google account. These applications are compatible with popular office software such as Microsoft Word and PowerPoint. Your Microsoft account also enables you to work with Office Online apps, including Word Online, Excel Online, PowerPoint Online, and OneNote Online. You can access these apps after signing in to Outlook.com or OneDrive (Microsoft's online file-sharing app).

» **Email clients:** When you log into Gmail or Outlook.com, you're using email software in the cloud. In addition, many email clients can access more than one email account, such as Yahoo! and Gmail.

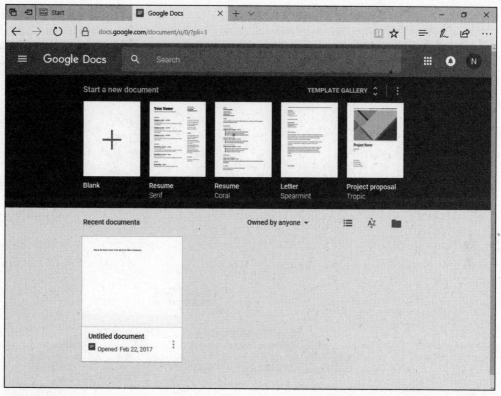

FIGURE 17-1

» **File-sharing sites:** Instead of attaching files to email messages, you have the option of uploading and sharing them on the file-sharing site. You can do that with Outlook.com and OneDrive, for example.

» **Photo-sharing sites:** Sites such as Flickr (`www.flickr.com`), shown in Figure 17-2, allow you to upload and download photos to them. A variation on this is a site such as Viewbook (`www.viewbook.com`), where you can create an online portfolio of art samples or business presentations to share with others.

» **Financial applications:** You might use a tool such as the Morningstar Portfolio Manager (`portfolio.morningstar.com`) to maintain an online portfolio of investments and generate charts to help you keep track of financial trends. You can also use online versions of popular money-management programs, such as Intuit's free online service Mint (`www.mint.com`), through which you can access your data from any computer or mobile device.

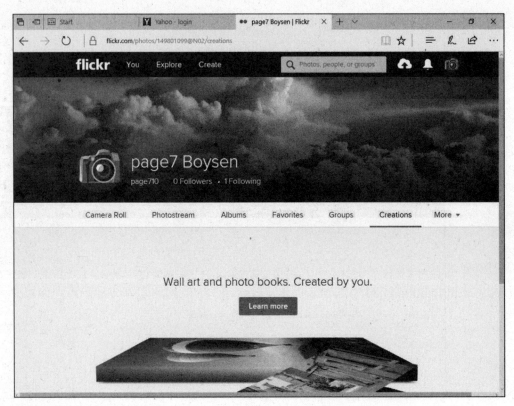

FIGURE 17-2

Understand How OneDrive Works with the Cloud

OneDrive from Microsoft is all about storing files and sharing them between your laptop and others via the cloud. In Windows 10, One-Drive storage folders in File Explorer on your laptop work together with the online version of OneDrive. (Sign in to `https://onedrive.live.com` with your Microsoft account to work with your online OneDrive.)

Any files you move or copy into a OneDrive folder in File Explorer automatically sync (or back up) to your OneDrive storage in the cloud. Any folder you create in OneDrive in File Explorer also magi-cally appears in your cloud OneDrive.

The first time you sign in to Windows, you might have noticed a Welcome to OneDrive window. Clicking the Get Started button takes you to a Setup OneDrive window where you can click Sign In to accept the terms of the service agreements and privacy statements that are required to use OneDrive. The next window that appears prompts you to confirm the default OneDrive folders on your laptop. Click Next, and then click Next again to accept the default setting of syncing all your OneDrive folders. Then click Done to close the window and begin using OneDrive. If you are prompted to enter an administrator password, type it and then click Yes.

After all that, you can open File Explorer and view your OneDrive folders. These are Documents, Music, and Pictures by default (see Figure 17-3). Click OneDrive in the Navigation pane to see these folders any time. Then just use your favorite technique to move or copy files into one of the folders (for example, click and drag or select a file and copy and paste it). From there, Windows uploads your files automatically.

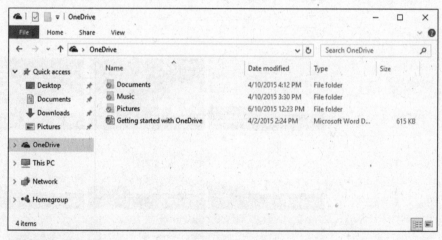

FIGURE 17-3

Add Files to OneDrive Online

1. You can easily add or upload files to OneDrive online at any time, from mobile devices as well as your laptop. Click the Microsoft Edge button on the taskbar.

2. Click in the Address field, type **https://onedrive.live.com,** and press Enter.

If MSN.com is your browser home page, you may see a button on that page that you can click to go to OneDrive.

TIP

3. Follow the process for signing in, if prompted, and use your Microsoft account user name and password. Your default folders appear (see Figure 17-4).

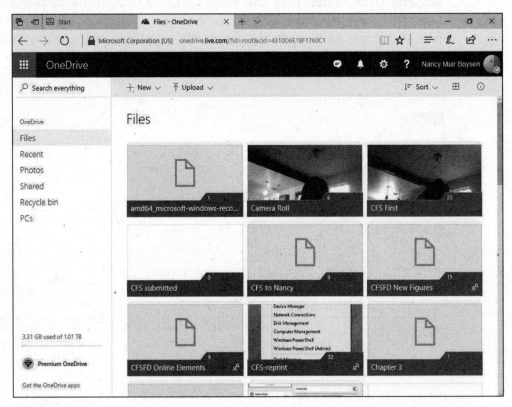

FIGURE 17-4

4. Click a folder (refer to 17-4) to open it.

After you click a folder, click Files in the left-hand pane to redisplay your default folders.

TIP

5. Click the Upload button in the OneDrive toolbar and then click Files or Folder.

6. Use the Open dialog box that appears (see Figure 17-5) to locate a file or folder.

Click a file

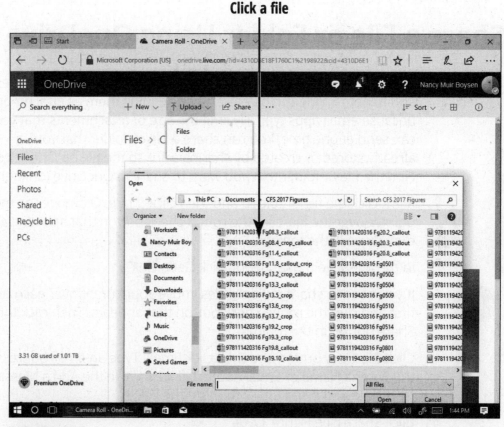

FIGURE 17-5

7. Click a file or folder.

8. Click Open.

TIP

You also can add a file to OneDrive by dragging it from the File Explorer window to an open OneDrive folder in your browser.

TIP

You may want to delete a file from OneDrive, as the free storage is typically limited to 15 gigabytes (GB), though you can purchase additional storage space or get more storage if you subscribe to Office 365, the online version of Microsoft Office. First, find the file that you want to delete in OneDrive. Right-click the file, and then click Delete.

Share a File or Folder Using OneDrive

1. The OneDrive service lets you share files with others. Sharing files and folders online can be easier than sending them as attachments because email apps typically limit the size of attachments that you can send at one time. You can share a file or folder that you've already stored or created by sharing a link to the file on OneDrive. Find the file or folder that you want to share in OneDrive (online).

2. Right-click the file or folder, and then click Share. Or, move the mouse pointer over the file, click the round check button that appears, and click Share in the toolbar.

3. In the Message that appears, click Get a Link.

TIP

If you need to share multiple files, move your cursor over each one first and click the round check button that appears. Then click the Share button in the toolbar.

4. Click the Copy button and then click Email. Type an email address in the Enter a Name or Email Address field. Click in the Add a Message Here field and press Ctrl+V to paste the link.

5. Click Share (see Figure 17-6).

6. The people you shared with receive an email message with a link for viewing the shared file.

Type an email address

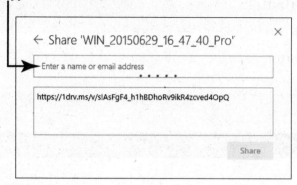

FIGURE 17-6

TIP

When you share a word-processing file with another person on OneDrive and grant permission to edit it, she can edit it in Word Online (a cloud version of Microsoft Word) or open the document in Microsoft Word on her computer. This is also the case with Excel and PowerPoint files.

TIP

You also can share a file or folder directly from the OneDrive folders on your computer (refer to Figure 17-3). Right-click the item to share, and click Share a OneDrive Link. This automatically copies the link to the Clipboard, and you can press Ctrl+V to paste it into an email message.

Create a New OneDrive Folder

1. You can keep your shared files in order by placing them in folders on OneDrive. After you've placed content in folders, you can then share those folders with others. This ability to share individual folders gives you a measure of security, as you don't have to share access to your entire OneDrive content with anybody. Open your browser, go to https://onedrive.live.com, and sign in with your Microsoft account if prompted.

2. If you want the new folder to be created within one of the three default folders, click a folder first.

3. On the toolbar, click New.

4. In the menu, click Folder.

5. Enter a name for the new folder (see Figure 17-7).

6. Click the Create button.

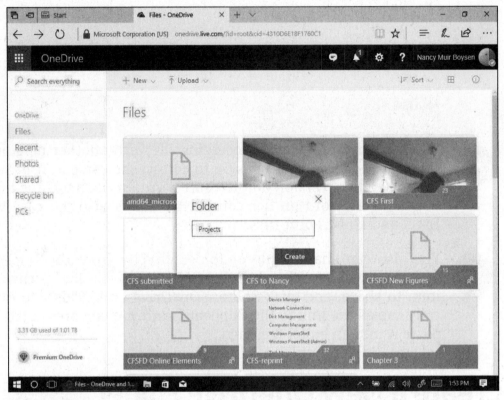

FIGURE 17-7

Turn On the Sync Feature

1. You can use the Sync feature to share your PC settings among Windows 10 devices so you don't have to redo the settings on each device. To sync, the Sync feature has to be turned on in settings, which it is by default. If, for some reason, it's been turned off, you have to turn it on. To turn on the Sync feature, start by pressing Win+I to display the Settings window.

2. Click Accounts, and then click Sync Your Settings.

3. Click the Sync Settings On/Off button (see Figure 17-8) if it is turned off to turn it on.

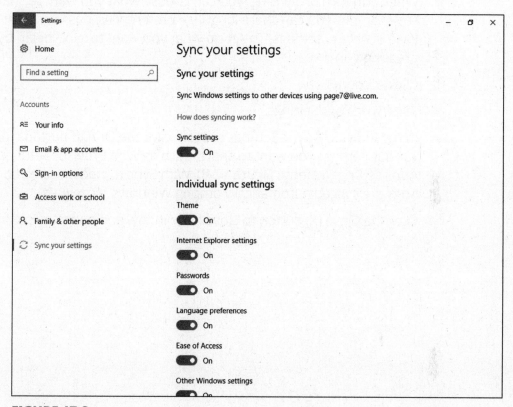

FIGURE 17-8

4. Click the window Close (X) button to close the Settings window and apply the settings. With the Sync feature turned on, sign in to your Microsoft account on another device, and all your settings will be synced from the cloud.

Syncing works only with Windows 10 settings and settings for apps that you buy from the Windows Store.

TIP

Choose Which Settings You Want to Sync

1. When you turn on syncing, you can choose what you want to share. For example, you can share language preferences, passwords, or Ease of Access settings. To set up what you want to sync, begin by pressing Win+I.

2. Click Accounts.

3. Click Sync Your Settings.

4. In the Individual Sync Settings section, click the On/Off buttons for the various settings you want to share, such as Web Browser Settings or Apps settings (refer to Figure 17-8). With Sync turned on selected settings are synced automatically among Windows 10 devices.

5. Click the Close (X) button to close the window and apply the settings.

Chapter **18**

Connecting with People Online

The Internet offers many options for connecting with people and sharing information. You'll find discussion boards, blogs, and chat on a wide variety of sites, from news sites to recipe sites, sites focused around grief and health issues, and sites that host political- or consumer-oriented discussions.

There are some great senior chat rooms for making friends, and many sites allow you to create new chat rooms on topics at any time.

Instant messaging (IM), on the other hand, isn't a website but an app. Using software such as the Skype app in Windows 10, IM allows you to chat in real time with your contacts. You can access instant-messaging programs via your laptop or your cellphone or use instant messaging features offered by some social networking services.

As with any site where users share information, such as social networks and blogs, you can stay safer if you know how to sidestep some abuses, including *data mining* (gathering your personal information for commercial or criminal intent), *social engineering* ploys that try to gain your trust and access to your money, ID theft scams, and so forth. If you're careful to protect your privacy, you can enjoy socializing without worry.

Finally, I provide an overview of playing downloaded or online games by yourself, or participating in multiplayer games online.

In this chapter, I look at some ways of sharing information and connecting with others and tell you how to do so safely.

Use Discussion Boards and Blogs

A *discussion board* is a place where you can post written messages, pictures, and videos on a topic such as home improvement. Others can reply to you, and you can respond to their postings. In a variation on discussion boards, you'll find *blogs* (web logs) everywhere you turn. Blogs are hosted on websites where the owner can post articles on a topic such as cooking or politics. You can also post your comments about those blog entries.

Discussion boards and blogs are *asynchronous*, which means that you post a message (just as you might on a bulletin board at the grocery store) and wait for a response. Somebody might read it that hour — or ten days or several weeks after you make the posting. In other words, the response isn't instantaneous, and the message isn't usually directed to a specific individual.

You can find a discussion board or blog about darn-near every topic under the sun, and these are tremendously helpful when you're looking for answers. They're also a great way to share your expertise — whether you chime in on how to remove an ink stain, provide historical trivia about button styles on military uniforms, or announce the latest breakthroughs in your given field. Postings are likely to stay up on the site for years for people to reference.

1. To try using a discussion board, enter this URL in your browser's address field: http://answers.microsoft.com/en-us. (Some discussion boards require that you become a member, with a username, and sign in before you can post. This site lets you sign in with the same Microsoft account that you use to sign in to Windows 10.)

2. On the lower-left corner of the screen, the default language and region is English. You can click that link and then click another language of your choice. Then click a topic area near the top under Browse the Categories, such as OneDrive.

3. In the topic list that appears, click another topic, such as Getting Started with OneDrive, to see more options. Continue to click until you get to a specific discussion thread, such as the one shown in Figure 18-1.

4. When you click a posting that has replies, you'll see that the replies are listed down the page in easy-to-follow threads, which arrange postings and replies in an organized structure. You can review the various participants' comments as they add their ideas to the conversation.

5. To reply to a posting yourself, first click the posting and then click the Reply link. For this site, you then type your comments in the Reply box (see Figure 18-2), scroll down, and click Submit.

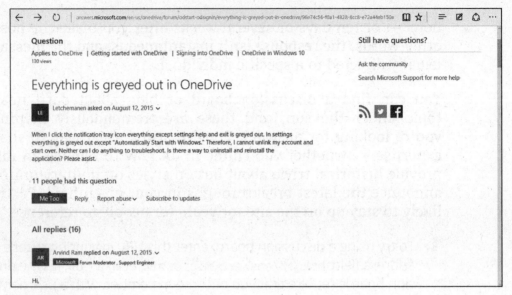

FIGURE 18-1

FIGURE 18-2

Participate in Chat

A *chat room* is an online space where groups of people can talk back and forth via text, audio, web camera, or a combination of media.

(See Figure 18-3, which shows a website that links to hundreds of chat rooms.) In chat, you're having a conversation with one or more people in real time, and your entire conversation appears in the chat window. You may have participated in chat with a customer service rep while browsing in an online store, for example. Here are some characteristics of chat that you should know about:

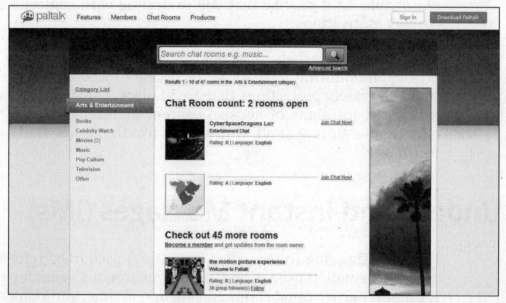

FIGURE 18-3

» When the chat is over, unless you save a copy, the conversation is typically gone.

» Interactions are in real time (synchronous), which means you can interact with others in the moment.

» On some sites, several people can interact at once, although this can take getting used to as you try to follow what others are saying and jump in with your own comments.

» When you find a chat you want to participate in, sign up to get a screen name, and then you simply enter the chat room, type your message, and submit it. Your message shows up in the stream of comments, and others may — or may not — reply to it.

When you're talking to someone in a chat room that hosts multiple people, you might be able to, if you'd like, invite a person to enter a private chat room, which keeps the rest of the folks who wandered into the chat room out of your conversation. Also, others can invite you into private chat rooms. Be careful who you interact with in this way, and be sure you understand the motivations for making your conversation private. This may be entirely reasonable, or it may be that you're dealing with someone with suspect motivations.

Before you get started, check out the website's Terms of Use and privacy, monitoring, and abuse-reporting procedures to understand the safety protections that are in place. Some sites are well monitored for signs of abusive content or interactions; others have no monitoring at all. If you don't like the terms, find a different site.

Understand Instant Messages (IMs)

Instant messaging (often called just *IMing*) used to be referred to as real-time email. It used to be strictly synchronous, meaning that two (or more) parties could communicate in real time, without any delay. It still can be synchronous, but now you can also leave a message that the recipient can pick up later.

Instant messaging is a great way to stay in touch with younger generations who rarely use email. IM is ideal for quick, little messages where you just want an answer without writing an email, as well as for touching base and saying hi. Text messaging on cell phones is largely the same phenomena: This isn't a tool you'd typically use for a long, meaningful conversation, but it's great for quick exchanges.

Depending on the IM service you use, you can do the following:

» Write notes to friends, grandchildren, or whomever.

» Talk as if you were on the phone.

» Send photos, videos, and other files.

» Use little graphical images, called *emoticons* (such as smilies or winks), *avatars* (drawn characters that represent you), and *stickers* (cartoony pictures and characters), to add fun to your IM messages.

» See participants via web cameras.

» Get and send email.

» Search the web, find others' physical location using Global Positioning System (GPS) technology, listen to music, watch videos, play games, bid on auctions, find dates, and more.

» Track the history of conversations and even save transcripts of them to review later.

Instant messaging programs vary somewhat, and you have several to choose from, including the Skype app that's included in Windows 10. Other messaging apps include Yahoo! Messenger (available at `http://messenger.yahoo.com`), and AOL Instant Messenger, also known as AIM (available at `www.aim.com`). Gmail also has a built-in IM feature.

TIP

IM is one place where people use shortcut text. Some of this will be familiar to you, such as FYI (for your information) and ASAP (as soon as possible). Other short text may be less familiar, such as LOL (laughing out loud) or AFAIK (as far as I know). Visit `www.pc.net/slang` for a table of common shortcut text terms. Knowing these will make communicating with younger folks more fun.

TIP

Consider what you're saying and sharing in IM and how you'd feel if the information were made public. IM allows you to store your conversation history, which is super-useful if you need to go back and check something that was said, but it has its downside. Anything you include in an IM can be forwarded to others. If you're at work, keep in mind that many employers monitor IM (and email) conversations.

TIP

If you run across illegal content — such as child pornography — downloading or continuing to view this for any reason is illegal. Report the incident to law enforcement immediately.

TIP

You can send IMs from a computer to a mobile phone (and vice versa) and from one mobile phone to another. If you include your mobile phone number as part of your IM profile, anyone who can see your profile can view it. This is useful information for both friends and criminals, so it's important to consider whether you want your number exposed — especially if you have many people on your contact list whom you don't personally know.

Explore Skype and Add Contacts

1. The Skype app enables you to send IMs to friends and make voice and video calls. To get started using Skype, open the Start menu and click the Skype tile.

2. You may be prompted to sign in with your Microsoft account or Skype Name.

TIP

You can also use the Cortana search box on the taskbar to search for and open Skype.

3. After finishing connecting to the service, click the Contacts button (see Figure 18-4). Existing contacts appear in the Contacts list. (You can add your friends and family in the Contacts app in order to easily message and call them from Skype. They have to be set up as Skype users, too.) A green check mark beside a contact's name indicates that the person is currently available for conversations and calls.

You can also invite new contacts not on your Contacts list. Click in the Search Skype Directory field and begin entering a name. Select a name on the list that appears and click the Add a Contact button (see Figure 18-5).

Skype lists your contacts here

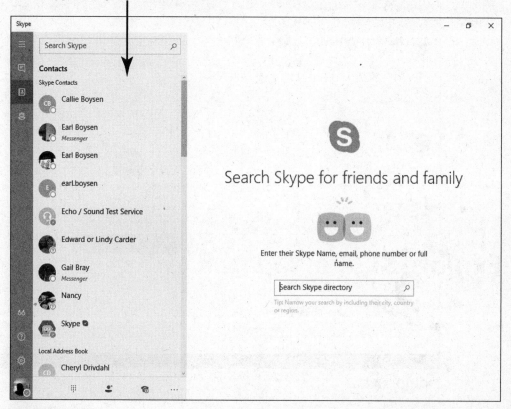

FIGURE 18-4

FIGURE 18-5

4. In the next window, click the Add to Contacts button.

5. Edit the brief message in the Type A Message field that opens at the bottom and click Send (see Figure 18-6). Once your contact receives your message and accepts the invitation, the question mark on the contact's photo or icon in your Contacts list changes to a green check mark. The green check mark also indicates when a contact is online, so the two of you can message and call on Skype.

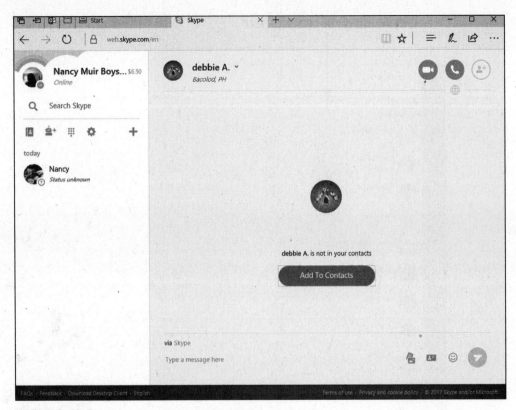

FIGURE 18-6

Send and Receive Instant Messages (IMs) in Skype

1. To instant message with a single user, just click Contacts in the left pane of the Skype window, and click an available (online) contact in the list (see Figure 18-7).

2. On the messaging screen, type a message in the field at the bottom of the screen (see Figure 18-8) and click Send. The message appears as the first message in the conversation. Read your friend's response when it appears, and type additional comments to carry on your conversation.

3. To return to the main Skype screen, click the Contacts button.

Click online contact to IM with

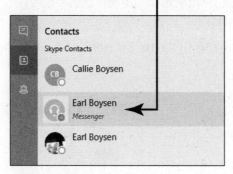

FIGURE 18-7

FIGURE 18-8

TIP

To start an IM with multiple contacts, click the Add People button on the contact screen (the plus symbol). In the list that opens, click each contact to IM with, and then click the Add button. Then type a message in the field at the bottom and press Send. After all the group members finish chatting, click the Contacts button to return to the main Skype screen.

TIP

Skype is also available as a mobile app. Install it on a smartphone or tablet to use those devices for IM.

TIP

Some online services call messaging *direct messaging* (DM) or *private messaging* (PM).

Make a Call

1. To make a call to a contact using Skype, you may have to connect a microphone and speakers to the system if they're not built in. Or, you can use a headset/microphone combination that's designed for making online calls. Follow the instructions that came with your laptop and the devices for connecting and setting them up in Windows.

2. In the main Skype screen, click Contacts in the left pane, then the contact to call in the Contacts list.

3. Click the Call button (see Figure 18-9) to the far right of the contact's name.

Click to place call

FIGURE 18-9

4. Your contact will see a pop-up box in Skype where they can click to accept or hang up the call.

5. Talk as you normally would using the built-in or headphone microphone. Move your mouse over the contact to display buttons for working with the call. You can click the Microphone button to (see Figure 18-10) mute and unmute your microphone.

6. Click the End Call button at the right below the contact photo to finish the Skype call.

7. Click Home in the left pane to go back to the main Skype screen. If you're finished using Skype, click the window's Close button.

TIP

To dial a phone number with Skype, click the Call Phones button (with the phone icon) on the main Skype screen, or use the onscreen keypad to enter a number, including the area code, and then click the round Call button at the bottom. Note that calling fees apply. In the United States, you can pay per minute as you go, or buy a low-cost monthly subscription.

TIP

If you simply close the Skype window, you are still signed in to Skype and will appear as Online (available for calls and messages) to your Skype contacts. If you receive any incoming IMs or calls, Skype will reopen to alert you. If you do not want to be available, you have two choices that you can make before closing the Skype window. You can either click your account picture in the lower left and then click Sign Out (in which case you will have to sign back in when you restart Skype), or you can click the On/Off button for Do Not Disturb or Do Not Share My Presence.

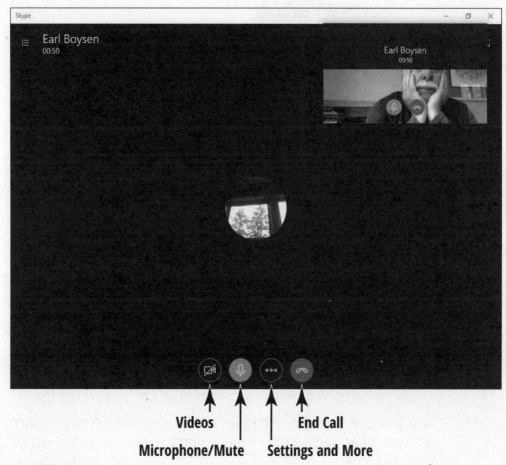

Videos

Microphone/Mute

End Call

Settings and More

FIGURE 18-10

Use a Webcam

Webcams are relatively inexpensive, and laptops now come with webcams embedded in their lids. (See Figure 18-11.) You can use a webcam with apps like Skype to make calls over the Internet, or other apps to have face-to-face, live meetings.

FIGURE 18-11

A webcam can be a great way to communicate with friends and family, but it can quickly become risky when you use it for conversations with strangers.

» Giving your image away, especially one that may show your emotional reactions to a stranger's statements in real time, simply reveals too much information that can put you at risk.

» If you use a webcam to meet online with someone you don't know, that person may expose you to behavior you'd rather not see.

» Note that webcams can also be hijacked and turned on remotely. This allows predators to view and listen to individuals without their knowledge. When you aren't using your webcam, consider turning it off or disconnecting it if it isn't a built-in model.

TIP

Teens in particular struggle to use good judgment when using webcams. If you have grandchildren or other children in your care, realize that normal inhibitions seem to fall away when they aren't physically present with the person they're speaking to — and many expose themselves, figuratively and literally.

In addition to having a conversation about appropriate webcam use with children and teens, it may be wise to limit access to webcams.

Get an Overview of Collaborative and Social Networking Sites

Although you may think kids are the only active group using social networking, that isn't the case. In fact, people 35–54 years old make up a large segment of social networkers.

There are several types of sites where people collaborate or communicate socially. The following definitions may be useful:

» **Wiki:** A website that allows anyone visiting to contribute (add, edit, or remove) content. Wikipedia, for example, is a virtual encyclopedia built by users providing information in their areas of expertise. Because of the ease of collaboration, wikis are often used when developing group projects or sharing information collaboratively.

» **Blog:** An online journal (*blog* is short for *web log*) that may be entirely private, open to select friends or family, or available to the general public. You can usually adjust your blog settings to restrict visitors from commenting on your blog entries, if you'd like.

» **Social networking site:** This type of website (see Figure 18-12) allows people to build and maintain a web page and create networks of people that they're somehow connected to — their friends, work associates, and/or other members with similar interests. Most social networking sites also host blogs and have social networking functions that allow people to view information about others and contact each other.

» **Social journaling site:** Sites such as Twitter allow people to post short notes online, notes that are typically about what they're doing at the moment. Many companies and celebrities are now *tweeting,* as posting comments on Twitter is referred to. You can follow individuals on Twitter so you're always informed if somebody you're a fan of makes a post.

FIGURE 18-12

TIP

Twitter has become a popular form of online communication. People can follow others and post responses to their tweets. Tweets are short, with a limit of 140 characters, so you have to keep your tweets and responses concise.

Sign Up for a Social Networking Service

Many social networking sites, such as Facebook or Pinterest, are general in nature and attract a wide variety of users. Facebook, which was begun by some students at Harvard, has become today's most popular general site, and many seniors use its features to blog, exchange virtual gifts, and post photos. Other social networking sites revolve around particular interests or age groups.

When signing up for a service, understand what is *required* information and what is optional. You should clearly understand why a web service needs any of your personally identifiable information and how it may use that information — before providing it. Consider carefully the questions that sites ask users to answer when creating a profile.

TIP

Accepting a social networking service's default settings may expose more information than you intend.

Walk through the signup process for Facebook to see the kinds of information it asks for. Follow these instructions to do so:

1. Type this URL into your browser's address line: **www.facebook.com**.

2. In the signup form that appears (see Figure 18-13), enter your name, email address, a password, your gender, and birthdate. Note that the site requires your birthdate to verify that you are old enough to use the service, but you can choose to hide this information from others later if you don't want it displayed. (I recommend hiding your birthdate to avoid senior-specific scams.)

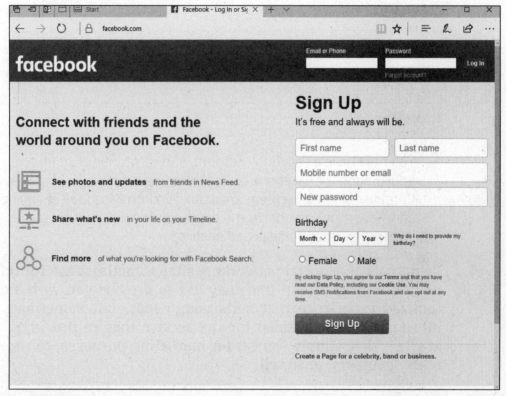

FIGURE 18-13

3. Click the Sign Up button. On the screen that appears (see Figure 18-14) click the Find Friends button if you want to find people from your contacts who are using the various services listed, or click Skip This Step and click Skip again in the dialog box that appears to move on without adding friends if you don't want to invite everybody on your contacts list to be your friend.

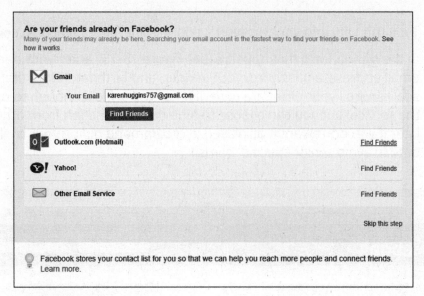

Are your friends already on Facebook?

Many of your friends may already be here. Searching your email account is the fastest way to find your friends on Facebook. See how it works.

M	Gmail	
	Your Email	karenhuggins757@gmail.com
	Find Friends	

O	Outlook.com (Hotmail)	Find Friends
Y!	Yahoo!	Find Friends
✉	Other Email Service	Find Friends

Skip this step

💡 Facebook stores your contact list for you so that we can help you reach more people and connect friends. Learn more.

FIGURE 18-14

4. You now have a Facebook account, and can continue to fill out profile information for Facebook on the following screens, clicking Save and Continue between screens. You can sign into Facebook at any time and view your personal home page, add friends, post messages, or view others' home pages and postings.

TIP

Remember that social networking sites sometimes ask for information during signup that they use to provide you with a customized experience that suits your needs. But sometimes the information isn't needed for the service they're providing you at all — they simply want it for marketing purposes, to show to other members, or to sell.

TIP

It's often very difficult to remove information from sites if you later regret the amount of information you've shared. It's best to be conservative in the information you share during the signup process; you can always add more later.

Understand How Online Dating Works

Many seniors are making connections with others via online dating services, and if you've been wondering if this route could be for you, here's how you can jump into the world of online dating:

» Choose a reputable dating site

» Sign up and provide information about your likes, dislikes, preferences, and so on. This often takes the form of a self-guided interview process.

» Create and modify your profile to both avoid exposing too much personal information and ensure that you're sending the right message about yourself to prospective dates.

» Use search features on the site to find people who interest you or other people who match your profile (see Figure 18-15). Send them messages or invitations to view your profile.

FIGURE 18-15

» You'll get messages from other members of the site, to which you can respond (or not). Use the site's chat and email features to interact with potential dates. You may also be able to read comments about the person from others who've dated him or her, if the site has that feature.

» When you're comfortable with the person and feel there might be a spark, decide if you want to meet the person offline.

TIP

Formal dating sites aren't the only places where people meet online, but they typically have the best safeguards in place. If you want to interact with people you meet on other sites, you should provide your own safeguards. Create a separate email account (so you can remain anonymous and abandon the email address if needed). Many dating sites screen participants and provide strong reporting measures that are missing on other types of social sites, so be particularly careful. Take your time getting to know someone first before connecting and always meet in a public setting.

Select a Dating Service

Select your online dating service carefully. Here are some tips:

>> Look for an established, popular site with plenty of members and a philosophy that matches your own.

>> Review the site's policy regarding your privacy and its procedures for screening members. Make sure you're comfortable with those policies.

>> Use a service that provides an email system (sometimes called *private messaging*) that you use for contacting other members. By using the site's email rather than your own email address, you can maintain your privacy.

>> Some sites, such as eHarmony (www.eharmony.com/senior-dating), offer stronger levels of authenticating members, such as screening to make you more confident that you know with whom you're interacting.

>> Visit a site such as www.consumer-rankings.com/dating for comparisons of sites. Whether you choose a senior-specific dating site such as DatingForSeniors.com or a general-population site such as FriendFinder.com, reading reviews about them ahead of time will help you make the best choice.

TIP

If you try a site and experience an unpleasant incident involving another member, report it and make sure the service follows through to enforce its policies. If it doesn't, find another service.

Play Games Online

Whether you want to play a game of solitaire, or want to interact with others in multiplayer games, there's a world of gaming for you to explore using your computer.

Instead of signing up with an online gaming service for single-player games like Solitaire or Bejeweled, I suggest you locate those apps in the Windows Store (see Figure 18-16) and download and play them on your computer. Some games are free and some will cost you a bit. Free online gaming sites may make these games available to play online, but they sometimes employ policies that allow them to sell information about your activities and identity to others.

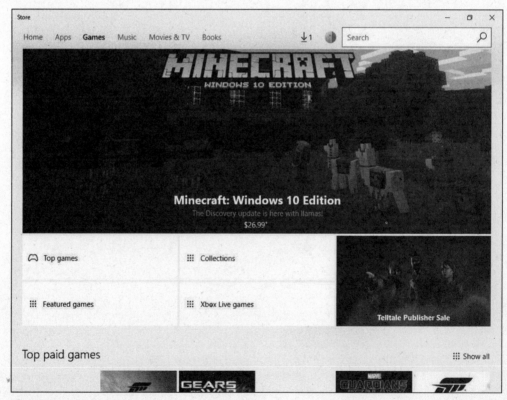

FIGURE 18-16

If you want to play an online game where you interact with others, such as Minecraft (which involves building realities and going on adventures), go to that website (in this case, `https://minecraft.net`), download any required app, and sign up. You can then log in to the game and use features to move around this virtual reality, interact with others, and build worlds.

TIP

Click the Xbox Live Games button when buying a game at the Windows Store to check out Xbox games for use with the Xbox device.

4

Having Fun

IN THIS CHAPTER

» Getting an overview of media apps

» Finding movies and TV shows in the Windows Store

» Streaming videos from other sources

» Uploading content from your digital camera or smartphone

» Taking photos and videos in the Camera app

» Viewing photos in the Photos app

» Editing and sharing photos

» Running a slide show in the Photos app

Chapter **19**

Getting Visual: Using Video, Photos, and Camera Apps

The world has discovered that it's fun and easy to share photos and videos online, and that's probably why everybody is in on the digital image craze. Most people today have access to a digital camera (even if only on their cellphones) and have started manipulating and swapping photos and videos like crazy, both online and off.

But today your phone, tablet, and computer not only let you upload and view pictures and videos: You can use a built-in camera and the Windows 10 Camera app to take your own pictures or record videos and play them back. You can also buy videos (movies and TV shows, for example) and play them on your laptop or other device, such as a tablet.

In this chapter, you discover how to buy and play video, including movies and TV shows. I also give you some guidelines for uploading photos from your digital camera or smartphone, and explain how to view and share your photos.

Get an Overview of Media Apps

Your laptop is a doorway into a media-rich world full of music, digital photos, and video. It provides you with all kinds of possibilities for working with media. Windows 10 has a useful media player built right into it: the Movies & TV app. The Photos app provides another option for viewing photos. In addition, the Camera app helps you to create and view photos and video.

Here's what you can do with each of these programs:

» **Movies & TV app:** Is just what its name suggests: As you see in Figure 19-1, it's a program you can use to watch movies, TV programs, or videos that you or others have recorded.

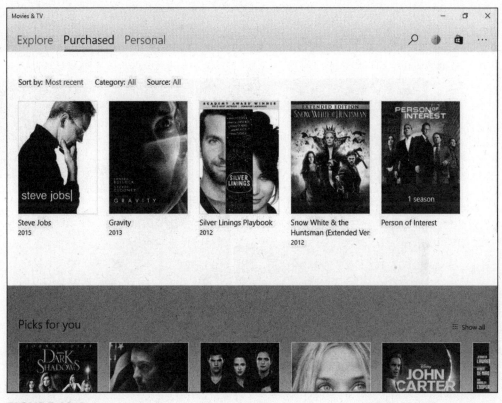

FIGURE 19-1

» **Photos app:** Enables you to view digital photos; it opens automatically when you double-click a photo (as shown in Figure 19-2) in File Explorer and when you click the Photos tile on the Start menu. You can also share photos from within the Photos app via social media sites.

» **Camera app:** Allows anybody who has a computer with a built-in or external camera or webcam to take photos and record videos.

FIGURE 19-2

Find Movies and TV Shows in the Store

1. The Windows Store offers a wonderful world of content that you can buy and play on your laptop. To shop for movies and TV shows, click the Start button and then click the Store tile. Click the Movies & TV link at the top of the window to get started.

2. Scroll down to view titles in categories such as Top-Selling Movies, Featured Collections, and Top Selling TV shows. Click a featured title to view details or watch a trailer.

TIP

If you're looking for a particular title or movies with a particular actor, enter a title or name in the search field at the upper-right corner of the window.

3. Click Buy (see Figure 19-3). If you click Rent at this point, you're taken through a similar sequence of steps. If requested, enter your Microsoft account password or PIN.

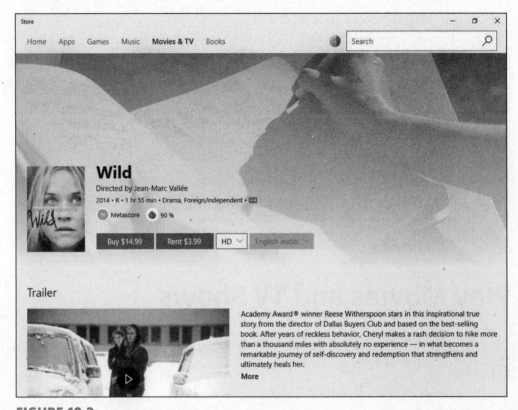

FIGURE 19-3

TIP

If you don't already have payment information associated with your Microsoft account, you'll be asked to enter payment information.

4. In the Buy Movie window, click the Confirm Purchase button (see Figure 19-4). The movie is added to Your Video Library in the Movie & TV app.

5. Click the Close button to close the Store.

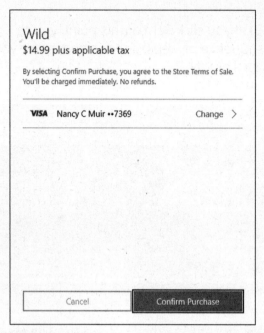

FIGURE 19-4

Play Movies and TV Shows

1. After you have bought a movie or TV show, from the Start menu, click the Movies & TV tile.

2. Click the Purchased tab.

3. In the window listing titles, click the title you want to play (as shown in Figure 19-5).

4. In the resulting window, click the Play button (if you've already played part of this video, the Play button will read Resume) to begin the playback (see Figure 19-6). If you've selected a TV series for which you own several episodes, select an episode before pressing the Play button.

TIP

Movies and TV titles will stream by default, but they also provide a download option (see Figure 19-6). Streaming refers to playing video using an online player rather than downloading content to your computer. To save space on your hard drive or solid state drive, you should download a title only if you'll be without a Wi-Fi connection for a time.

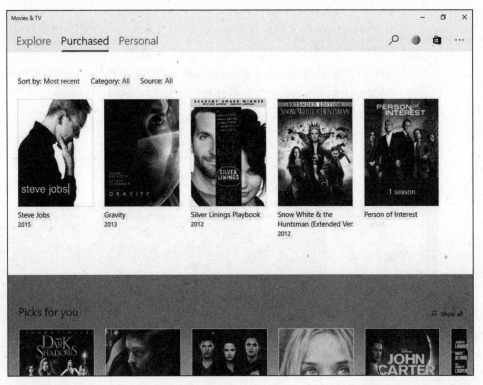

Movies & TV

Explore **Purchased** Personal

Sort by: Most recent   Category: All   Source: All

Steve Jobs
2015

Gravity
2013

Silver Linings Playbook
2012

Snow White & the
Huntsman (Extended Ver.
2012

Person of Interest

Picks for you

Show all

FIGURE 19-5

5. Use tools at the bottom of the screen (see Figure 19-7) to do the following (if they disappear during playback, just move your mouse or tap the screen to display them again):

- **Adjust the volume** of any soundtrack by clicking the Show Volume Menu button to open the volume slider and dragging the slider left (to make it softer) or right (to make it louder). Click the megaphone-shaped volume icon to the left of the slider to mute the sound (and click it again to turn the sound back on).

- **Pause the playback** by clicking the Pause button in the center of the toolbar.

- **Enable captions** by clicking the Show Menu to Subtitles and Audio button and then clicking the language you prefer.

- **Change the display size** of the movie. Display the movie in a smaller window by clicking the Play in Mini View button.

- **View the movie on full screen** by clicking the Full Screen button. When the movie is displayed in full screen, the Full Screen button becomes an Exit Full Screen button. Click this button to view the movie in a smaller window.

- **View the movie on a Bluetooth enabled TV** by clicking the Show More Options button and then clicking Cast to Device.

6. Click the Close button to close the Movie & TV app.

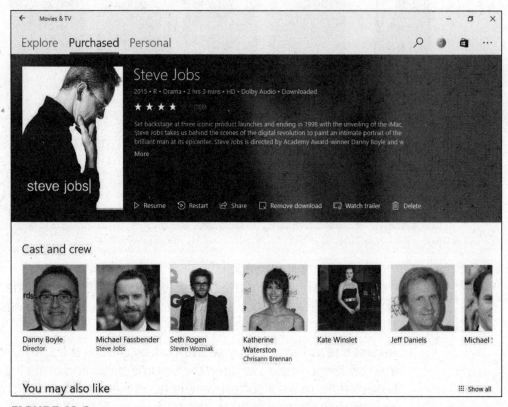

FIGURE 19-6

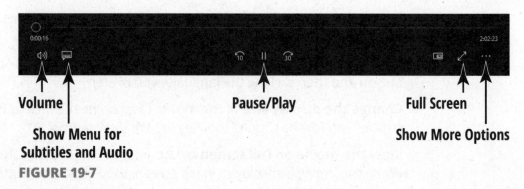

Volume

Show Menu for
Subtitles and Audio

Pause/Play

Full Screen

Show More Options

FIGURE 19-7

TIP

You can also use the Movie & TV app to play your own video content. Just click the Movie & TV tile on the Start menu, locate the video in the Videos section, and click to play it. The playback controls are almost identical to those discussed for playing movies.

Stream Videos from Other Sources

Today many people prefer to stream video rather than purchase or rent and download it. Playing a video on the YouTube website (a site where people can post their own videos) is one example of streaming, but you can also stream from sites such as Amazon or Netflix (sites that typically require a purchase or subscription to view movies or TV shows), just as you can from the Windows Store.

The advantage to streaming is that you don't have to store large video files on your device, especially important on a smartphone or tablet with smaller storage capabilities. The downside to streaming: When you have a weak Internet connection, the playback can be glitchy, stopping and starting often.

If you have a strong Internet connection and want to try streaming, go to a site such as Amazon.com and locate a movie or TV show, rent or buy it, and start viewing.

Upload Content from Your Digital Camera or Smartphone

Uploading photos and videos from a camera or phone to your laptop is a very simple process, but it helps to understand what's involved. (Check your manual for details.) Here are some highlights:

» **Making the connection:** Uploading photos and videos from a digital camera or phone to a laptop requires that you connect the camera to a USB port on your laptop using a USB cable that typically comes with the device. Power on the camera/phone or change its setting to a playback mode as instructed by your user's manual.

Some cameras are Wi-Fi enabled, which eliminates the need for a USB cable when you are in range of a Wi-Fi network.

» **Installing software:** Digital cameras also typically come with software that makes uploading photos to your laptop easy. Install the software and then follow the easy-to-use instructions to upload photos and videos. If you're missing such software, you can simply connect your camera to your laptop and use File Explorer to locate the camera device on your laptop and copy and paste photo or video files into a folder on your hard drive. (Chapter 3 tells you how to use File Explorer.)

» **Sharing photos from your phone:** Many people today use their smartphones as their primary camera. You can transfer content using a USB connection, dragging content from your device to a file folder in File Explorer. You can also share photos and videos via a messaging app or email, and then open them on your laptop.

» **Printing photos straight from the camera:** Digital cameras save photos onto a memory card, and many printers include a slot where you can insert the memory card from the camera and print directly from it without having to first upload pictures. Some cameras also connect directly to printers. However, if you want to keep a copy of the photo and clear up space in your camera's memory, you should upload the photos to your laptop or an external storage medium such as a DVD or USB stick, even if you can print without uploading.

TIP

Story Remix is a new app in Windows that allows you to use photos and videos to create a video and even add 3D objects to an image or draw on a photo to add commentary or emphasis. Story Remix works in the Cloud so that you can use content from a variety of devices, including Android and Apple iOS devices.

Take Photos with the Camera App

1. If your laptop has a camera, you can use the Camera app features to take both still photos and videos. Click the Start button, click All Apps, and then scroll down and click Camera.

2. Click the Settings button. The Settings pane opens; click the Aspect Ratio drop-down box and choose a setting. Click outside the Settings dialog box to close it.

3. If the Camera button is larger than the Video button (see Figure 19-8), you're in photo mode. If the Video button is larger than the Camera button, click the Camera button to go to photo mode. Aim your laptop toward the subject of your picture and click the Camera button. The photo is captured.

4. Click the Camera Roll button in the lower-right corner to view the photo.

TIP

When you take a photo, you can click the Photos App button and make use of the photo editing or sharing tools. See the "Edit Photos" and "Share Photos" sections below for more details.

Video

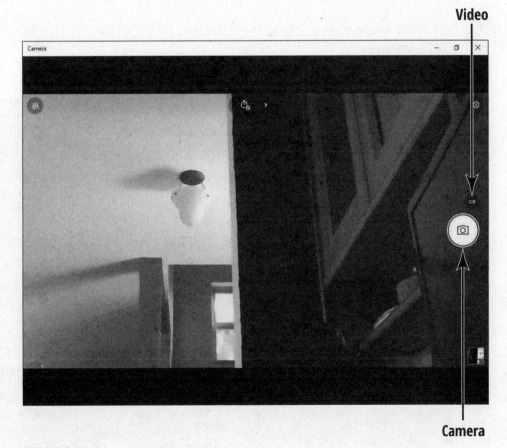

Camera

FIGURE 19-8

Record Videos with the Camera App

1. If your laptop has a built-in camera (and most do), you can use the Camera app to take both still photos and videos. Click the Start button, click All Apps, and then scroll down and click Camera.

2. Click the Settings button. The Settings pane opens (see Figure 19-9). Scroll down to the Video Recording and Flicker Reduction drop-down boxes and adjust the resolution, frame rate, and flicker reduction frequency settings if necessary (most people leave these at their default settings). Click outside the Settings dialog box to close it.

3. Click the Video button (see Figure 19-10) to switch to video mode.

4. Click the Video button to begin the video recording.

5. Click the Video button again to stop recording.

TIP

To view your video, click the Camera Roll button in the lower-right corner.

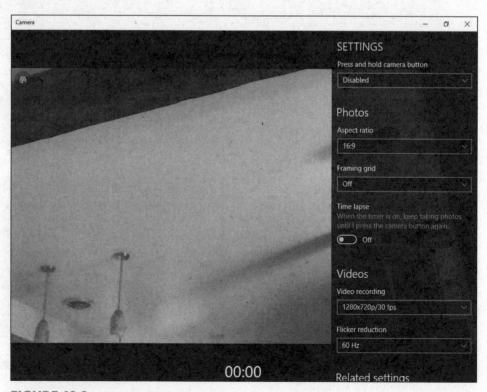

FIGURE 19-9

FIGURE 19-10

View Photos in the Photos App

1. To peruse your photos and open them in the Photos app, click the Photos tile on the Start menu. The Photos app opens with a thumbnail for each photo in your collection, as shown in Figure 19-11. Browse the thumbnails and click any thumbnail to open a photo.

2. In the Photos app, click the Albums button and then click an album, such as Camera Roll. The resulting screen shows your photos organized by date. Click a photo and move the mouse on the picture; arrows appear on the sides (click these arrows to see the next or previous photos in the album). Click the Zoom button in the toolbar at the top to enlarge the photo (see Figure 19-12). Click these to zoom in and out. To delete a photo, click the photo and then click the Delete button (the trashcan-shaped button at the bottom).

FIGURE 19-11

FIGURE 19-12

Edit Photos

In the Photos app, click a photo, and then click the Edit button. An Editing panel appears on the right side of the screen. You can use the tools shown in Figure 19-13 to do any of the following:

FIGURE 19-13

» Click the Enhance tab and then click the Crop and Rotate button. Click a corner of the photo and drag inward to crop the image. You can also click the Aspect Ratio button and choose a ratio, which will crop your photo automatically. Click the Rotate button to rotate the image.

» In the Enhance Your Photo area, click the left side of the photo to darken it, or click the right side of the photo to brighten it.

» The Filters button allows you to choose between thumbnails of the image with different filter effects applied.

» The Adjust tab allows you to adjust settings such as brightness, color, clarity, and red eye.

» The Light button lets you choose to adjust Contrast, Exposure, Highlights, or Shadows.

» Clicking the Color drop-down arrow lets you make Tint and Warmth settings.

Share Photos

1. Click the Photos app tile on the Start menu. Open a photo you want to share and then click the Share button.

2. The Share screen opens showing the apps that you can use to share the file (see Figure 19-14). Click any app you want to use, such as Facebook or Mail.

FIGURE 19-14

To share a photo you need to download the appropriate social media app, such as Facebook. From the Store, open the social media app and sign in and you can then use that social media app to share photos.

3. In the form that appears (see Figure 19-15), enter your message.

4. Click the appropriate button such as Post or Send. The photo and message are posted on your Facebook page or sent to another selected destination such as Mail.

FIGURE 19-15

If you want to set an image for your lock screen, click the See More button at the upper-right corner of the screen. A menu appears that allows you to set the image to be used on the lock screen, or to copy or print the image.

Run a Slide Show in the Photos App

1. You can use the Photos app to play a slide show, which continues to run until you stop it. Click the Photos tile on the Start menu and then click a photo album to open it.

2. Click the Slideshow button shown in Figure 19-16. All photos and videos are displayed in sequence.

3. Click anywhere on the screen to stop the slide show.

FIGURE 19-16

Chapter **20**

Playing Music in Windows 10

M usic is the universal language, and your laptop opens up many opportunities for appreciating it. Your laptop makes it possible for you to listen to your favorite music, download music from the Internet, play audio DVDs, and organize your music by creating playlists. You can also access your music library on your other Windows 10 devices, such as your phone or tablet.

You can set up your speakers and adjust volume, and then use the Groove Music app to buy music, play music, and manage your music library.

Set Up Speakers

1. Attach headphones or speakers to your computer by plugging them into the appropriate connection (often labeled with a little earphone or speaker symbol) on your laptop.

2. Right click the Volume button (which looks like a little speaker) in the notifications area of the taskbar and in the menu that opens, click Playback Devices.

3. In the resulting Sound dialog box (see Figure 20-1), click the Speakers item and then click the Properties button. *Note:* depending on your speaker and headphone models, these settings might vary.

Click Speakers

FIGURE 20-1

4. In the resulting Speakers Properties dialog box, click the Levels tab, shown in Figure 20-2, and then use the Output slider to adjust the speaker volume. *Note:* If you see a small red circle with a slash through it on the Speaker button, click it to activate the speakers.

Click and drag the slider

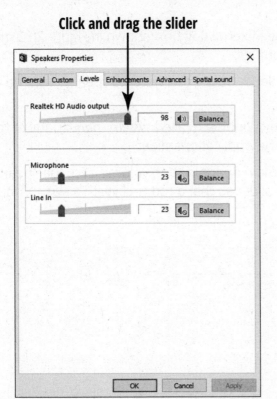

FIGURE 20-2

5. Click the Balance button. In the resulting Balance dialog box, use the L(eft) and R(ight) sliders to adjust the balance of sounds between the two speakers.

6. Click OK three times to close all the open dialog boxes and save the new settings.

TIP

If you use your laptop to make or receive phone calls, check out the Communications tab of the Sound dialog box. Here you can make a setting to have Windows automatically adjust sounds to minimize background noise.

Adjust System Volume

1. You can set the master system volume for your laptop to be louder or softer. Right click the Volume button in the notifications area of the taskbar and in the menu that opens, click Open Volume Mixer.

2. In the resulting Volume Mixer dialog box (shown in Figure 20-3) make any of the following settings:

- Move the Device slider to adjust the system's speaker volume up and down.

- For sounds played by Windows (called *system sounds*), adjust the volume by moving the Applications slider.

- To mute either the main or application volume, click the speaker icon beneath either slider so that a red circle with a slash through it appears.

3. Click the Close button.

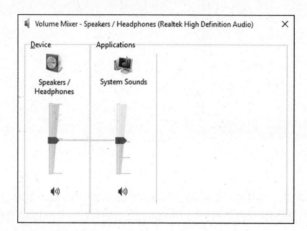

FIGURE 20-3

TIP

Here's a handy shortcut for quickly adjusting the volume of your default sound device. Click the Volume button (the gray speaker) in the notification area on the right side of the taskbar. To adjust the volume, use the slider on the Volume pop-up menu that appears, or click the Speaker button to mute sounds.

TIP

Today, many keyboards include volume controls and a mute button to control sounds from your computer. Some even include buttons to play, pause, and stop audio playback. Having these buttons and other controls at your fingertips can be worth a little extra in the price of your keyboard.

Use Windows Media Player to Rip Music

1. If your laptop has a DVD drive and you place a CD/DVD disc in that drive, Windows Media Player can *rip* the music from the disc to your laptop's Music folder. Ripping copies all the tracks on the DVD to your laptop. That music is then available to play with Windows Media Player or the Groove Music app. Open Windows Media Player from the All Apps list in the Start menu. You may be presented with a window where you can click Recommended Settings to set up the player and then click Finish. To control how ripping works, click the Organize button and choose Options.

2. Click the Rip Music tab to display it.

3. In the Options dialog box (see Figure 20-4), you can make the following settings:

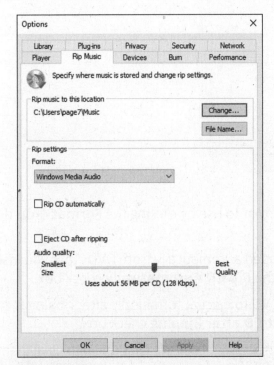

FIGURE 20-4

- Click the **Change** button to change the location where ripped music is stored; the default location is your Music folder.

- Click the **File Name** button to choose the information included with file names for music that is ripped to your laptop (see Figure 20-5).

FIGURE 20-5

- Choose the audio format to use by clicking the **Format** drop-down list.

- If you want music ripped automatically from DVDs that you insert in your drive, select the **Rip CD Automatically** check box.

- If you want the CD/DVD to eject automatically after ripping is complete, select the **Eject CD after Ripping** check box.

4. When you finish making settings, click the OK button to save them and close the Options dialog box.

TIP

Use the Audio Quality slider to adjust the quality of the ripped music. The Smallest Size setting will save space on your laptop by compressing the file, but this causes a loss of audio quality. The Best Quality setting will provide optimum sound, but these files can be rather large. The choice is yours based on your tastes and your computer's capacity.

TIP

If you don't have a DVD drive in your laptop, consider buying your music online and downloading it to your computer. With services such as Amazon.com's Cloud Player or Apple's iTunes, any music you buy is stored online so you can play it from any computing device. See the task "Buy Music" for more details about buying music online.

TIP

If you have a collection of music on CDs or DVDs and you don't have a CD/DVD drive in your laptop, consider buying an external CD/DVD drive that you can plug into a USB port. You can then use the CD/DVD drive to rip your music from disks onto your laptop.

Find Music in the Store

1. The Store's search feature provides a great way to search for new music. With the Store open (click the Store tile in the Start menu), click the Music tab then type an artist name or song title in the search box.

2. Press Enter. Results appear as shown in Figure 20-6.

3. Hover your mouse anywhere in the row of Albums and arrows will appear on one or both ends of the row. Click an arrow to scroll to the left or right to view additional albums. Click and drag the scrollbar on the right to scroll down and view more songs, and when available, apps, movies, or TV shows (in some cases even games) related to the artist or title.

4. Click an item to view more details about tracks and artist, to play a preview using the Groove Music app player, or to buy it (see Figure 20-7). You can click the triangle-shaped button to play a preview of the song.

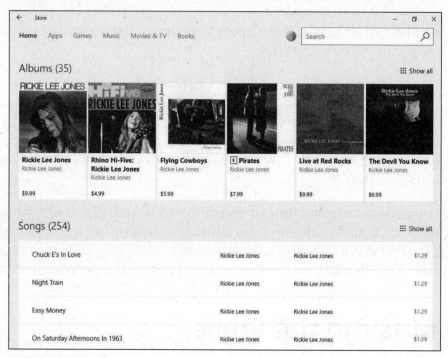

FIGURE 20-6

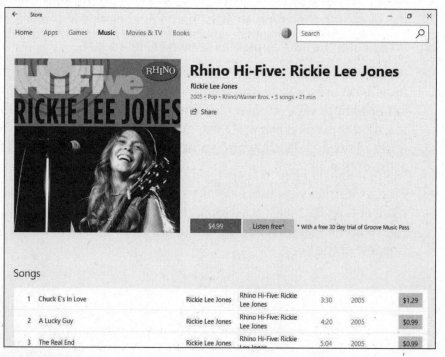

FIGURE 20-7

Buy Music

1. Purchasing music from the Windows Store involves making your selection, entering payment information if you don't already have payment information associated with your Microsoft account, and then completing your purchase. With a music selection displayed (see the previous task), click the Buy or Price button (the button showing the cost of the item) for an album or individual song. If requested, enter your Microsoft account password or PIN.

2. In the screen that appears, click the Add a Credit Card link and then fill in a payment method for your account; click Next.

3. In the following screen (see Figure 20-8), click the Buy button. The album downloads to your laptop and is available for you to play using the Groove Music app.

FIGURE 20-8

TIP

You can purchase a Groove Music Pass that allows you, for a monthly fee, to stream or download as many titles as you like in the Music Store.

Search for Music with Cortana

1. Enter a term in the Cortana Search field or click the Microphone button and speak a word or phrase to have Cortana search for an artist, album, or song. Results for the search for the song "Georgia on My Mind" appear in Figure 20-9.

FIGURE 20-9

2. In the search results, you might find:
   - Videos of performances
   - Other online stores where you can purchase the music
   - Information about the song or artist
3. Click any of the items to view the results.

Create a Playlist

1. A *playlist* is a saved set of music tracks you can create yourself — like building a personal music album. From the Start menu, click the Groove Music tile. You may be asked to purchase a pass or say No Thanks. The Groove Music app appears.

2. Click the Menu button and then click the Create New Playlist button (the plus symbol next to the Playlists setting shown in Figure 20-10). In the dialog box that appears (see Figure 20-11), click Name This Playlist and type a name for the playlist. Click the Create Playlist button.

Click to create new playlist

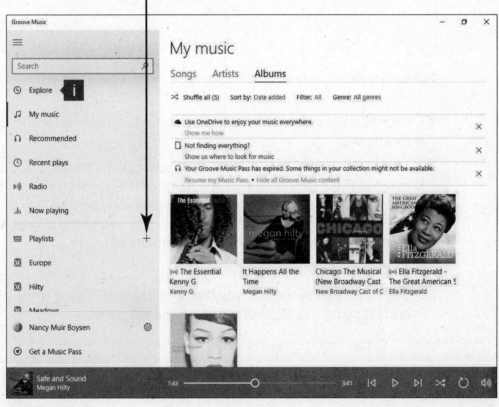

FIGURE 20-10

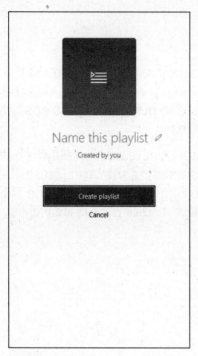

FIGURE 20-11

3. Click Add Songs from My Collection or Find Something New to search for music.

4. Move your cursor over an item and then click the Add To button (shaped like a plus sign); click the name of the playlist you want to add the song or album to from the list that appears (see Figure 20-12). Repeat this step to locate additional titles to add to the playlist. When you're done, click the Playlists button on the left.

5. To play a playlist, click its name.

6. You can organize music in playlists by clicking on a song in the playlist and dragging it to another playlist in the left panel.

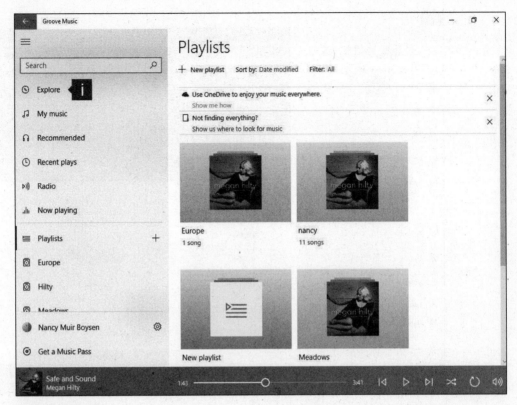

FIGURE 20-12

Play Music

1. Open the Groove Music app by clicking the Groove Music tile in the Start menu.

2. The Groove Music app opens. Click My Music in the left panel to get a view of the albums in your collection. Click a library tab such as Artists or Songs; the library contents appear. If you choose Albums or Artists, click an item to show a list of songs.

3. Click a song and then click the Play button that appears (see Figure 20-13).

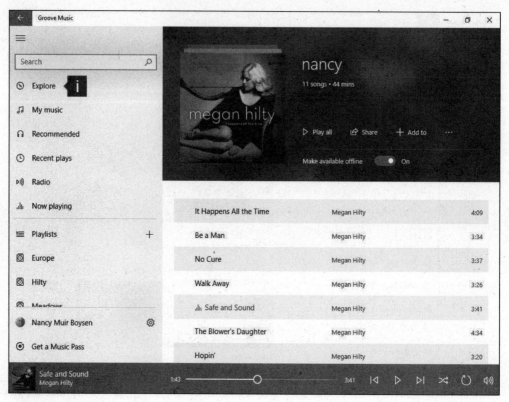

FIGURE 20-13

4. Use the buttons on the bottom of the Music app (as shown in Figure 20-14) to do the following:

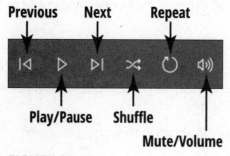

Previous   Next   Repeat

Play/Pause   Shuffle

Mute/Volume

FIGURE 20-14

- Click the **Play** button to play a song. When a song is playing, this button changes to the **Pause** button.

- Click the **Next** or **Previous** button to move to the next or previous track in an album or playlist.

- Use the **Repeat** button to repeat an album or playlist.

- Use the **Mute/Volume** control to turn the sound up or down without having to modify the Windows volume settings.

TIP

Tired of the order in which your songs play? You can click the Shuffle button (it sports wavy arrows) to have the Groove Music app move among the songs in your album randomly. Click this button again to turn the shuffle feature off.

TIP

To jump to another track, rather than using the Next and Previous buttons you can double-click a track in a list in the Groove Music app. This can be much quicker if you want to jump several tracks ahead or behind the currently playing track.

5
Windows Toolkit

IN THIS PART . . .

Connect to a network.

Work with Bluetooth technology.

Improve computer security with Windows Firewall and Defender.

Create a strong password.

Troubleshoot computer problems.

Improve performance by optimizing your hard drive.

Chapter **21**

Working with Networks

A computer network allows you to share information and devices, such as a printer, among computers.

You can connect your laptop to other computers by setting up a wired or wireless network. Devices connected to a group of computers on a network called a Homegroup can share hardware, files, an Internet connection, and more.

In addition to a computer network, you can use Bluetooth technology to connect to devices without wires at a short range. For example, you might use your laptop's built-in Bluetooth capability to connect to a Bluetooth mouse or headphones.

You can also use your mobile phone's 3G or 4G cellular network to go online through a process called *tethering*.

In this chapter, you'll explore several options for getting connected to other devices and sharing information.

Join a Homegroup

1. When you set up a network, you have to arrange to include each computer on the network in a Homegroup so that they can connect to each other, a single Internet connection, and shared hardware such as printers. If somebody has set up a Homegroup on another computer, you can join that network with a few steps. Start by pressing Win+I.

2. Click Network & Internet.

3. With the Wi-Fi category selected on the left, click Homegroup in the right panel under the heading Related Settings, click the Join Now button, and then click Next.

4. Click the various drop-down lists to choose what to share with the Homegroup on the network (see Figure 21-1).

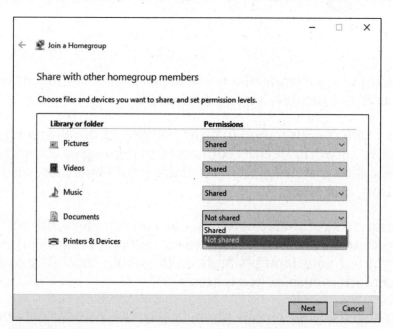

FIGURE 21-1

5. Click Next and enter a Homegroup password. Click Next again to make your laptop part of that Homegroup.

TIP

To locate the password for the Homegroup, you need to sign in as a user with administrator status. Then, open the Start menu and choose Settings ⇨ Network and Internet ⇨ Homegroup. Click View or Print the Homegroup Password.

Make a Connection to a Network

1. If you take a laptop with you around town or on the road, it's handy to be able to connect to networks in locations such as airports, coffee shops, or hotels. These public network connections are called *hotspots*. When you're in range of a hotspot, click the Network Settings button on the taskbar.

2. Click an available network in the list shown in Figure 21-2.

FIGURE 21-2

3. Click the Connect button, as shown in Figure 21-3.

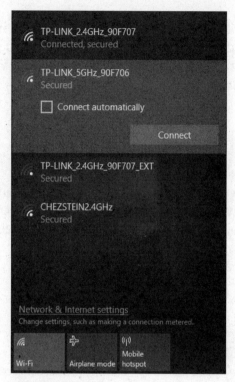

FIGURE 21-3

4. If you want your laptop to disconnect from a network, you can select the connected network and click the Disconnect button for that network. Note that just by moving out of range of the network you'll be disconnected from it.

TIP

In many cases, you're asked to enter a password for a network after you click Connect in Step 3. You have to ask somebody for this password; it may be publicly posted — for example, in a coffee shop — or you may have to ask for the password when you check into a hotel.

Specify What You Want to Share over a Network

1. Many people use networks to share content such as word-processing documents or pictures, or even a printer connection. When you're using a network to go online, you might not want to share your valuable data with others, so you may want to modify your sharing settings. Be sure you are part of the Homegroup (see the previous "Join a Homegroup" task) and then press Win+I.

2. Click Network & Internet.

3. Click Homegroup, and then click Change What You're Sharing with the Homegroup.

4. Click the drop-down list for any item that is currently Shared and click Not Shared to change the setting (see Figure 21-4).

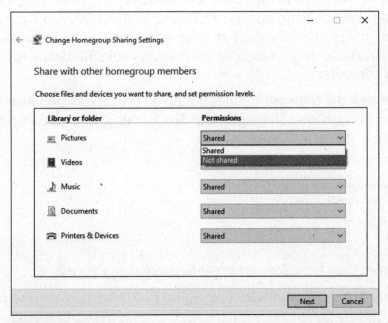

FIGURE 21-4

TIP

If you decide you don't want to participate in the network anymore, you can leave it by scrolling down in the Homegroup window that appears in Step 3 above and clicking the Leave the Homegroup link.

TIP

You can also share documents using a service such as Microsoft's OneDrive. You can upload and share files using this service, and a small amount of online storage is free. You can then access this content from any computer, whether it's connected to your network or not. See Chapter 17 for more about OneDrive.

Set Up a Wireless Network

1. If you have several computers in your home, you'll find you can save yourself steps by connecting them to each other through a wireless network. No more will you have to walk upstairs to print from a single laptop; all your computers on every floor and in every room can share that printer, as well as an Internet connection and documents. Start by connecting a router or other access point hardware to one of your computers.

2. Right-click the Network Settings button on the taskbar and then select Open Network and Sharing Center on the menu that appears (see Figure 21-5).

> Troubleshoot problems
> Open Network and Sharing Center

FIGURE 21-5

3. Click Set Up a New Connection or Network (see Figure 21-6).

4. Click Set Up a New Network (see Figure 21-7) and then click Next.

5. Click the router or access point to be set up and then click Next.

6. In the window that appears, enter the PIN number located on the router label and then click Next.

7. Enter a network name and then click Next. Windows completes your network setup. Click the Close button to close the window.

Click this option

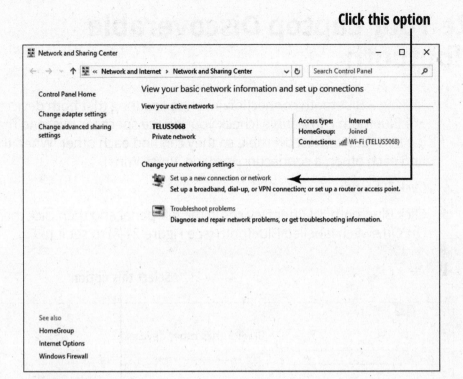

FIGURE 21-6

Click this option

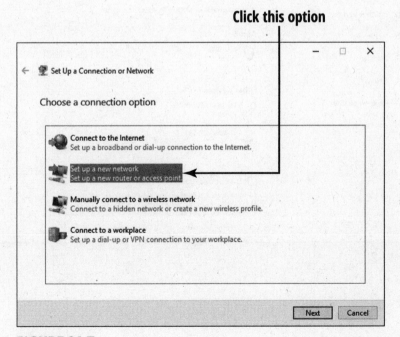

FIGURE 21-7

Make Your Laptop Discoverable to Bluetooth

1. Making a Bluetooth connection involves ensuring that both devices are Bluetooth compatible (check your device specs for this) and making both devices discoverable so they can find each other. When they find each other, a connection is made. Press Win+I.

2. Click Devices.

3. Click Bluetooth & Other Devices in the left panel and then click the On/Off switch labelled Bluetooth (see Figure 21-8) to set it to On.

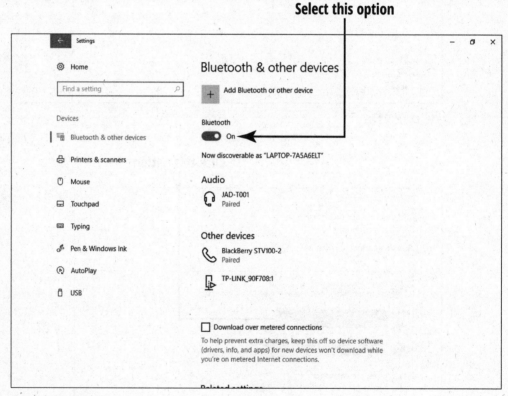

FIGURE 21-8

TIP

If you're travelling out of your home with your laptop, under Related Settings click More Bluetooth Options. In the resulting Bluetooth Settings dialog box (shown in Figure 21-8), make sure the check box for Allow Bluetooth Devices to Find this PC is not selected. This step protects your laptop's contents or settings from people who might try to connect and steal your data via Bluetooth. Another option is to leave your laptop discoverable but select the Alert Me When a New Bluetooth Device Wants to Connect check box in the Advanced Bluetooth Settings dialog box.

Connect to Bluetooth Devices

1. After you make your laptop discoverable, you can connect to another Bluetooth device that is turned on. Begin by pressing Win+I.

2. Click Devices.

3. In window that appears, click Bluetooth & Other Devices in the left panel and then check that Bluetooth is set to On.

4. Your laptop searches for nearby Bluetooth devices. When the one you want to pair your laptop with appears, click it and then click Pair. With some devices a code will appear on your computer and device screen asking you to verify the pairing. With other devices, such as a Bluetooth mouse, the device is simply paired. The word *paired* appears below the device name (see Figure 21-9).

5. Click Close.

TIP

Bluetooth devices are improving, but you may find that connections are spotty. If a Bluetooth device such as a headset isn't dependable, consider having a USB or wireless version of the device available as a backup.

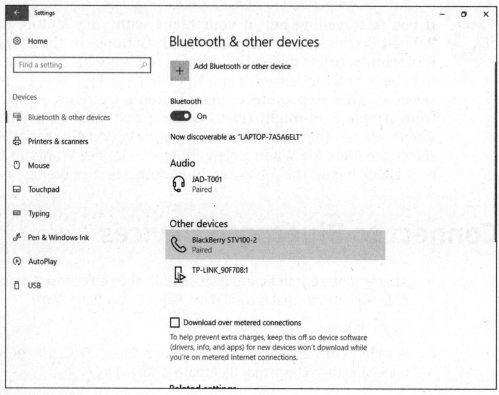

FIGURE 21-9

Go Online Using Your Cellular Network

1. It's possible to use a smartphone's 3G or 4G connection to connect to the Internet. You may have to pay your phone service provider a monthly fee for this service, called *tethering* or *personal hotspot*. In addition, your laptop has to be Wi-Fi capable (newer laptops all are). Start by turning on the hotspot feature on your phone (typically this is found in Network settings).

2. On your laptop, press Win+I, and then click Network & Internet.

3. Click Show Available Networks and then click your phone's Wi-Fi connection, as shown in Figure 21-10.

Click your phone's connection

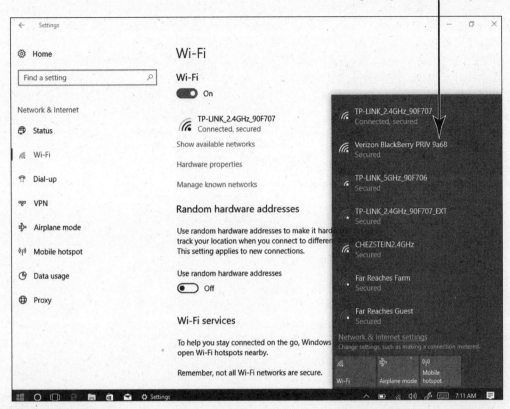

FIGURE 21-10

4. Click Connect and enter the security key.

5. Click Next.

TIP

Be aware of the drain on your phone's battery when tethering. Connect your phone to a power source when tethering, if possible, and turn off hotspot when you're not using it.

Chapter **22**

Protecting Windows

Your laptop contains software and files that can be damaged in several different ways. One major source of damage is from malicious attacks that are delivered via the Internet.

Microsoft provides security features within Windows 10 that help to keep your laptop and information safe, whether you're at home or travelling with your laptop. In addition, there are software programs you can purchase or find for free online to monitor, block, and repair unwanted attacks on your computer.

In this chapter, I introduce you to the major concepts of laptop security and cover Windows 10 security features that allow you to do the following:

» Run periodic updates to Windows, which install security solutions and patches (essentially, *patches* fix problems) to the software.

» Enable a *firewall,* which is a security feature that keeps your laptop safe from outsiders and helps you avoid several kinds of attacks on your data.

» Change the password used to protect your laptop from others.

» Protect yourself against spyware.

» Use devices such as a laptop lock or fingerprint reader to stop bad guys from stealing or breaking into your laptop.

» Protect your laptop from physical damage.

» Find your laptop or protect the data on it from thieves if it's lost or stolen.

Understand Laptop Security

Every day you carry around a wallet full of cash and credit cards, and you take certain measures to protect its contents. Your computer also contains valuable items in the form of data, and it's just as important that you protect it from thieves and damage.

Some people create damaging programs called *viruses* specifically designed to get at your laptop's hard drive and destroy or scramble data.

Companies might download *adware* on your laptop, which causes pop-up ads to appear, slowing down your laptop's performance. Spyware is another form of malicious software that you might download by clicking a link or opening a file attachment; *spyware* sits on your laptop and tracks your activities, whether for use by a legitimate company in selling products to you or by a criminal to steal your identity.

Your laptop comes with an operating system (such as Microsoft Windows) preinstalled, and that operating system has security features to protect your valuable data. Sometimes the operating system has flaws or new threats emerge, and you need to get an update to keep your laptop secure. You can also use Windows security tools such as Windows Defender to protect your laptop from dangerous computer programs collectively known as *malware.* See Chapter 15 for more detail about threats and protections from malware.

Use Other Software Protection

You can use third-party antivirus or antispyware programs (see Figure 22-1) to protect your computer, instead of relying solely on Windows 10 security tools. Several products on the market, such as Kaspersky and Norton Security, charge a yearly subscription fee. One advantage of these products is that their business is to track and catalog all the latest threats. When you perform an update to this software before running a scan, you're up to the minute in defending your computer from threats. Another benefit is that they often offer additional security tools that help you avoid sites with bad reputations or scan your computer more deeply for threats.

Free security products are also available. Search the web for "best free antivirus programs" to locate one. Many of these free programs are excellent, but you get what you pay for, and may find that a program with a subscription fee keeps you a bit safer.

FIGURE 22-1

Understand Windows Update Options

When a new operating system such as Windows 10 is released, it has been tested for many months; however, when the product is made available for general use, the manufacturer begins to get feedback about a few problems or security gaps that it couldn't have anticipated. For that reason, companies such as Microsoft release updates to their software, both to fix those problems and deal with new threats to computers that appear after the software release.

Windows Update is a tool you can use to make sure your laptop has the most up-to-date security measures in place. Today most updates happen automatically, but using Settings, you can control how frequently those installations happen. You can set Windows Update to install updates and restart to complete the installation at certain times or days by following these steps:

1. In the Start menu, click Settings ⇨ Update & Security ⇨ Windows Update.

2. Click the Restart Options link. In the resulting Restart Options dialog box (see Figure 22-2), you find these settings:

- **Automatic On/Off switch:** Click this setting to turn the feature on, and then choose when you want updates installed.

- **Pick a Time/Pick a Day:** You can make settings to choose a time of day to install updates, or pick a day to install. In most cases a daily update is sufficient.

Click here

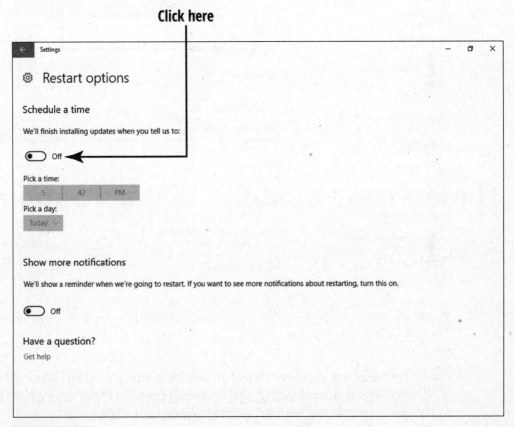

FIGURE 22-2

Check for Windows Updates

1. In the Start menu, click Settings ⇨ Update & Security ⇨ Windows Update.

2. In the resulting window, as shown in Figure 22-3, click the Check for Updates link to see all updates.

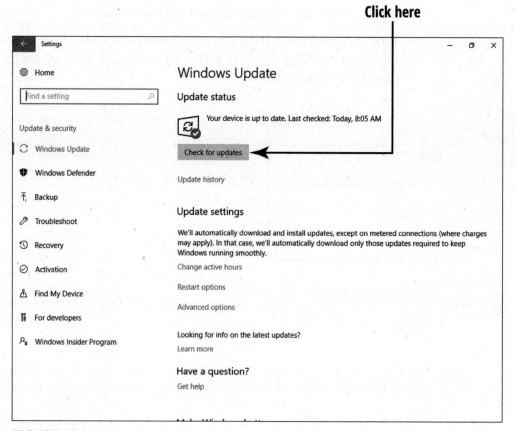

Click here

FIGURE 22-3

3. The following window shows all available updates (see Figure 22-4) and begins downloading and installing them in most cases. If instead you're presented with an Install Now button, click it.

4. If a restart is required a screen opens that allows you to either choose a restart time or click a Restart Now button.

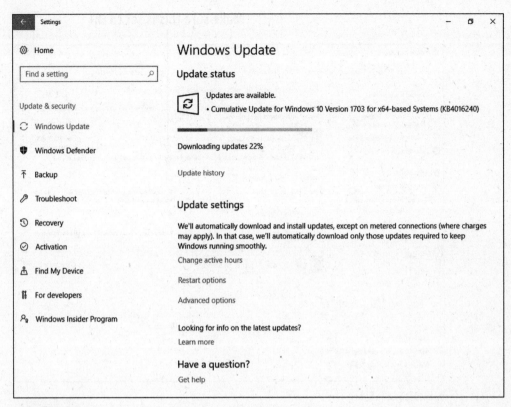

FIGURE 22-4

Enable Windows Firewall

1. A firewall keeps outsiders from accessing your laptop via an Internet connection. A firewall is built into Windows 10. In the Cortana search box, enter **Firewall**.

2. Click Windows Firewall in the search results.

3. In the Windows Firewall window that appears (see Figure 22-5), make sure that Windows Firewall is On. If it isn't, click the Turn Windows Firewall On or Off link in the left pane of the window.

Make sure this is set to On

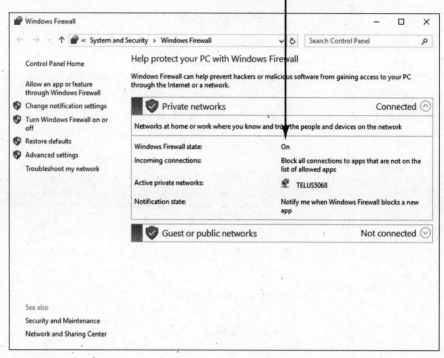

FIGURE 22-5

4. In the resulting Customize Settings window (see Figure 22-6), select the Turn on Windows Firewall radio button for Private Networks (such as your home network) and/or Public Networks (such as a coffee shop) and then click OK.

5. Click the Close button to close the Windows Firewall dialog box.

TIP

A *firewall* is a program that protects your laptop from the outside world. This is generally a good thing, unless you access a Virtual Private Network (VPN), often used in a corporate setting. Using a firewall with a VPN can restrict you from sharing files and using some other VPN features.

TIP

Antivirus and security software programs may offer their own firewall protection and may display a message asking if you want to switch. Check their features against Windows and then decide, but usually most firewall features are comparable. The important thing is to have one activated.

Select one or both of these

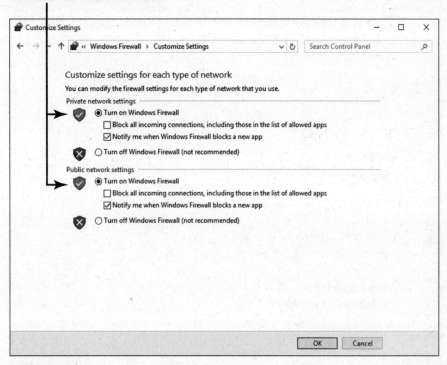

FIGURE 22-6

Run a Scan with Windows Defender

1. In the Settings window, click Update & Security, and then click the Windows Defender option on the left side.

2. In the Windows Defender dialog box that appears, click Open Windows Defender Security Center. In the window that appears, click the Virus and Threat Protection button on the left side (it's shaped like a shield).

3. Click the Quick Scan button. Windows Defender scans your computer and reports any findings.

4. Click Advanced Scan in the Windows Defender Security Center window shown in Figure 22-7 to choose among a full scan, a custom scan, or an offline scan. Windows Defender scans your laptop according to your choice and reports any findings.

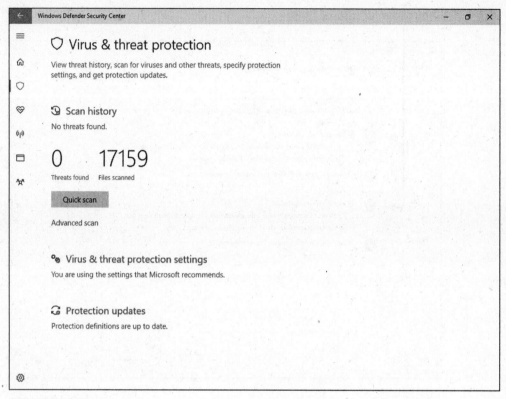

FIGURE 22-7

Change Your Laptop Password

1. If you log into Windows using an online account, your password is the password associated with your Microsoft account. If you set up a local account not associated with an online account, you create a password when you set up the account. To change a password, in the Start menu, click Settings, and then click Accounts.

2. In the Accounts window, click Sign-in Options in the left pane. In the resulting window, shown in Figure 22-8, click the Change button under Password. You may be asked for your password before proceeding to the next step. If so, enter your password and click Next.

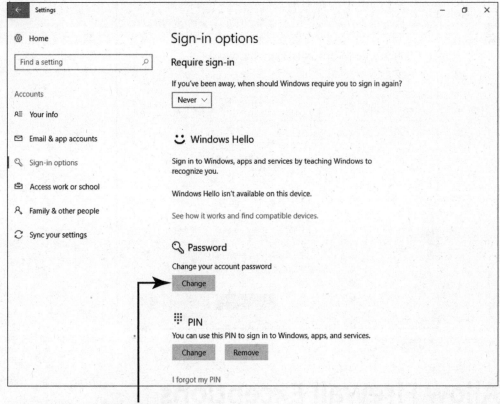

Click this link

FIGURE 22-8

3. In the Change Your Microsoft Account Password screen, shown in Figure 22-9, enter your current password, and then enter the new password and confirm it.

4. Click Next.

5. Click Finish.

TIP

After you create a password, you can change it at any time by going to the Sign-in Options in the Account settings and clicking the Change button under the Password setting.

FIGURE 22-9

Allow Firewall Exceptions

1. When you have a firewall active, you can allow certain programs to communicate through that firewall. For example, you might want to allow live apps such as Weather or Video to send information or content to your computer. In the Cortana search field, enter **Firewall**. Then click the Windows Firewall setting and press Enter.

2. In the resulting Windows Firewall window (see Figure 22-10), click Allow an App or Feature through Windows Firewall.

3. In the Allowed Apps window that appears (see Figure 22-11), click the Change Settings button, and then select the check boxes on the left for apps on your computer that you want to allow to communicate over the Internet without being stopped by Firewall.

Click this option

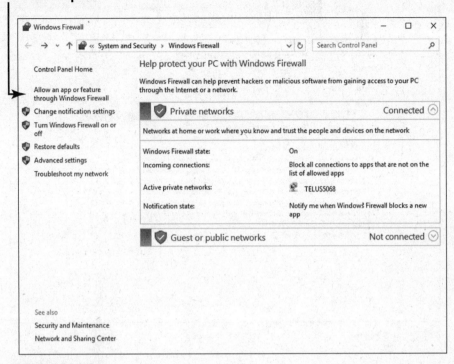

FIGURE 22-10

4. Click the Private and Public check box to narrow down whether you want just networks that are secure to allow this communication, or also public and nonsecure networks to do so.

5. Click OK and then click the Close button to close the Windows Firewall window.

TIP

If you allow apps to communicate across your firewall, it's very important that you do have antivirus and antispyware software installed on your laptop, and that you run updates to them on a regular basis. These types of programs help you avoid downloading malware to your laptop that could cause advertising pop-ups, slow your laptop's performance, damage computer files, or even track your keystrokes as you type to steal your identity and more. If you don't want to pay for such a program, consider a free solution such as Spyware Terminator (www.spywareterminator.com).

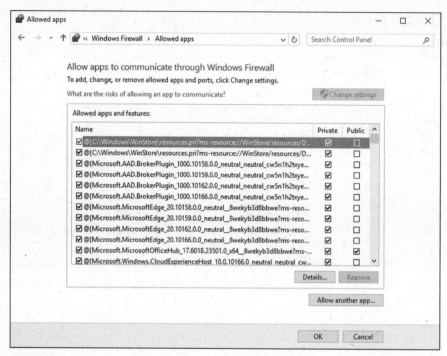

FIGURE 22-11

Use a Lock to Deter Thieves

When you travel with your laptop, you may have to leave it alone for a few moments now and then — perhaps in a cubicle in a branch office or a table at an Internet café while you step away to grab your latte. When that happens, a lock that you clip into a slot in your laptop (usually located on the back or side, and often identified by a lock icon) and a cable that you wrap around a table or desk leg might make you more secure. These are similar to the lock you use to keep your bicycle safe as you wander into a store or gym.

Don't count on a laptop lock to keep your laptop safe during a lengthy absence. They are relatively easy to circumvent. But for a short period of time in a non-high-risk area, they can be useful.

Locks are relatively cheap, from about $5 to $30 or so. They're also usually pretty easy to tuck into a laptop case without adding much bulk.

Use a Fingerprint Reader

Fingerprint readers use *biometric* technology that identifies you by a unique physical characteristic. Here's what you should know about laptop fingerprint readers:

TIP

» Many laptops include a built-in fingerprint reader for security. This is useful to keep anybody but you from accessing data on your laptop because your fingerprint is unique. See your manual for instructions on using the reader.

An option to using your fingerprint is using your finger to draw your password. Windows 10 has a picture password feature that works with touchscreen laptops and tablets. You enter onscreen gestures on a picture to log in to Windows.

» If your laptop doesn't have a built-in fingerprint reader, you can buy an external model such as the Microsoft Fingerprint Reader. These come in a wide price range (from about $40 to $200), but they are relatively portable. Figure 22-12 shows one such device from Zvetco Biometrics.

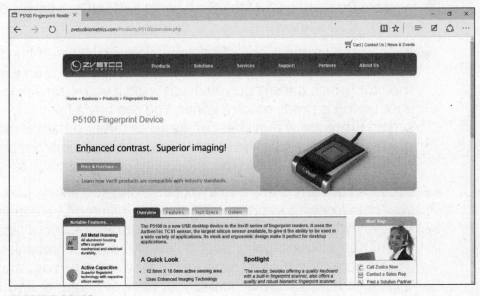

FIGURE 22-12

>> Some fingerprint readers allow you to log in to your laptop by simply swiping your finger over the reader, and some can also store passwords for your online accounts. Laptops or tablets with a touchscreen may allow you to press your finger to the screen to read your fingerprint.

TIP

Don't forget Windows Hello, a feature available on certain computers with compatible hardware that allows you to use facial recognition to provide access to your computer without ever entering a password. Many computers that have a fingerprint reader can also use facial recognition.

Protect Your Laptop from Damage

Here are a few tips for protecting your laptop from physical damage, or recouping some losses if damage does occur:

>> A well-made laptop case is really a must when moving about with your laptop. It helps to protect the laptop if you drop it and protect it from things falling on it. Look for one with both good padding and pockets for storing USB sticks and cords and DVDs, a power cord, and possibly a fingerprint reader or lock.

>> Your laptop screen is one of its biggest vulnerabilities. If it gets scratched or damaged in some way, short of attaching an external monitor (which doesn't do you much good if you're on a plane), your laptop is pretty much a goner. You can buy a fairly low-cost screen protector, a thin sheet of plastic or tempered glass that you place across your monitor that can help prevent scratches and, as a bonus, keep your screen from picking up dust or smudges.

>> Because you can't prevent every possible disaster, always *back up* your data (copy it to storage other than your laptop's hard drive) so you don't lose it — and consider getting insurance for your laptop. If your homeowner's policy doesn't already cover it, companies such as Safeware offer special laptop insurance against damage and theft. If your laptop is essential to your work or hobby, or if you travel with it a great deal, you might want to get an insurance quote to see whether coverage is within your budget.

Use a Service to Find a Lost Laptop

Laptops are lost or stolen on a frighteningly regular basis. The biggest concern, aside from having to buy a new laptop (which may or may not be covered by your insurance), is what a thief might do with the data on the laptop. Stored passwords for financial and retail shopping accounts could be used to steal your identity or run up debt in your name.

Luckily, there are software applications such as Absolute LoJack (www.lojack.absolute.com/en) (see Figure 22-13) for

» Pinpointing where your laptop is whenever it connects to the Internet

» Remotely disabling the computer, deleting files from it, or locking out any would-be user

» Issuing a warning to the thief that the computer is now protected and useless

» Observing what activities the thief is performing on your computer in real time

FIGURE 22-13

IN THIS CHAPTER

» **Shutting down a nonresponsive application**

» **Creating a system restore point**

» **Restoring your laptop**

» **Resetting your laptop**

» **Optimizing your hard drive**

» **Freeing up disk space**

Chapter **23**

Maintaining Windows

All the wonderful hardware that you've spent your hard-earned money on doesn't mean a thing if the software driving it goes flooey. If any program causes your system to *crash* (meaning it freezes up and you have to take drastic measures to revive it), you can try a variety of steps to fix it. You can also keep your system in good shape to help avoid those crashes. In this chapter, you find out how to take good care of your programs and operating system in these ways:

» When a program crashes, you can simply shut that program down by using Windows Task Manager. This utility keeps track of all the programs and processes that are running on your laptop.

» Use the System Restore feature to first create a *system restore point* (a point in time when your settings and programs all seem to be humming along just fine), and then restore Windows to that point when trouble hits.

» You can clean up your system to delete unused files, free up disk space, and schedule maintenance tasks.

Shut Down a Nonresponsive Application

1. If your laptop freezes and won't let you proceed with what you were doing, press Ctrl+Alt+Delete on your keyboard.

2. In the Windows screen that appears, click Task Manager.

3. In the resulting Task Manager dialog box, click More Details, click the Processes tab (see Figure 23-1), and then select the application that you were working in when your system stopped responding.

Click this tab

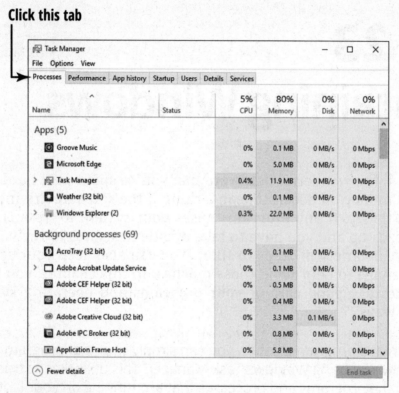

FIGURE 23-1

4. Click the End Task button.

5. The app shuts down. Click the Close button to close Task Manager.

TIP

If pressing Ctrl+Alt+Delete doesn't bring up the Task Manager, you're in bigger trouble than you thought. You might need to press and hold your laptop's power button to shut down. Note that some applications use an AutoSave feature that keeps an interim version of the document that you were working in. You might be able to save some of your work by using the auto-saved version. Other programs don't have such a safety net, and you simply lose whatever changes you made to your document since the last time you saved it. The moral? Save, and save often.

TIP

You may see a dialog box appear when an application shuts down that asks if you want to report the problem to Microsoft. If you say yes, information is sent to Microsoft to help it provide advice or fix the problem down the road.

Create a System Restore Point

1. You can back up your system files, which creates a restore point you can later use to return your laptop to earlier settings if you experience problems. Enter **Create a restore point** in Cortana's search field and then press the Enter key on your keyboard.

2. In the System Properties dialog box that appears (see Figure 23-2) on the System Protection tab, click the Create button. (You may have to select the drive, click Configure, and then click Turn On System Protection before the Create button becomes available.) Click OK.

3. In the System Protection dialog box that appears, enter a name to identify the restore point, such as the name of a program you are about to install, and click Create.

4. Windows displays a progress window. When the restore point is created, the message shown in Figure 23-3 appears. Click Close to close the message box and click the Close button to close the System Properties dialog box.

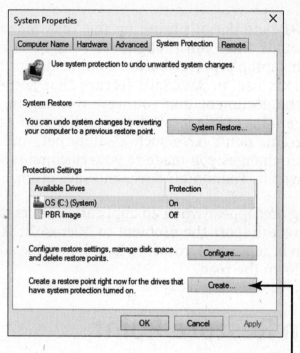

Click this button

FIGURE 23-2

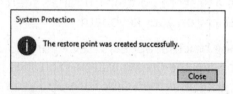

FIGURE 23-3

TIP

Every once in a while, before you install a piece of software or make some new setting in Windows, even though things seem to be running just fine, create a system restore point. It's good computer practice, just like backing up your files, only you're backing up your settings. Once a month or once every couple of months works for most people, but if you frequently make changes, create a system restore point more often.

Restore Your Laptop

1. Enter **Create a Restore Point** in Cortana's search field and then press Enter.

2. In the System Properties dialog box that appears, click the System Protection tab and then click the System Restore button, as shown in Figure 23-4.

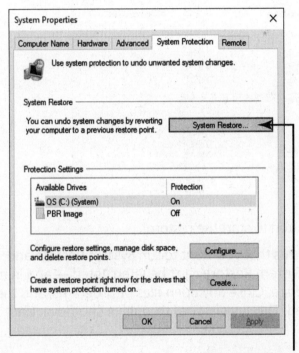

Click this button

FIGURE 23-4

3. In the System Restore window, click Next. In the window that appears, choose the date and time of the restore point (see Figure 23-5), and then click Next.

Choose a restore point

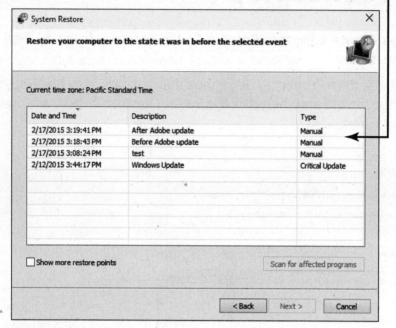

FIGURE 23-5

4. Click the Finish button to start the restore.

5. A dialog box confirms that you want to run System Restore and informs you that System Restore can't be interrupted — and in most cases can't be undone. Close any open files or programs, and then click Yes to proceed. The system goes through a shutdown and restart sequence.

TIP

System Restore doesn't get rid of files that you've saved, so you don't lose your Ph.D. dissertation. System Restore simply reverts to Windows settings as of the restore point. This can help if you or some piece of installed software made a setting that's causing some conflict in your system, making your laptop sluggish or prone to crashes. If you're concerned about what changes will happen, click the Scan for Affected Programs button shown in the window displayed in Figure 23-6.

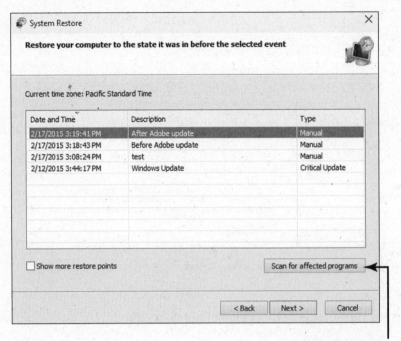

Click this button

FIGURE 23-6

Reset Your Laptop

1. Whereas refreshing a computer resets system files to factory defaults and retains all your files and some apps, resetting not only resets system files, it gets rid of all your personal files and apps you installed. Resetting is for those times when nothing else has gotten your laptop working again. To begin, in the Start menu, click Settings, and then click Update & Security.

2. In the resulting Update & Security window, click Recovery in the left pane. Under Reset this PC in the right pane (see Figure 23-7) click Get Started.

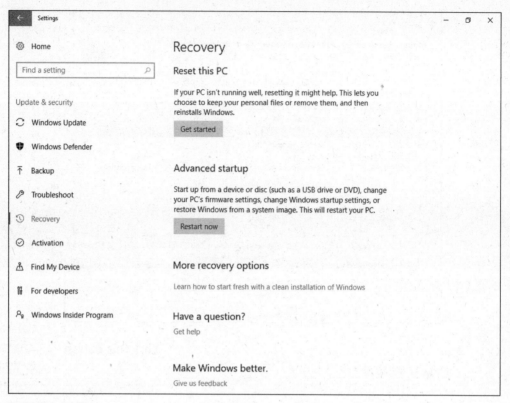

FIGURE 23-7

3. In the following screen, shown in Figure 23-8, choose either Keep My Files, Remove Everything, or Restore Factory Settings.

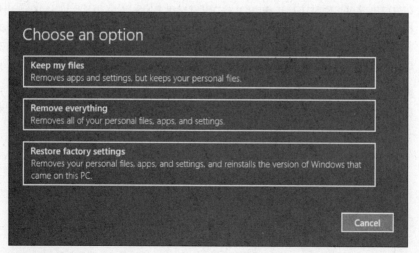

FIGURE 23-8

4. In the following screen, if you're positive you want to proceed, click the Next button.

WARNING

The Reset procedure is a somewhat drastic step that will remove any apps you installed and files you saved. Remember, you can back out of the Reset procedure at any time up until you hit the Reset button. Just click Cancel.

Optimize Your Hard Drive

1. To clean up files on your hard drive, enter **Optimize** in Cortana's search field and then click Defragment and Optimize Drives and press Enter.

2. In the resulting Optimize Drives window (see Figure 23-9), to the left of the Optimize button is the Analyze button. Choose a disk and then click the Analyze button to check whether the disk requires defragmenting. When the analysis is complete, click the Optimize button. A notation appears (see Figure 23-10) showing the progress of optimizing your drive.

3. When the optimizing process is complete, the Optimize Drives window displays 0 days since last run, indicating that your drive no longer requires optimizing. Click Close to close the window.

WARNING

Disk optimizing can take a while. If you have energy-saving features active (such as a screen saver), they can cause the optimize feature to stop and start all over again. Try running your optimization overnight while you're happily dreaming of much more interesting things. You can also set up the procedure to run automatically at a preset period of time — such as once every two weeks — by using the Change Settings button in the Optimize Drives window and choosing a frequency in the dialog box that appears.

Click this button...

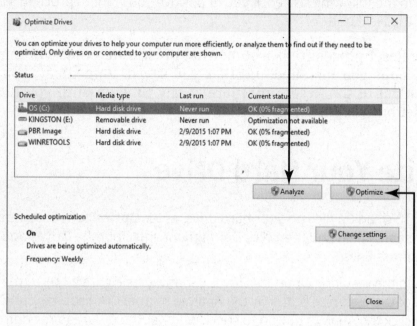

FIGURE 23-9

then this button

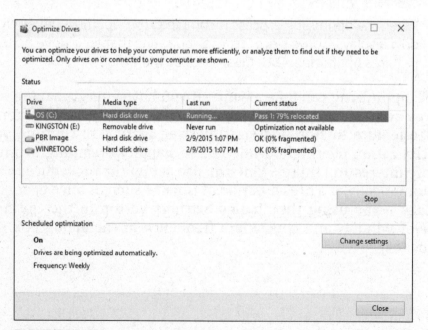

FIGURE 23-10

Free Disk Space

1. To run a process that cleans unused files and fragments of data from your hard drive to free up space (don't worry, this won't delete any personal files) enter **Disk Cleanup** in Cortana's search field and then press the Enter key on your keyboard.

2. In the Disk Cleanup: Drive Selection dialog box that appears (see Figure 23-11) choose the items you want to clean up from the list. The amount of space that will be freed up is indicated to the right of each item. Click OK. Disk Cleanup confirms that you want to delete files of the type you selected. Click Delete Files to proceed.

TIP

If your laptop only has one drive, the Disk Cleanup: Drive Selection dialog box will not appear. Your computer will go straight to calculating how much space you will be able to free up.

3. The selected files are deleted.

FIGURE 23-11

TIP

Click the View Files button in the Disk Cleanup dialog box to see more details about the files that Windows proposes to delete, including the size of the files and when they were created or last accessed.

Index

About the Author

Nancy C. Muir is the owner of a writing and consulting company that specializes in business and technology topics. She has authored more than 100 books, including *Laptops For Seniors For Dummies* and *iPhone For Seniors For Dummies*. Nancy holds a certificate in Distance Learning Design and has taught technical writing and Internet safety at the college level.

Dedication

To my husband, Earl, for going above and beyond in supporting me while writing these books. Honey, you're the best.

Author's Acknowledgments

Thanks to Katie Mohr, who has been a loyal and supportive acquisitions editor through the years. Also my gratitude to Elizabeth Kuball, for very ably handling all the many details of two of my books this year. Thanks also to Sharon Mealka for tech-editing the book to keep me on track.

Publisher's Acknowledgments

Acquisitions Editor: Katie Mohr

Project Editor: Elizabeth Kuball

Copy Editor: Elizabeth Kuball

Technical Editor: Sharon Mealka

Sr. Editorial Assistant: Cherie Case

Production Editor: Tamilmani Varadharaj

Cover Image: © Johnny Greig/iStockphoto

Leverage the power

Dummies is the global leader in the reference category and one of the most trusted and highly regarded brands in the world. No longer just focused on books, customers now have access to the dummies content they need in the format they want. Together we'll craft a solution that engages your customers, stands out from the competition, and helps you meet your goals.

Advertising & Sponsorships

Connect with an engaged audience on a powerful multimedia site, and position your message alongside expert how-to content. Dummies.com is a one-stop shop for free, online information and know-how curated by a team of experts.

- Targeted ads
- Video
- Email Marketing

- Microsites
- Sweepstakes sponsorship

20 **MILLION**
PAGE VIEWS
EVERY SINGLE MONTH

15
MILLION
UNIQUE
VISITORS PER MONTH

43%
OF ALL VISITORS
ACCESS THE SITE
VIA THEIR MOBILE DEVICES

700,000 NEWSLETTER
SUBSCRIPTIONS
TO THE INBOXES OF
300,000 UNIQUE **INDIVIDUALS**
EVERY WEEK

# of dummies

Custom Publishing

Reach a global audience in any language by creating a solution that will differentiate you from competitors, amplify your message, and encourage customers to make a buying decision.

- Apps
- Books
- eBooks
- Video
- Audio
- Webinars

Brand Licensing & Content

Leverage the strength of the world's most popular reference brand to reach new audiences and channels of distribution.

For more information, visit dummies.com/biz

PERSONAL ENRICHMENT

Staying Sharp
9781119187790
USA $26.00
CAN $31.99
UK £19.99

Facebook
Carolyn Abram
9781119179030
USA $21.99
CAN $25.99
UK £16.99

Guitar
Mark Phillips
Jon Chappell
9781119293354
USA $24.99
CAN $29.99
UK £17.99

Investing
Eric Tyson, MBA
9781119293347
USA $22.99
CAN $27.99
UK £16.99

Beekeeping
Howland Blackiston
9781119310068
USA $22.99
CAN $27.99
UK £16.99

Digital Photography
Julie Adair King
9781119235606
USA $24.99
CAN $29.99
UK £17.99

Meditation
Stephan Bodian
9781119251163
USA $24.99
CAN $29.99
UK £17.99

Pregnancy
9781119235491
USA $26.99
CAN $31.99
UK £19.99

Samsung Galaxy S7
Bill Hughes
9781119279952
USA $24.99
CAN $29.99
UK £17.99

iPhone
Edward C. Baig
Bob "Dr. Mac" LeVitus
9781119283133
USA $24.99
CAN $29.99
UK £17.99

Crocheting
Karen Manthey
Susan Brittain
9781119287117
USA $24.99
CAN $29.99
UK £16.99

Nutrition
Carol Ann Rinzler
9781119130246
USA $22.99
CAN $27.99
UK £16.99

PROFESSIONAL DEVELOPMENT

Windows 10
Andy Rathbone
9781119311041
USA $24.99
CAN $29.99
UK £17.99

AutoCAD
Bill Fane
9781119255796
USA $39.99
CAN $47.99
UK £27.99

Excel 2016
Greg Harvey, PhD
9781119293439
USA $26.99
CAN $31.99
UK £19.99

QuickBooks 2017
9781119281467
USA $26.99
CAN $31.99
UK £19.99

macOS Sierra
Stephen L. Nelson, MBA, CPA, MS in Taxation
9781119280651
USA $29.99
CAN $35.99
UK £21.99

LinkedIn
Joel Elad, MBA
9781119251132
USA $24.99
CAN $29.99
UK £17.99

Windows 10
Woody Leonhard
9781119310563
USA $34.00
CAN $41.99
UK £24.99

SharePoint 2016
Rosemarie Withee
Ken Withee
9781119181705
USA $29.99
CAN $35.99
UK £21.99

Fundamental Analysis
Matt Krantz
9781119263593
USA $26.99
CAN $31.99
UK £19.99

Networking
Doug Lowe
9781119257769
USA $29.99
CAN $35.99
UK £21.99

Office 2016
Wallace Wang
9781119293477
USA $26.99
CAN $31.99
UK £19.99

Office 365
Rosemarie Withee
Ken Withee
Jennifer Reed
9781119265313
USA $24.99
CAN $29.99
UK £17.99

Salesforce.com
Liz Kao
Jon Paz
9781119239314
USA $29.99
CAN $35.99
UK £21.99

Coding
Nikhil Abraham
9781119293323
USA $29.99
CAN $35.99
UK £21.99

Learning Made Easy

ACADEMIC

9781119293576
USA $19.99
CAN $23.99
UK £15.99

9781119293637
USA $19.99
CAN $23.99
UK £15.99

9781119293491
USA $19.99
CAN $23.99
UK £15.99

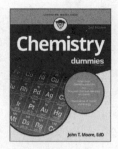

9781119293460
USA $19.99
CAN $23.99
UK £15.99

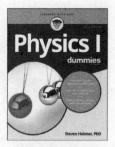

9781119293590
USA $19.99
CAN $23.99
UK £15.99

9781119215844
USA $26.99
CAN $31.99
UK £19.99

9781119293378
USA $22.99
CAN $27.99
UK £16.99

9781119293521
USA $19.99
CAN $23.99
UK £15.99

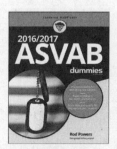

9781119239178
USA $18.99
CAN $22.99
UK £14.99

9781119263883
USA $26.99
CAN $31.99
UK £19.99

Available Everywhere Books Are Sold

dummies.com

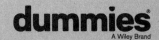